The Backpack Years
Two Memoirs, One Story

STEFANIE WILSON
&
JAMES WILSON

To most of the people in this book
and some of the ones who aren't.

CONTENTS

ACKNOWLEDGMENTS

There are many important people in our lives, and whom we met on our travels, who are not mentioned in this book. We were trying to tell a specific story, and unfortunately not everyone fit into that narrative. We want them to know they are still very important to us.

Every event in this book happened. However, some timelines were condensed for clearer storytelling. All names were changed.

Stef's chapters use American spelling, grammar, and punctuation conventions (Chicago Manual of Style). James's chapters use British. (Oxford Guide to Style).

Huge thanks to Patti, Shawn, Carol, Charlotte, Randy, Garrett, Michelle, Cathy, Scott, and Jean for your amazingly helpful feedback.

PART ONE:

A WORLD APART

(2000 – 2002)

CHAPTER 1
JAMES

I leaned against the bar, empty pint glass slipping through my fingers.

'Double vodka, please. Neat,' I shouted to the barman, my voice barely audible over the 'Grease Megamix.' My friends were scattered around the club, chatting up random birds. Flashing lights illuminated smiling faces on the dance floor.

What the fuck is everyone so happy about?

They sang along to the same shit songs that played here last night and the night before and every other fucking night for fuck knows how long.

I looked down at the twenty-pound note in my hand and the credit card I inserted into a cash machine earlier to withdraw sixty pounds on credit. I'd marched a twenty into the bank and used it to pay off the card's minimum balance for the month. *Well, that's another sixty quid in debt.*

The vodka went down in one.

I peered at my watch through blurry eyes. I always stood in this exact spot, at this exact time, surrounded by these exact people. At work, I liked the rules, regulations and boundaries of accounting, but its rigidity had infiltrated my social life.

A steroid-inflated bouncer stared me down as I left the club alone. *Wanker.*

The late-night crowd lumbered along the pavement, seemingly lured by the smell of frying grease. Their vacant eyes looked through me as I weaved between them in the opposite direction, past the queue outside the chippy, past the brawling outside the taxi rank and towards the edge of town. One route home was direct, along a brightly lit dual carriageway lined with retail parks. The other was bleak and littered with dilapidated warehouses. I found myself taking the latter.

My short-sleeved shirt was no match for a January night in Northern England. My teeth chattered, and my breath condensed to mist. I thought of Spain and its sunshine, beaches and cocktails. In the summer, I'd go there and escape the monotony of my life for two whole weeks. But then I'd be back, tanned, blond and broke again. I'd grind away at my shitty job for another year until the next brief escape.

I shuffled towards my parents' semi-detached house on a council estate in Warrington, a small town near Manchester where I grew up. My dad hadn't worked in years, not since they closed the coal mines, and my mum had to quit her cleaning job due to a heart condition. They relied heavily on government benefits. I needed to pay my way, but I earned less than minimum wage at my accounting apprenticeship.

A large portion of my wages went to my parents for board and lodgings and a third of the cable and electricity. They itemised the dial-up internet and phone bills, so I paid for my portion of those, too. Then there was a car loan, petrol and insurance.

As I stumbled under a decrepit railway bridge, I envisioned a future I had no control over. I'd pass my exams and become a fully qualified Chartered Accountant at age twenty-two. Next up, a pay rise. I'd spend it on a new car, clothes and flat to reflect a professional life I was already disillusioned with. Debt repayment would devour the rest. Many kids from my neighbourhood ended up either addicted to drugs or selling them. I escaped an inevitable path, just to replace it with another one.

Near an abandoned factory, I imagined my future family. My missus and I work all week and spend Sundays round my mum's, where she cooks in the tiny kitchen until Dad comes home from the pub, bringing with him the smell of sweat, beer and cigs. He sits on the sofa because I'm in *his* chair. He won't look at me or speak to me. Instead, he clears his throat repeatedly with increasing volume until I vacate it. After a tense dinner, we say ta-ra and go back to the house we can't afford.

My vision continued on and on, as I walked past the rusty gas tower and the collapsing brick chimney stack. An indistinguishable blur of work, sleep, holiday, drunken nights out and more debt. The debt. My mind always came back to the debt. Suddenly short of breath, my heart picked up speed like it was trying to escape through the walls of my tight chest.

The credit cards, the store cards, the car loan, the interest, the late fees, the guilt, the shame. The fucking debt.

I looked to the sky and inhaled sharply.

'Fuuck! Fuuuuck! Fuuuuuuck!'

I screamed until my throat burned, looked to the empty night sky again and fell into the road. The blaring horn of a speeding taxi startled me back onto the pavement. The screaming stopped.

I cut through the park where a dark, empty field stretched out in front of me. Wet grass stuck to my perfectly polished shoes. In the playground, the trousers my mum had ironed for me now dragged through a thick layer of damp dirt. My shoes were now partly submerged in mud. On any other day, this would have bothered me, even with no one around.

I tried to yell, 'Get me out of here!' but my voice broke, and the words caught in my throat. No one could hear me. No one was listening.

Finally, the field gave way to pavement. With each step, the mud from my shoes dried and crumbled, leaving a trail on the concrete. Grass shook loose until only a few stubborn blades remained. I walked in silence, hands in pockets and head down, the hairs on my bare arms at full stretch, searching desperately for a source of warmth. Road signs became clear, and streetlamps shone brightly against a lightening sky.

At home, I sat up in bed, shivering under my duvet. I covered my face with my cold hands and gasped for air amid shallow breaths. Tears streamed down my cheeks and through my fingers. There, in the dawn light, something had changed.

CHAPTER 2
STEF

I followed Seema, my roommate and an actual model, into a dark bar called La Candelaria. Steamy warmth blurred the windows and soothed my frozen cheeks. Young Spaniards chatted in groups, sipping beer or wine, or danced on the crowded floor, clapping overhead to a Latin beat.

The world buzzed. Y2K Global Meltdown narrowly averted, the air was now filled with the hope and potential of a new millennium.

I dumped my peacoat on a stool, adjusted the spaghetti strap on my tank top, and leaned over the bar to order myself a *ginebra con limón*—a gin and Lemon Fanta mix that glowed under the blacklight. I'd won a scholarship for a study abroad program and chose to take these extra classes pass/fail, locking in my 4.0 GPA before graduation. I wasn't really studying abroad but partying abroad—making up for lost time. I'd only started drinking alcohol once I turned twenty-one, because an underage drinking citation could have: A.) Kept me from getting a teaching job and B.) Disappointed my parents.

I loved making my parents happy. As a nurse and mechanic, they worked long hours to provide me and my sister Cassie with a safe and stable life in Pittsburgh, and I owed it to them to be good and work hard, too.

For as responsible as I was, I'd also craved adventure for as long as I could remember. When I was two, I'd often climb my bookshelf to enjoy the view of my bedroom. The next year, my dad came into my room to find I'd cranked open the window and climbed outside to hang out on the ledge.

As a teen, Dad's stack of old *National Geographic* magazines called to me from the basement. I'd sit on the floor, pouring through musty back issues in wonder. I was very aware that Pittsburgh was just one speck on the globe, and there was a whole world out there, where people lived life in entirely different ways. I wanted to eat their food, listen to their music, and immerse myself in their cultures. Every afternoon after school, I watched *Globe Trekker*, envious of the travelers and longing to feel the awe of unfamiliarity.

We never went abroad, and I knew few people who had. Our childhood vacations were a week at Virginia Beach, or visiting Great Uncle Aleksy in Gerardville, where we toured a coal mining museum and drove by the Mrs. T's pierogi factory. I loved those vacations, and I was lucky to have parents who could and would take us on vacation at all. But those trips didn't satisfy my curiosity about the rest of the world.

I sipped my gin and scanned the room. Spanish people seemed rude by American mores—nobody made eye contact or smiled on the sidewalk. But if you chat for a few minutes in a bar, they'll invite you to their home for dinner. Stop a stranger in the street for directions, and they'll *escort you there*. I loved meeting Spaniards, and since nobody in the city of Valladolid spoke English, I considered my nocturnal excursions an integral part of my education.

Seema smoothed her dark hair and reapplied her lip gloss. Immediately, an eager young man appeared by her side. "*Hola.*"

"*Hola,*" Seema said, without a hint of her Indian-English accent. "*Me llamo Seema.*" She leaned in to kiss his cheeks.

"What do you want to drink, *bonita*?"

She ran her fingers through her hair again. "*Tequila, gracias.*"

He delivered a tall, thin highball glass brimming with golden liquor. Seema's doe eyes grew bigger

"*¡Un chupito!*" I teased, demonstrating the size of a shot glass with my pointer finger and thumb. "She just wanted a shot!"

He nodded, delicately took the glass from Seema, and tossed half the tequila on the floor. He handed it back. "*Aquí*, now it's a shot."

We cracked up and Seema took the shot. I noticed two guys joking around at the bar. The tall one's smile lit up his handsome face.

I pulled Seema to the dance floor and positioned myself in Hot Guy at the Bar's line of sight, attempting to dance seductively to a techno remix of Bob Marley's "Sun is Shining." I shimmied to illuminate the body glitter on my chest.

He and his friend stared but didn't approach. As a blond, blue-eyed American, I was considered alluring in Spain, and this allure gave me an assurance I never had before. Or it could have been the gin.

I asked his friend, "Do you want to dance with us or just watch?"

6

They laughed and replied, "Just watch!"

Hot Guy's name was Miguel. He placed his kisses close to the corners of my lips, and his subtle touch made my skin tingle. We met his brother and friends and talked and danced until closing time.

Seema and I grabbed our coats and stepped onto the sidewalk. The overcast sky reflected the city lights, giving the night a yellow glow. A few snowflakes drifted onto the empty street.

Miguel followed us outside. "I want to make dinner for you sometime," he said. He entered our apartment phone number in his cell under the name *mi niña*—my girl.

"Is that because you don't remember my name?" I joked as he pushed the glowing buttons.

He feigned offense. "*¡Claro que no, Estefanía!* I will call you tomorrow." He leaned in for two more kisses to say goodbye while a gust of wind swirled the snowflakes around us like glitter in a snow globe. As Seema and I walked home, I couldn't feel the cold on my flushed skin.

CHAPTER 3
JAMES

My older brother, Archie, his wife Liz and their kids stood next to me in the London Heathrow airport terminal. I hugged everyone tightly.

'Don't carry anything for anyone! They could be planting drugs on ya,' Archie reminded me again.

I rolled my eyes. 'I won't.'

'Bye, Uncle James!' the kids shouted, waving me off as I joined the airport security queue. I waved back with a forced grin.

It took an age to get through security. Archie and his family watched the whole time, but I wished they would leave because I couldn't hold it together much longer. With one final wave, I passed through the metal detectors and out of sight.

I held my boarding pass in my shaky hands. Bombarded with emotions of sadness, regret, excitement, anxiety, fear, self-loathing, guilt and joy, huge tears ran down my face. I wiped my cheeks with my jacket sleeve, adjusted the straps on my bag and headed for the gate.

As I boarded the plane, I realised how much I'd miss Archie and the kids. I liked being an uncle. The kids always got excited looks on their faces when I walked into Archie's house; they used me as a climbing frame and we always laughed together. I enjoyed babysitting even though they had recently got me into trouble.

'Be careful with me new plant,' Liz said as she and Archie left for the evening. As soon as the front door closed, the kids grabbed all the pillows from the sofa and launched them at each other.

'Stop it off, now,' I said, glancing at the delicate plant tied to a wooden stick for support.

They joined forces, aiming a barrage of pillows at my head, their cheeks red and smiles wide. I caved, launching my own attack and making them giggle.

We heard a snapping sound and fell silent. The plant was broken.

'I'll tie it back to the stick, and no one tells your mum, right?'

'OK, Uncle James.'

When Archie and Liz pulled into the driveway, I gave the kids a 'remember what we talked about' look. They smiled and nodded. The door opened.

'Uncle James broke the plant!' they shouted in unison and squealed with laughter as I chased them down the hall.

My relationship with my brother and his family was a bright spot in my life, and it was hard to leave them.

For the past year, I'd been stressing about money. Weekends of drinking, clubbing and hangovers distracted me from the heavy feeling in my chest. Monday morning always saw its return. Letters from the bank and credit card companies arrived more frequently, worded more ominously.

I couldn't take the anxiety anymore and sold everything I owned: TV, game console, mobile phone, computer, CD player, CDs, clothes. I scraped together the money for a twelve-month work visa and a one-way flight to Australia, which was as far as I could get from my job, my debts and my dad.

On the eve of my flight, I sat in my empty childhood bedroom with a pen and pad and a few envelopes.

To whom it may concern,

I am writing to regretfully inform you that I can no longer afford to pay my debts. I am leaving this address permanently, so please do not try to contact me here.

Yours faithfully,

James Wilson, a worthless piece of shit

I didn't actually write that last part, but I wanted to.

I'd extended my layover to stay a few days in Bali before arriving in Darwin. I arrived in Kuta with an aching body and a fluttering stomach, grabbed my new backpack from the luggage carousel and placed it on the floor. The backpack my brother bought for me. The one filled with clothes my mum ironed, folded and packed for me.

In the seconds it took to get my other bag, the backpack had vanished. I frantically scanned the crowd and spotted an older Balinese man dragging it across the terminal. 'Where the fuck are *you* going?' I demanded as I snatched my backpack from him.

He recoiled and pointed at a badge clipped to his shirt pocket: Official Airport Baggage Carrier.

'Shit. Sorry, mate.' Relieved, I gave him my other bags, and we made our way into the humid late-night air. He loaded my bags into a taxi, and I tipped him with a 50,000 Indonesian rupiah note, worth four quid, which I plucked from the money belt under my sweat-soaked T-shirt. I studied my new surroundings from the backseat of the cab, but outside, it was mostly dark. Exhaustion and intimidation pushed me straight to bed.

The following day I awoke to chirping birds and the distant splashing of water. Outside, palm trees swayed in the breeze. Three local women sat cross-legged in wide-brimmed woven hats, manicuring a lawn using office scissors.

I yearned for the swimming pool and a sun-lounger, but I needed to find accommodation. I had only booked two nights at this budget-busting hotel, and one of them was already over.

Beyond the hotel compound, the plush lawns and palm trees gave way to an uneven dirt road, the rubbish lining the street reminiscent of the council estate I'd grown up on. The road led me to an open-air market. Locals filled the street, moving quickly from one stall to the next. T-shirts hung from wire hangers, *Bintang Beer* written across them. Brightly coloured fabrics adorned the stalls above neatly arranged rows of handbags.

Vendors rushed up, shaking their merchandise in my face. My heart beat faster as they closed in.

'You want watch?'

'You want bag?'

Two women grabbed my hands, pulling me towards their shop. I snatched my hands away. 'Get off me!'

When I turned to leave, four scowling men blocked my path. I froze. The women grabbed me again, and I relented. They plopped me down in a chair and painted my fingernails and toenails with clear nail polish. 'Make nails strong,' one said. She lifted her arms to flex her muscles and laughed loudly. A third woman appeared and massaged my shoulders. Resistance was futile.

I gave them a 50,000 rupiah note and headed towards the exit with fortified nails and relaxed shoulders. They frowned. They shook their heads and held out their hands for more. I handed over another 50,000.

'We need more,' one woman said.

'That's all I have left,' I explained.

'I take you to hotel for more,' she replied, buckling up her scooter helmet.

I ran back to the hotel, through the tall gates, up a flight of stairs and into my room. I collapsed onto my bed, panting, and sank into the comfy mattress, wishing I could stay there.

'You can do this!' I told my reflection in the hotel bathroom mirror and set off again mid-afternoon. Avoiding Nail Polish Alley, I found the main drag, Jalan Legian, a bustling street with bars, shops, restaurants and internet cafes, where I walked amidst a crowd of seasoned backpackers and rookie tourists. With my brand-new sandals and three-quarter length trousers, there was no doubt which one I was.

A young Balinese woman squatted down outside a shop. She arranged flowers inside a bowl made from a palm leaf and added nuts and shiny coins. She lit a stick of incense and delicately placed it in the bowl. The smoke danced above the flowers, subduing the smell of exhaust fumes. Kneeling, she put her hands together, closed her eyes and bowed her head. Somehow, she drowned out the scooter horns and found peace, right there on the crowded pavement.

For the next few hours, I scoured the streets for new digs. Sweat oozed from every pore of my reddening skin. Deep cuts formed along the stiff straps of my sandals. No rooms were available anywhere. *What the fuck was I thinking?*

I noticed a piece of cardboard in a bush, with the word *vacancy* and an arrow scrawled on it. I followed it down an alley and found an old man in a stained shirt sat reading a newspaper. A huge grin adorned his face when he saw me. 'I have room. Good price for you, my friend. Only 50,000.'

He led me to a hut and pushed open its creaky door. The room had one tiny window and a rickety fan. Disgusting bugs scurried around the floor, and a lizard scaled the wall and disappeared into a hole in the ceiling.

'I'll take it!'

On the walk back to my hotel, a bare-chested Balinese man stepped out of the shadows. A white T-shirt hung from the waistband of his ripped jeans. "You want poof-poof?" he asked, pointing to the cigarette in his mouth.

'No, thank you,' I replied and stepped around him.

He followed me. 'You want ecstasy? You want opium?'

I shook my head. 'No, thank you.'

'You want girl?'

'No, thank you.'

'Ah! You want boy?'

I turned around. 'No! I don't want *anything*.' I walked away again. Something hit me on the back of the head. A large coin rolled past my feet. I faced him. 'What the fu—?'

He'd been joined by five of his friends. Each with the same dangling T-shirt and half-smoked cigarette balanced loosely on his lips. I picked up the pace. Every few steps, another coin struck me with more force than the last, followed by bouts of laughter. After six or seven hits, I ran across the street, avoiding scooters, taxis, flower baskets, locals, tourists and more coins.

I ducked into a brightly lit internet cafe and sat at a computer. The excited faces of my brother and his family consumed my thoughts. I'd wanted this, but right then, I couldn't remember why.

Dear Archie,

Thanks for seeing me off at the airport. Bali is beautiful, I love it here, and all is well.

I held down the delete key and started my email over.

Dear Archie, I fucking hate it here!

I told him that I was miserable and my first day was rubbish. Why would he expect anything less from a boy whose mum cooked his meals and washed his clothes? I had to toughen up because I wasn't going back now.

After a nap back at the nice hotel, a shower and a generous dollop of after-sun lotion, I headed back to Jalan Legian in search of beer. The sun had set. Traffic was quieter, but the bars were louder.

A building shaped like a pirate ship rose high above the others. When I entered The Bounty, a local man gestured for me to sit at the bar. 'Bintang. Two for one.' He instructed the barman to get me one and leave the other chilling in the fridge.

'Where are you from?' he asked.

'Manchester.'

'Ah! Manchester United!' he declared. 'David Beckham!'

I smiled and nodded politely.

Two lads walked in. The barman greeted them and brought them over to me. 'He is English too. Talk to him,' he said and walked away.

After an awkward silence, we shook hands.

'It's OK, lads, you don't have to talk to me,' I assured them.

'That's alright, mate. I'm Martin, and this is Shaun,' the taller lad said. 'We'll have a beer with ya.'

'We've just come from a month in Thailand and Vietnam,' Shaun said. 'You?'

'Ah, that's quality. It's actually me first day. I've never been anywhere on me own before.' I showed them my glistening nail polish. 'I've got me nails done and coins lobbed at me 'ead.'

The lads laughed. When we finished our beers, they invited me to a club called Double Six. A taxi took us along a dark road, away from the lights of Kuta, where we passed empty fields and half-built houses.

'Erm, how do you know about this place?'

'An Aussie bloke we met in Vietnam told us about it. It's a locals' club,' Martin explained.

We walked into the open-air club, the only place lit for miles. My blond hair stuck out in a crowd of black-haired locals. I stood behind Shaun. 'This place looks well dodgy.'

'We'll be alright. The Aussie said that one time, a local stole a tourist's wallet in this club, so the others stoned him to death and dumped his body in the sea.'

'What the fuck?' I replied, wide-eyed.

'They don't want the bad publicity.' He grinned.

I was just about to suggest we leave when Martin carried over a fishbowl filled with a bright yellow cocktail. 'This is jungle juice.' He handed me a straw.

The lads and I shared a few drinks in the corner and kept ourselves to ourselves until the jungle juice kicked in. Then we moved confidently through the staring crowd onto the dance floor. The music reverberated through my chest. The locals watched, giggling as we danced. But then they joined us, playfully mimicking our moves and shaking our hands. I had no idea where I was, what time it was or who these people were, and I couldn't have been happier.

In the early morning, still buzzing, we took a taxi back to Legian. While we paid the driver, another cab pulled alongside.

'Where you go?' the driver asked.

'You just saw us get out of a taxi. Why would we need another one?' Shaun said.

'Where you go?' he persisted.

'Manchester,' I shouted, and he drove off, muttering under his breath.

Legian was dark, and the bars had closed. The chirping of crickets had replaced the music, and only a few stumbling tourists remained.

Baskets of wilted flowers lay in the street. The dried leaves and burnt-out incense bore the effects of a day in the sun. After the care with which the girl had prepared her offering earlier, there was a sadness in seeing it worn, discoloured and unappreciated. It reminded me of the girls back home, all dressed up for a big night out. Makeup perfect, hair done, nice heels. Then sometime in the early morning, they'd stumble home pissed, carrying their shoes, mascara smudged and hair dishevelled.

'Where are you staying, James?' Martin asked me.

'As of tomorrow, in a shithole with a lizard.'

'What? No. Follow me,' he insisted. He led me to their guesthouse reception, where he booked me a lizard-free, air-conditioned room for the grand sum of 50,000 rupiah.

13

CHAPTER 4
STEF

Seema and I walked to the university in the morning, ambling down a pedestrian walkway, where bare trees sprouted from squares of dirt. An ornately carved church guarded the corner. We turned down a narrow cobblestone street, just wide enough for a man on a Vespa to rumble past. I looked up, still awed by the beautiful balconies we passed each day.

"Stef, hurry up!"

I hustled, never taking my eyes off the intricate ironwork above me. I tripped, scuffing my chunky-heeled boots and angering a pigeon who warbled and flapped away. A woman in a pencil skirt and stilettos tutted and clicked past me, swinging a leather purse and trailing expensive perfume.

"Smooth," Seema said.

I laughed. "Always."

That was far from the truth. I was what you'd call "incident-prone." My most recent embarrassment being part of my physical exam just before coming to Spain. A nurse handed me large traffic controller headphones, said something about humming, and sat behind me to administer a hearing test. I hummed what I heard, trying my best to match each pitch. When I doubted I could hit a high note, I turned around to ask for guidance. "Did you say, 'Hum what you hear?'"

The nurse stared at me—twenty percent amused and eighty percent incredulous that I got accepted into college at all. "No. Raise your hand when you hear a hum."

I'm sure she told the whole office after I left.

I ran into my friend Nat by the vending machines at school. I'd first seen her at JFK airport, awkwardly dragging a long ski bag back and forth through the cordoned-off line at check-in. I saw her next when she sat beside me on the plane. We spent the whole flight to Spain chatting about outdoor sports, career plans, and ex-boyfriends, and we'd been inseparable since.

"We should plan a ski trip," Nat said, flashing her easy, gap-toothed grin.

"I met the hottest guy at the Candelaria last night!" I blurted at the same time.

"Nice!" She watched my can of Lemon Fanta land with a thump. "Who drinks pop at 10 a.m.?"

I ignored her and cracked it open. "He said he's gonna call me."

"Awwww," Nat teased as we walked down the hall. "Do you have butterflies in your stomach?"

"It's like the monarch migration in there."

Nat wrinkled her nose. "Don't say that nerdy shit to him."

I laughed and ducked into my classroom. "Okay. Later!"

I loved learning. I always made honor roll and won a foreign language award and future educator scholarship. But not everything came easily. I struck out in softball with improbable frequency, and I faked playing the clarinet in band by moving my fingers randomly without blowing into it.

I was teased for my thrift store coat and a bad perm and called Poopyshoes for years after I stepped in dog crap at the bus stop. When Craig leaned in for my first real kiss at sixteen years old, I went in full-pucker, and his tongue deflected up my nose.

So, while I looked forward to sharing my passion for culture and languages, I really wanted to be a teacher so I could help kids through a tough stage of life. Plus, teaching was a steady job with insurance, retirement, *and* time to travel. It was the perfect plan.

I watched the red hand on the classroom clock tick off every second of class. I speed-walked home, dumped my messenger bag on the floor, and perched on the edge of the couch, looking out the window at the apartment buildings across the courtyard. Their hung laundry fluttered in the breeze like bullfighters' capes.

I jumped when the phone's ring pierced the silence. I shook the nerves out of my arms, prepped a laid-back voice, and answered after the third ring.

"*Díme.*"

"*¿Estefanía?*"

"*Sí, ¿cómo estás?*"

"*Bien.* Would you like to go for a coffee? I can pick you up in twenty minutes."

Fifteen minutes later, the apartment was a disaster. Unacceptable outfits lay flung across my bed, and makeup and brushes littered our bathroom. Seema would understand. I ran down the stairs in a cloud of Country Apple body spray and sat on the cement steps outside my apartment building.

Across the narrow street at the *pescadería*, a man laid fish on a display tray of ice next to a whole octopus. Two teen girls in pleated skirts walked down the sidewalk, linked at the elbows, sharing candy from a white paper bag. They squealed when a young man walked a pack of five fluffy puppies around the corner. An elderly woman slowly pushed a cart of produce from the *frutería*. She stopped to chat to a gentleman in a tweed cap. No Miguel yet.

I caught my breath and tried to appear nonchalant. Based on my dating record, chances for embarrassment were high. Once I locked a guy's keys in his car at midnight while it was running in my parents' driveway. And the afternoon I met my college boyfriend Alex, I was hiking with new friends and slid off a rock into a river. Soaking wet, I rode back to campus in the trunk of our buddy's Jeep.

Miguel pulled up in a miniature gold Renault. I jumped in the front seat, feigning calm and confidence. A Shakira CD played.

"How were classes today?" he asked.

"Fine, thanks!"

"Good." He sang with the CD, goofily mimicking Shakira's vibrato and putting me at ease. We drove to a café, went inside, and ordered a coffee and a Coca-Cola Light.

"Where do you see yourself in the future?" Miguel asked, sipping from a miniature cup.

"What's my five-year plan?" I joked, thinking his question sounded like a job interview.

Miguel gave me a blank look.

"Never mind. I'm going to be a teacher. And I'm going to travel a lot."

"You sound very certain," Miguel said.

"Yeah. I never want to regret not doing something I always wanted to do."

He nodded contemplatively. "Maybe if you would meet the right man, your plans could change."

"Oh, I forgot," I said, quickly diverting. "I want two dogs."

"I have two dogs!" he exclaimed.

The conversation flowed effortlessly. He leaned in as if every word I spoke captivated him. Coffee cups cooled, and ice cubes melted.

"Hey, would you like to go see the dogs?" he asked.

"*Absolutamente.*"

We drove into the countryside as the sun dipped behind rolling hills and arrived at his family's country home, a white stucco cottage he called the *chalet*. Miniature Grecian statues accented the front yard, and trellises braided with ivy covered the house.

Two large dogs sprinted to the wrought iron gate. We petted them until they settled down, and then we strolled around the lawn under gleaming moonlight. Bare trees left shadows on the grass. The still of winter enveloped us—no buzz of insects, no chirp of birds. I gazed up at his handsome face, sure he'd hear my heart pounding.

"*Bueno*," he said. "It's late. I should take you back."

"*Claro*." We rode quietly. Shakira sang a simple, aching melody, and the moon followed us home.

I lay in bed that night wondering why Miguel didn't kiss me. I decided it was for the best. I didn't need or want a boyfriend, and I would be leaving in three months anyway. I didn't want a repeat of what happened with Alex.

Even so, the next morning, I shot out of bed and ran down the hall when the phone rang.

"*Díme*."

"*¿Estefanía?*"

We made plans to go for a drink that evening. Miguel picked me up in the little gold car and greeted me with a big smile.

"I need to stop by my office quickly," he said. "I forgot my house keys."

We parked outside a large metal hangar. "I sell trucks," Miguel explained as I followed him inside and up a set of metal steps. His office overlooked a dim expanse of tractor-trailers. He sat in the leather chair behind his desk, leaning back like a big shot. "Would you like to see some of our fabulous models?"

I laughed. "*¡Claro que sí! Gracias, señor.*"

He snatched his keys off the desk, and we ambled back down the steel stairs, each step echoing across the vast cement floor. Miguel climbed up and opened the cab door to one of the trucks. I hauled myself into the driver's seat and gleefully pretended to yank the air horn. I glanced behind the front seats.

"Beds? Cool!" I climbed onto the top bunk in the dark.

Miguel chuckled at my excitement and lay on the bottom bunk, looking up at me.

We talked for hours in our cozy nook. I rubbed the nape of my neck, sore from looking down so long.

Miguel slid off the bottom bunk and stood up close to me. He leaned forward with a nervous smile and brushed my hair gently with his fingers.

17

I couldn't breathe. Finally, his lips touched mine, and for a minute, I forgot I was lying in the cab of a Mack truck. He pulled away a moment later. "I should probably take you home. Sorry we did not go anywhere else."

I couldn't have imagined a better night.

That Saturday, Nat and I went to a *discoteca*. Seema was out with Tequila Shot Guy. I got home late, changed into my sweats, and collapsed on my bed. A few hours later, the bedroom door creaked open. A sliver of yellow light streamed in around Seema's slim body. "Stef!" she whispered loudly from the hall.

"Mmm. What?" I pulled my blanket over my head to block the light. "What time is it?"

"Six."

"What the hell, Seema?"

"Miguel's here!"

My eyes flew open, and I yanked the blanket down.

"We saw him at La Candelaria," she continued. "He came back with us!"

It was *way* too soon for him to see me like this. Raccoon mascara, bedhead, morning breath. Sweatpants and no bra under a baggy Dave Matthews Band concert T-shirt. And no way out.

Miguel's silhouette appeared in the light behind Seema's, and she went back to the living room.

"*Hola, mi niña*," he whispered and flicked on the bedroom light. "How are you?"

"Tired." I winked and quickly smoothed my hair.

He sat next to me on my bed. "Sorry." He suddenly looked like he realized this might not have been a good idea. "It's that, I wanted very much to see you."

I smiled reassuringly. "*Está bien.*"

From the shelf above my headboard, Miguel took down a framed photo of the skyline of Pittsburgh. "Peets-boorg?"

"*Sí.*"

"*Es fantástico.* I will see it someday."

I grinned and imagined introducing him to friends and family, ignoring the fact he wouldn't be able to talk to anyone.

As if reading my mind, Miguel said, "I need to learn English."

"Okay! What first?"

"*Tú tienes los ojos bonitos.*"

I smiled and translated: "You have beautiful eyes." I found a notepad, drew a line down the middle of the paper, and wrote the Spanish on one side, the English on the other.

"Yoo haf bew-tee-full ice," he pronounced. He caressed my cheek and kissed me sweetly. Time passed, unacknowledged.

A quick knock on the door jolted us back to reality. White sunlight peeked around the edge of my curtain.

"Are you ready to go?" Tequila Shot Guy asked from the hall.

"*Sí, un momento.*" Miguel grabbed my notepad and wrote a sentence on the Spanish side. He handed it to me nervously. "How does one say?"

"*Creo que me estoy enamorando,*" I read aloud with shallow breath. I wrote the translation on the paper and pronounced, "I believe I am falling in love."

Miguel walked to the door and repeated, "I beleef I ahm fallink een loff." Then he slipped out before I could respond.

CHAPTER 5
JAMES

I travelled from Bali to Australia. I wasn't there for an adventure, as I didn't deserve it. But my year-long work visa would allow me to hit pause on the mess awaiting me back home. I tried not to think about what I'd do after it expired, but I hoped in the meantime I could earn enough that I could eventually pay back some of my debt.

In a downtown Melbourne hostel, I befriended Valerie, a short Irish girl with spiky purple hair and an infectious laugh. Though I didn't always understand her Cork accent, I enjoyed its lyrical lilt and the way most of her sentences ended with the word 'so,' making me wait for more words that never came. Also, she did my laundry once.

I didn't ask her to. I'd walked into the large laundry room one day, and it was filled with backpackers who all knew what they were doing. I didn't even recognise half the machines. We never had a tumble dryer at home, and I had no clue what clothes were even allowed in it, so I turned around and went back to the dorm. Valerie heard me talking about it and offered to wash them for me, and I accepted.

Baby steps, James.

I had to get a job, so I bought the local newspaper every day to sift through the employment section. Most of the ads were for cooks in restaurants or waiters with experience. I grimaced as an accounting vacancy caught my eye.

One day Valerie invited me to go fruit picking with her friends in a town called Euston. Knowing nothing more than we'd be on a grape farm in the middle of nowhere for two months, I accepted.

'G'day. How ya going?' our new boss Mike said softly. He was a short, muscular man in his mid-twenties. A loose singlet emblazoned with a company logo barely covered his torso. Mike ran the family farm, started by his Italian immigrant parents.

'Jump in.' He pointed to his ute. Weary from a twelve-hour bus ride, the five of us threw our bags in the back and climbed on.

The cool morning air whipped past us as we drove out of the small town and onto a dusty road. The desolate land reminded me of the movie *Texas Chainsaw Massacre*. We didn't know this man or exactly where he was taking us. None of us owned mobile phones, though I doubted we could get a signal anyway.

We stopped in front of a rickety shed and climbed off the truck amidst a cloud of dust.

'The house has got running water, but it's from the river, so don't drink it,' Mike said.

'What house?' I asked.

'There, mate.' Mike pointed to the shed. 'Fill up ya water bottles from the rain tank. Work starts at 6am tomorrow.' He waved and left.

We stood in silence for a long moment.

'It'll be grand, so.' Valerie declared and pushed open the door.

It smelled like cow shit inside. A layer of dirt and fine gravel lined the concrete floor. Ill-fitting windows clattered in their frames. When I pushed one open, a breeze blew in with a loud whoosh and swirled the gravel. The corrugated tin roof moaned.

I imagined myself as an archaeologist discovering an ancient tomb as I examined the artefacts: an old TV with a crooked antenna and perhaps the first refrigerator ever made. The living room had a wonky table and six rusty chairs. Ripped vinyl cushions exposed their yellow stuffing. Peeking into one of the two tiny bedrooms, I declared, 'This bed's mine,' and dove onto the squeaky mattress. *Home Sweet Home.*

We walked into town. Town being a few houses, a caravan park, a shop, a petrol station, a pub and grapes. Lots of them. A boat ramp to the Murray River sat at the end of the main street. We planted ourselves on the grass under a cloudless sky. A flock of white, squawking cockatoos flew overhead, and at first, I thought they'd all escaped from a pet shop.

As the others swam, I thought about my old job. In a stagnant office, my desk stood buried under a sea of invoices and bank statements. Hidden amongst them, my fourth cup of coffee left a stain on a folder. People in drab suits talked around me. 'Balance sheet, profit and loss, audit, stock control,' they mumbled with glum faces. With every client's accounts finished and filed away, a piece of myself got filed away too.

On my way out of the office on my last day, the boss of the firm stopped me in the hall. 'So, James. Australia. What will you do there?'

'I don't know, to be honest.'

He frowned. 'And how will you make money?'

'Don't know that either,' I said with a big grin and walked out the door.

Valerie joined me on the grass. 'You OK, James?'

Her question dragged me out of my old office and back to the river. 'Yeah, just thinking about my former life.' Though I wasn't looking forward to picking grapes for ten hours a day, anything was better than what I'd left behind.

Early the next morning, Mike presented each of us with razor-sharp shears. 'Make sure you cut the bunches. Don't pull 'em. Turn 'em over, trim off the bad ones and put 'em in your bucket.'

'Then what?' I said.

'You do it again. You get paid per bucket, so fill as many as you can. Lunch is at twelve. You knock off at five.' And with that, he left.

We each chose a row of grapes and began.

Standing at roughly five foot nothing, Valerie was the perfect height for grape picking. She zoomed up and down the rows. At six feet, I was the wrong height. Constant bending sent my back into spasm, and squatting burned my muscles. Kneeling on the hard dirt shredded the skin off my legs. I rotated the three techniques all day before limping to the shack, exhausted and dehydrated, with lines of dried blood down my shins.

We removed our shoes and tended to our cuts in fatigued silence. We took turns showering in the river water, though we didn't feel truly clean. Valerie set about chopping vegetables and cooking chicken on a gas stove while the rest of us swept the floors and filled bottles from the rain tank outside. Valerie served dinner, and we sat on tetanus-riddled chairs, devouring her delicious stir fry. We discussed our picking numbers for the day, and as the meal went on, smiles slowly crept back onto our weary faces.

The vines provided little shade, and over the next few weeks, my translucent British skin baked and peeled. Cuts crisscrossed my palms, and calluses covered my fingertips. Everything ached. Despite the harsh working conditions, I knuckled down, picked the grapes, filled the buckets, swept the floors and cashed a paycheque. My back longed for the comfort of my old office chair, but for the first time, in a long time, I had a healthy mind.

I'd learned the value of hard work from my mum. She raised me and my brother and sister, cooked, cleaned, did the shopping, washed and ironed our clothes, worked two part-time jobs and held the family together on her low wages while my dad drank or gambled most of his away.

Antagonizing Valerie was my only source of entertainment. I'd bend down under the vines and hurl grapes at her bare legs on a daily basis.

'Ouch. Fuck off, will ya?' she'd scream from amongst the vines.

'Sorry, shitty-arse.' I'd reply, knowing full well that one, she wouldn't believe the sincerity of my apology and two, she hated my new nickname for her.

'You're a shitty arse, so.'

'So...please throw another grape at me?'

'What?'

'OK, then.' I launched another grape.

Once, while serving dinner, she poured a glob of gravy on me and burst into laughter. When she walked away, I grabbed my fork and poked her in the arse. She let out a high-pitched squeal and glared at me. I flew off my chair and out the door.

She chased me relentlessly like she always did. Just as she got close, she fell, grazing her knee on the hard dirt road. I looked down at her, wracked with guilt.

'You OK, mate?'

She replied with a shriek followed by giggles. I helped her up, and we walked back laughing.

On one 43°C day, the hot wind caked us in dust. Tired and thirsty, I resorted to pulling the grapes from the vines to save time. Though Mike warned against it, I held my shears up and yanked a stem onto the sharp blades.

Blood sprayed from my hand like in a scene from a low-budget horror movie. I dropped to my knees and rested against a grapevine. Sweat rolled down my dirty forehead, filtering through my eyebrows and dripping into my eyes. Feeling woozy, I closed them. I heard loud shouting in Italian, and Mike's dad grabbed my trembling hand. I felt a cold liquid on my wound, and my eyes bolted open. Through sweat and tears, I saw the remedy pouring from the old farmer's hip flask, revealing a deep cut on the bone of my swollen thumb.

I found Mike and showed him. 'You need an x-ray, mate. You'll have to get the bus to Mildura.'

'Why not here?' I asked.

'You can only get x-rays on Tuesdays out here.'

The following morning on the bus ride to Mildura, the sparse countryside whizzed by my window. My thumb throbbed under the bandage Valerie had wrapped it in. My thoughts were never far away from money, and the prospect of losing this job made me nervous. Again. Nervous about going home. Nervous about facing my debts.

I was supposed to go to uni and get a good job. I'd tried.

At age seventeen, while taking my A-Levels, I worked part-time in a busy bar as a glass collector on Friday and Saturday nights and in a timber yard all day on Saturdays. It was exhausting, and I barely had time to study. To the disappointment of teachers who knew I could do better, I scraped through with very low marks and was barely accepted into a metropolitan university.

The government had gotten rid of university grants, and I didn't want to put a financial strain on my parents, so I took a year out to work and save up. I took on more hours at the timber yard and eventually went full-time at a supermarket warehouse, working ten-hour shifts filling large cages in cold storage.

One day I saw an ad for a new government initiative called a modern apprenticeship. I would work four days in an office, and one day I'd attend a local training centre for an accounting qualification. I wrote to the university to decline my place and swapped my gloves and steel-toed boots for a shirt and tie. I worked just as much and earned just as little.

After a long day at the clinic, thankfully, I found out no bones were broken in my thumb, but I did have to take a few days off from grape picking. I sat in the shed, switching back and forth between the two TV channels, one of which was black and white. I was adjusting the antenna when Valerie walked in to check on me.

'How's your day off, so?' she said.

'Super!' I replied sarcastically. 'Actually, I'm used to being off sick.'

'Really?'

'Yeah, I was sick a lot last year. I got tonsillitis about once a month.' I said. 'I had fever dreams, night sweats and chronic fatigue. I was knackered all the time. I had so many antibiotics they stopped working.'

Valerie looked sad. 'You seem OK, now.'

'I had 'em removed a couple of weeks before I left England.'

'Sounds awful.'

'It was. It made me miserable, to be honest.'

'Sorry to hear that. Glad you're OK, now!" Val smiled. "See you later. I need to get back to work.'

At the end of the season, Mike invited our group to dine with his family as a thank you for our hard work. We sat around a long wooden table with Mike's dad at the head. His family waved their hands, punctuating a lively conversation we didn't understand.

It reminded me of Christmas dinner growing up, the only time my family ate together. My brother would bring a long fold-up table over from the community centre, and we'd set it up while mum cooked. We'd eat off the good plates, watching the Queen's speech and James Bond movies. That was until my dad banned Christmas dinner, citing too much hard work for my mum. Not true. She was heartbroken. He just wanted her to himself. For a spell when I was very young, he forbade her to leave the house unless it was for work or food shopping.

I slurped up a massive bowl of pasta and homemade sauce and sat back in my seat, full and thankful for the delicious meal. When Mike's mom cleared the table and brought out some freshly baked bread, I secretly opened the top button on my shorts. Roasted chestnuts, more pasta, goat. I could hardly breathe.

After the last of the dishes had been devoured, Mike's dad returned from the barn with a large glass jar filled with red grapes in a clear liquid. He strained to lift it onto the table, speaking in Italian while Mike translated.

'This is grappa that's been fermenting for two years. He's been saving it for a special occasion and wanted to share it with us.'

'What's grappa?' I asked.

'Strong liquor made from grapes,' he said. 'Dad carries it around the farm in a hip flask.'

I shook my head. 'Please tell your dad this is too much.'

But the lid was already off. Pungent alcohol fumes overpowered the garlic.

He passed the jar to Mike's mum. She stabbed several large grapes with her fork, eating them whole with no visible reaction. She pushed the jar to me and smiled.

Fuck.

The others looked on with open mouths. Valerie bit her lip to keep from laughing. I leaned over the jar, and the vapours stung my eyes. Mike's dad gestured with his fork. I skewered the smallest grape and placed it gingerly into my mouth.

I let it sit there for a moment. The room went silent. I bit down and gagged on half of the grape while the other half dribbled down my shirt, and everyone burst into laughter. I faked a smile as my throat burned. Mike's mum nodded in approval.

After the grappa, we thanked Mike's family and shook Mike's hand. Though this job was gruelling, I enjoyed the labour. The physical suffering was far easier than the alternative.

The next morning, I stood at the bus stop. Valerie came to wave me off. Two months of living in a shed was enough. I'd earned sufficient money to keep travelling for a bit longer. I didn't know what I wanted out of life, but I definitely knew I didn't want to go home.

I turned to Valerie. 'Why are you staying again?' I asked.

'I got a job as a barmaid at an Irish pub in Mildura.'

'I feel sorry for them.'

Valerie scowled and punched me on the arm before laughing.

'You gonna miss me throwing grapes at ya?'

'No!' she said with watery eyes.

I leaned down to hug her. 'I'll miss you too, shitty-arse.'

CHAPTER 6
STEF

I lounged on my towel on a black sand beach, letting the tropical sun toast my winter skin. Nat and I had flown to the Spanish-speaking island of Tenerife with two other classmates, Myah and Erica.

Miguel and I had been inseparable for a few weeks, but when Erica suggested we go to the Canary Islands, I couldn't pass it up.

"I'm excited to hang out with those guys from the hotel tonight," Myah said, running a comb through her short raven hair.

"Make out with them, you mean," Erica said.

Myah hurled a flip-flop at her.

Erica blocked it and lay back on her towel, topping up her tanning bed glow with actual solar rays. Her belly button ring glimmered.

I pulled my tankini down over my pale belly and ran my fingers through the dark, warm sand. Ash Wednesday, the start of Lent, was a few days away. "Remember that you are dust," the priest would say as he dipped his thumb in a pot of ash and smeared a cross on my forehead.

Raised Catholic, I'd observed Lent—a spiritual preparation for Easter—my entire life. Forty days of prayer, sacrifice, and fish sandwiches. I never imagined I'd celebrate Carnaval, the bawdy festival preceding it. Drinking, dancing, and debauching were not only accepted but encouraged. Do it now, while you still can.

"The guys told me everyone dresses in costumes," I said. "We should throw something together."

Dad would have been disappointed I hadn't researched "Tenerife Carnaval traditions" and packed two costumes, just in case. Conversations spanning my childhood often ended with Dad urging Cassie and me to do something "just in case," like taking a jacket everywhere and always peeing before getting in the car.

"Look at this ocean, guys. The palm trees!" I raved.

"The tits," Myah said. European women of all ages and body types lay topless along the beach. "You girls want to?"

Erica sat up. "I'll do it!"

I looked down at my tankini, suddenly embarrassed by my modesty. I looked at Nat, and she shrugged.

Erica whipped off her top, revealing a hoop through each nipple.

My eyebrows flew off my forehead. "Erica!"

"Oh yeah, my door knockers."

The rest of us pulled off our tops. My heart raced, and I scanned the beach. Nobody cared. I lay back on my towel and shut my eyes, amused by the feeling of the breeze on my boobs.

A bit later, I put my top on to walk down the beach. A young man sat in a long T-shirt at the emptier far end, staring at the water. He seemed lonely.

"*Hola*," I said and sat next to him, trying to be kind.

From my new line of sight, I could see his T-shirt was *all* he was wearing. There lay his penis and testicles, nestled in the soft pewter sand. I fumbled out a few more words, holding very direct eye contact. Then I politely said goodbye and ran away.

"Are you gonna tell Miguel you were looking at other guy's dicks on vacation?" Myah called from our hotel bathroom.

Nat cackled.

"Shut up!" I frowned at her but couldn't help laughing.

Erica sat on the couch, smoking a cigarette in her underwear. Myah smoothed the fringe on a plastic hula skirt she'd bought at a souvenir shop and held out a matching skirt for Erica. "Bitch, let's go!"

Erica sneered and stood up to get dressed.

Nat wore a tie-dyed Peace Frog T-shirt. "Can you help me draw a peace sign on my cheek?" she asked, handing me a blue eyeliner pencil.

I pieced together a funky outfit of turquoise pants, a sparkly fuchsia tube top, Erica's blue sunglasses, and blond pigtails. I glanced in the mirror. I looked like Baby Spice.

Myah jingled the car keys. "*¡Vamos!*"

Myah parked our rental car on a palm tree-lined road near the beach. A colorful halo radiated over the town center, leading us like a beacon to the party. We turned a corner into a plaza filled with light and music. On a large stage, drag queens sashayed in glittering gowns and massive feathered headdresses.

I stood still and quiet, taking it in. I never wanted this party to end.

Soon I'd return home, student teach, and graduate college. Then work. Forever.

I'd always been the sober one at the frat party. The church-going good girl. I followed the rules because I wanted to please people—especially my parents. Misbehaving didn't give me a rush. It gave me diarrhea. But now, I stood on the cusp of adulthood, having never experienced a crazy adolescence.

Do it now, while you still can.

"Babe." Nat grabbed me by the arm and snapped me out of my trance. "Wine?"

"Wine," I agreed.

The plaza heaved with Carnaval revelers. Glamorous cabaret dancers showed off fishnet stockings. Two Eves wrapped themselves in giant toy snakes. A posh Marie Antoinette, lips lined in a permanent pucker, strutted in a pink gown. They all were men, celebrating the Tenerife Carnaval tradition of dressing in drag. I danced with them and insisted they all take photos with me.

We found the Spanish guys from our hotel. They'd dressed as a pirate, Jesus, and a particularly disheveled woman. Myah locked lips with Pirate immediately. Jesus and Disheveled Woman attended to the rest of us, welcoming us into their group and making sure we had full cups of wine.

"So, you're looking very voluptuous," I said to Disheveled Woman.

He swept back the synthetic hairs of his straggly wig. "*Gracias*. I think I look ravishing with my new *tetas*," he replied, jiggling his crooked fake knockers.

I laughed and then noticed we were missing someone. "Dammit. Where's Erica?"

Nat and I wove through the packed plaza, scanning hazy faces until we found our hula girl flirting with a random guy. I dragged her to our adopted corner of the square. "Erica, we should stay together."

Myah and Pirate were still making out. The makeup from his drawn-on beard had smeared all over Myah's face.

Jesus welcomed us back. "You're like the mom of the group," he told me. He bought a parrot-shaped helium balloon from a street vendor and tied it to Erica's wrist as a tracking device. "Better?"

I gave him a thumbs-up. "*Sí*."

Jesus took my hand and spun me round and round to the music. He broke into an oblivious grin as he stomped on my feet, dancing with a fervor that required several loincloth adjustments.

Hours later, city workers swept plastic cups from the cobblestones as the early morning crowd thinned out. Half-costumed merrymakers milled about, carrying wigs and accessories that now annoyed them. Musicians packed instruments into battered cases. We scanned the plaza for a floating parrot.

We found Erica munching on a candy apple, unaware she was lost.

"Erica, we gotta fly home in like, an hour." I dragged her, parrot balloon trailing behind, back to Myah and Pirate. "Myah, let's go!" I awkwardly tapped her on the shoulder.

Myah and Pirate finally peeled their lips apart, and she gazed up at him. He ran his fingers through her hair, ignoring her new goatee.

Nat, Erica, and I hugged our new friends and walked out of the city toward the rental car. Soon we'd be back to winter, back to school. I was buzzing. From wine, from excitement, from feeling less like—me. Rebellion burst out of me, regrettably, in the form of an Obnoxious Drunk American Tourist.

"Hey girls," I said, "let's go topless in Tenerife one last time!"

We pulled off our tops and ran down the dark, empty street shouting, "Topless in Tenerife!" I laughed so hard I doubled over, clutching my bare stomach. The sidewalk blurred.

"Let's go!" Nat called back. A big blue smear covered her right cheek.

I sprinted to our rental car, waving my pink tube top like a flag, and jumped into the backseat.

Myah yanked the car into the street, still adjusting her bikini top. She was sober—it's hard to drink wine with a pirate's tongue down your throat.

Myah and Nat chattered up front, but Erica passed out instantly, snoring in the backseat next to me. I reflected on the day as the dawn sky blushed. I felt free. I rolled down the window and stuck my arm into the warm, briny air. "Woohoo! ¡Carnaval!"

When I returned from Tenerife, Miguel and I spent every moment we could together. One day in March, he took me to the chalet to meet his family. The yard had exploded in green. Leafy trees provided shade for napping dogs. Clusters of colorful blossoms dotted the grass, and the breeze carried their delicate scent. My chest felt tight as we approached the door.

Miguel stepped inside, and I followed closely behind. His mom gave me a hug before he'd finished introducing me. His brother, his sister, and her fiancé welcomed me kindly, and an assembly line of cheek kissing commenced. The tension in my chest melted away.

His mom returned to the kitchen, and the rest of us settled in the living room on overstuffed couches. A rustic fireplace dominated the room, and a lifetime of fragrant smoke permeated the terra cotta walls. Smells of meat and garlic wafted in from the kitchen. "Food is ready!" his mom called out.

I walked into the kitchen. "Let me help you."

She loaded our arms with platters. On the way to the table, she dropped one. Food and ceramic smashed on the floor.

"*¡Me cago en la leche!*" she exclaimed.

I looked at Miguel, face blank with confusion, sure I misunderstood. Everyone burst out laughing.

"I shit in the milk?" I repeated.

"It is a weird expression," Miguel agreed.

"I love it," I said. "I'm going to say it as often as possible."

We cleaned up, sat at a long, rustic wooden table and began feasting on herbed olives, shrimp with garlic, chicken croquettes, and paper-thin slices of cured ham. His mom brought out a dish with octopus tentacles sprinkled in paprika. It was chewy and gelatinous, like nothing I'd ever tasted before. I loved it.

"This food is amazing!" I gushed, and Miguel's mom grinned.

We talked at the table for hours. Before we left, his siblings and mom gave me hugs and kisses as if I were already part of the family. His sister touched me on the arm. "You should fly back for the wedding in September."

"Wow, I'd love to, *gracias*."

I beamed with relief when we got into the car. "Your family was so nice to me."

"Of course! You make me happy. So that makes them happy."

"You make me happy, too."

As we drove home, I watched country fields morph into city streets. Miguel dropped me off with a kiss, and I walked up to my apartment. Seema was out with a new guy. I shut the door, draped my jacket over a chair, and sat on the couch in the dark, silent room. I slumped forward, chin in my hands.

I loved Miguel. I'd just met his family, and we'd discussed him meeting mine in Pittsburgh in August. It was a natural step. But our situation wasn't natural. We'd done a great job of ignoring the fact that I had to finish my degree and start a career soon—in the United States.

I'm sure his family wondered why we were getting so serious. Suddenly, I did too. We'd only known each other for a few weeks. Our relationship was barreling ahead like a runaway train, even though in two months, we'd run out of track.

The next day, Miguel came over to cook me dinner. He carried a bag from the market and presented a Styrofoam tray of what looked like gray spaghetti.

"What is it?" I asked, curious about the spaghetti's teensy black

31

eyeballs.

"*Angulas.*"

Miguel dumped the baby eels into a pan with garlic and a splash of olive oil.

Seema peeked her head in the kitchen. "*¡Hola!*"

Miguel smiled. "*Hola, Seema.* Would you like some eels?"

Seema frowned. "*No, gracias.*" She waved and continued down the hall.

"I saw the movie *The Beach* with Seema today," I said. "It made me want to go to Thailand. I may add it to the list after New Zealand."

"I am not even sure where Thailand is." He held out a fork with one little sizzling eel. "Here, try."

I tasted it and nodded in approval. "*Delicioso.*"

Miguel looked intently at me as if trying to decide what to say next. "So, I have started thinking of jobs I could get you for the summer. You could live with us in the city apartment."

He looked into my eyes, nervously awaiting the answer to his unspoken question. I stepped closer and kissed him. Then I grabbed a plate and loaded it up with eels.

I lay in bed that night, thinking. Suddenly, I was crying. I didn't recognize myself. I'd always liked to have fun, but being good, responsible, and predictable had also been a big part of my identity. Now, I rarely studied and I went out several times a week. And I was considering staying in Spain instead of going home to work at my old summer camp like I'd planned.

I didn't quite know who I was anymore. The quick change threw me off-balance, but it wasn't that I didn't like who I was becoming. I did.

Nat and I met at the train station for our ski trip to the French Alps at the end of March. I threw my duffel over my shoulder and boarded. Nat struggled with her luggage. She'd shoved all her clothes and toiletries into her ski bag, plumping it up and adding twenty pounds to it. It was like watching Steve Irwin wrestle a crocodile.

"What the hell were you thinking?" I asked, laughing.

"I don't know. I thought it would be easier with just one bag."

"Is it?"

She shot me a deadly look and dumped the beast in the aisle. My new cell phone, an old Nokia of Miguel's, vibrated with a text.

> *Miguel: When you leave, it is going to be very hard.*
> *Stef: I know. What should we do?*
> *Miguel: Take me on your travels with you.*
> *Stef: Okay, next stop—New Zealand!*

I smiled, but I knew he didn't mean it. Miguel didn't seem to have much interest in traveling. I tucked my phone in my backpack.

"Miguel?" Nat asked. "Sucks you're leaving soon."

"Yeah. He's going to try to find me a job for the summer, though."

"Aww! He's a keeper."

I nodded. "It's funny. It never occurred to me that I could just—not go home."

"Really?" Nat feigned shock.

I elbowed her. "Shut up."

Nat laughed. "Well, I think it would be great."

"Yeah. It would," I said, though since Miguel's suggestion, I hadn't thought much about the details. What kind of job would I do? I certainly couldn't sell tractor trailers. I hadn't shifted into planning mode yet, which was unlike me, but I was enjoying the idea of staying a few more months.

After a layover lunch, Nat and I got lost in the pastel maze of Toulouse. The French town's distinctive pink stone buildings closed in around us, three or four stories high, covered in shutters of sky blue or mint green. Lantern-shaped streetlights dangled from twirling wrought iron brackets on the front of each building.

"*¡Me cago en la leche!*" I exclaimed, worrying about missing our next train.

"Ask that guy where the station is," Nat said.

"We'd know where it is if you didn't insist on dragging that freaking bag all over looking for a McDonalds."

She slurped her chocolate milkshake through a straw. "You know you love me."

I approached a French man standing on the corner. "*Excusez-moi, où est la gare, s'il vous plaît?*"

"*Quoi?*" He wrinkled his nose and furrowed his eyebrows in mock Gallic confusion.

"*La gare?*"

The man stared across the street and casually sucked on a cigarette.

Nat jumped in, exchanging vocabulary for volume. "Train? Choo-choo!" she blared. She hunched under the weight of her giant bag, bent her knees and made a chugging motion with the hand holding her milkshake.

The French man watched her with pity. "Oh, *la gare!*" he said, like he'd deciphered the babbling of a one-year-old. He smirked and pointed down the lane.

Nat and I finally found the station, boarded the train, and after sixteen hours and three more train transfers, we arrived at our destination. Outside the small station in Bourg St. Maurice, my English buddy Pete leaned his lanky frame on a hotel van. I'd worked with him the summer before at a camp in Pennsylvania, near where his brother lived.

I gave him a big hug. "This is Nat. And her bag."

His mouth dropped open. "Bloody hell. What is this devil sausage?" He picked up the bag, groaned comically, and heaved it into the van. "Let's go, ladies."

Pete drove us up a narrow mountain road that carved through a thick layer of white, switchbacking as it climbed—so many times I lost count. We passed small clusters of gray and tan stucco buildings, their sloping wooden roofs capped with snow.

Pete brought us to the hotel bar that night to meet his friends. Large windows offered expansive views of the mountains and alpine villages. I sank into a squishy couch next to a guy named Kenneth.

"You were at the summer camp with Pete, right?" he asked. "You should come up in May. We run a camp for English senior school groups."

A new adventure. If I were going to delay going home, wouldn't it be better to do something different? That's why I was traveling—to soak up as much newness as possible. Working at an Alpine camp with British people would be amazing.

Miguel barged into my thoughts. Stirring baby eels, asking me to stay.

Were we just denying the inevitable? My future was in America. Miguel was a keeper, but we'd only been together six weeks, and I wasn't ready to keep anybody yet.

"Yeah! I'm interested!" I blurted without hesitation. I instantly felt excited and guilty at the same time.

Nat looked over at me, wide-eyed. Sensing her surprise, I avoided her glance. I was surprised, too. I'd just jumped at the chance to spend my summer in France—not in Spain, not with my doting boyfriend.

The following day while Pete and Nat skied, the camp director interviewed me and hired me on the spot. I walked out of the office in shock and quickly dialed Miguel's number. Any hesitation would allow me to back out. I unconsciously picked at the hem of my sweater while I waited for him to pick up.

"¡Hola mi niña!"

I stopped breathing for a second.

"¡Hola!" I told him about the long journey, the crisp air, and the dazzling scenery. "Um . . . they—they run a summer camp and offered me a job."

No response.

"It would be an amazing opportunity, and I'd get to practice my French with some of the staff and people in town," I quickly explained, pacing in a tight loop.

"Whatever you want, *mi niña*."

"Nothing has to change. I still want you to visit me in the States," I said.

"*Claro*."

"And I still want to come to your sister's wedding. I'm sorry. It's just a really amazing opportunity," I said again.

Pete rapped on the door. "Stef?"

"Okay. I'm going to go—my friend is back. *Adiós*."

"*Adiós*."

I hung up and opened the door with a shaking hand.

"Nat's still skiing, but I wanted to see how the interview went." Pete plopped onto the bed.

I noticed I'd unraveled some of my sweater. "Good. I'm hired," I said flatly.

"Brilliant. I knew you would be."

I bit my lip and stared out the window. Heavy snow whitewashed the view of the mountains.

"The boyfriend?" Pete asked.

"Yeah." I sat next to him. "I mean, if I'm going home eventually, what's the point? Right?" Pete just listened, aware I wasn't really asking him. "Why invest all your time and emotion into something that's not going to work, probably," I continued.

"Well, people do move to different countries to stay together. You met my brother in Pennsylvania—he did. You just don't want to."

I put my head in my hands. "Why am I such an asshole?"

Pete chuckled. "I've heard this from you before."

"I know. I know!" I shook my head vigorously, as if I could dissolve the memory like a drawing from an Etch-a-Sketch.

Alex. My sweet college boyfriend. My first real relationship. We'd started dating a few months before I went to summer camp. He was sweet but content to never leave Pennsylvania. At camp, I had a blast with adventurous counselors from around the world. I didn't miss Alex like I should have. I realized he wasn't forever, and I broke up with him when I returned home.

I stood in Alex's apartment that fall semester, in the living room with scratchy carpet and a thin mandala tapestry thumb-tacked to the wall. The sky was dull that day. A gust of wind blew crispy brown leaves past the window. Alex looked at me with watery eyes and said, "I feel like I waited all summer for you to come home, and you never did."

The memory always made my stomach hurt. "What's wrong with me?"

"Hey. You're *not* an asshole." Pete nudged me in the side. "You just know what you want."

"I shouldn't be in relationships."

Pete stood up. "I doubt that's true. Shall we go get some lunch?" He held out his hand.

I grabbed it, and he pulled me off the bed. "Yes. Please."

CHAPTER 7
JAMES

After grape-picking, I stopped at a distant relative's home in a coastal town called Warrnambool. Distant as in my brother's wife's dad's cousin Chris, and his family. Whom I'd never met before. They welcomed me into their home, cooked me a meal, served me home-brewed grog and invited me to stay with them for a while.

I only planned on staying for a few days, but their hospitality made it hard to leave. I especially enjoyed a comfortable bed and daily steaming hot showers in clean water. I hid my fruit picking trainers, their rancid smell a reminder of my lowly backpacker status.

'We could help you find a job if you wanna stick around for a bit.' Chris's Scouse accent was still strong, even after thirty years of living Down Under.

'Doing what?' I asked.

He thought for a moment. 'You could work at the abattoir in town. They're always looking for workers.'

I cringed. 'You're joking. I'm not butchering animals.'

'It won't be blood and guts and all that,' he assured me. 'I worked there once, and they just had me scanning barcodes.'

The idea still repulsed me, but I liked staying with Chris's family and felt guilty about doing nothing but sitting around eating their food and drinking their beer. 'I guess I could handle that.'

Chris woke me at 4am with a hot cup of coffee and two slices of toast. I rubbed my hands together and breathed warm air into them as we walked to the car. Windscreen wiper blades carved arches in condensation while the headlights penetrated the misty morning air. I turned on the radio, and we headed to the abattoir.

In a dimly lit reception, a short man handed me a cracked biro and a clipboard stacked with forms to fill in. Form One: name, address, phone number, etc. Form Two: If you accidentally die, you can't sue us. Form Three: If you contract black lung or bubonic plague, you can't sue us.

'What's taking so long?' Chris said.

'What the hell is black lung?' I glared at him. 'I'm signing me bloody life away, here.'

'Don't worry about those James, you'll be away from all that. It's just procedure.'

I completed the forms declaring I was OK with dying for minimum wage and handed them back.

A tall, burly man entered, dressed in a white boiler suit that pulled tight over his belly. He wore bright green Wellington boots and a fluffy white hairnet. He scowled. "I need three today," the big, angry clown announced, scouring the room for potential workers.

I sat up straight and pushed out my chest.

He picked two men before looking my way. 'You! Let's go.'

He led us down a dingy hallway to an equipment room. An attendant threw our outfits at us along with long green rubber gloves. I pictured a veterinarian birthing a cow before remembering animals didn't come here to live.

We followed the man down a series of corridors with buzzing yellow fluorescent lights and exited into the dark morning, crossed a courtyard and climbed a flight of stairs into another building. A burst of white light hit me. I raised my arms and squinted.

Then my eyelids were prized open like a boxer being revived with smelling salts. *What the fuck is that smell?* It wasn't meat, and it wasn't shit. It was chemicals. I assumed it had to be industrial strength to mask whatever happened in this room.

My eyes finally adjusted. Skinned cattle carcasses entered the room dangling from an assembly line of hooks. A worker slit a cow from top to bottom; its innards spewed onto the white floor. I gagged and looked away. 'Don't worry,' the man said. 'You fellas won't be working in here.'

'Thank fuck for that,' I whispered to one of my coworkers.

After two left turns and a couple of rights down identical hallways, the man stopped and pointed into an open room. 'This is you, James. Go in and wait for Kelly. She'll tell ya what to do.' He left with the other two men.

I stood by a pristine, stainless-steel workbench facing a white wall. Loud, clinking metal echoed around me. I shivered in the cold room, taking sharp, shallow breaths.

A large tray with jiggly brown lumps was placed in front of me.

'I'm Kelly.'

I looked over to see a pale, freckled woman with ginger hair that poked through the holes in her hairnet. 'These are pig's livers. The arteries are still attached, so you gotta cut 'em.'

'Wait, what?'

She placed a Y-shaped device with sharp blades onto the bench, picked up a slimy liver with one hand and held out its long, cream-coloured, stringy artery with the other. Bringing them down forcefully into the point of the Y, she separated them. 'Put the livers in this other tray and throw the arteries in the bin.'

'Excuse me…'

'Make sure you inspect 'em good, coz some livers got black spots on 'em, and they get thrown away too.'

She left me there motionless. *Barcodes my arse!*

I picked up a cold liver, its squishy texture apparent even through rubber gloves. After fumbling to grab the clinging artery, I sliced it free. It clung to my glove. I shook my hand, and it flew off, leaving a gooey residue. My stomach churned. My throat tightened. My mouth filled with saliva.

Kelly barged me out of the way and set down another tray. 'These are sheep hearts.' She picked up a hose from a nearby sink and sprayed them. Blood splattered all over my bright white boiler suit, some drops hitting my cheeks.

I jumped back a few feet. 'What the fuck?'

Kelly didn't flinch.

I surveyed the room. 'How do I get out?'

'Why?' She rolled her eyes.

'I need to get out.' I was light-headed.

'Do you need some fresh air?'

'No, I'm done. I'm off.'

She pointed to a door and I ran, my feet slipping on the floor. I peeled off my slimy glove and wiped my face, hurried through the labyrinth of hallways and followed exit signs back to the equipment room, where I yanked my uniform off and threw it into a pile on the floor.

'You won't get paid anything,' the attendant announced from behind her newspaper.

I didn't care that I wouldn't get paid. Hopefully, I'd find something else soon, and my fruit picking money would tide me over for a month or so if I was careful. I used the payphone in reception to ask Chris to pick me up.

'You OK, James?' Chris asked as I got in the car.

'I don't wanna talk about it.' I wound my window down to let the air purify my nostrils. I turned the radio off, and we sat in silence for the duration of the ride home. I felt terrible about quitting after five minutes, considering Chris set the job up and drove me there at the crack of dawn. But I hoped he'd understand once I could bring myself to describe what happened. I could now add 'liver artery cutter' after 'accountant' to the official list of jobs I would never do again.

Back at the house, Carolynn, Chris's wife, cleaned the breakfast dishes while Emily, their youngest, sat at the table drawing. Carolynn leaned on the counter. 'Your face is white as a sheet. You alright, James?'

'No, I'm not actually,' I replied.

'No barcodes then?' Chris asked, furrowing his brow.

I shook my head. 'Nope. Not one.'

He grimaced. 'Sorry, mate.'

I joined Emily at the table. She handed me a white sheet of paper and some crayons, and I calmly coloured a lush, open field with cheerful pigs, sheep and cows under the beautiful Australian sunshine.

CHAPTER 8
STEF

Miguel pulled up alongside my apartment building to drop me off after an evening at the chalet.

"*Adiós*," I said and leaned over to give him a kiss goodbye.

"Wait," Miguel said. He looked at me, steeling himself. "I think we should decide to just be friends after you leave next month. So we are prepared."

Tears sprung to my eyes, but I knew it made sense. I nodded. "*De acuerdo.*"

Then we made plans for the next afternoon, in denial that the day I'd leave would ever actually come.

I also needed to make the most of my time in Spain, though, and my drive to explore pulled me away just once more. For spring break in April, Nat and I roamed around Andalucía—the Spain of my imagination. Bull-shaped billboards guarding dusty hillsides. Fragrant orange trees lining sidewalks. Flamenco dancers in billowy polka-dotted dresses, stomping their feet and clapping staccato rhythms.

One morning, we toured the Alhambra, a Moorish hilltop palace. Birds chirped in manicured gardens while courtyard fountains bubbled. Every inch of tawny stone bore carvings in geometric patterns and sinuous Arabic script. I walked down an open, arched corridor and pictured it as it was 700 years ago. The sultan's family and children wandered leisurely around me, chatting and laughing. I imagined a warm breeze rustling my bright, airy robes. Through the curved windows, below a rocky outcropping, lay our kingdom of Granada.

Nat and I descended the long road from the palace toward town. Trees lined the street and shaded us from the midday sun. "You wanna get some food?" I asked.

"Always."

"I was telling my professor last week how much I love Spanish food, and I told him there are too many *preservativos* in American food," I said.

"That's true."

"Nope. It turns out *preservativo* means condom."

Nat howled. "That's awesome."

Two brunette Romani women approached us, wearing teal eyeliner and colorful, flowing skirts. Most Spaniards called them *gitanas*. Gypsies. One grabbed my wrist without invitation and inspected the lines on my palm. I froze, captivated, as she pressed a sprig of rosemary into my open hand. She locked her brown eyes onto my blue ones, searching.

"There is a dark-haired man who loves you very much," she said in Spanish.

My heart stopped.

She smiled kindly. "You have beautiful eyes. You are very beautiful, very intelligent. You are American." She studied my palm again and traced a crease with a silver-ringed finger. "You will return here in one year, and you will have two children together. One girl. *Ojazos como suyos.* Beautiful eyes like yours."

I stood paralyzed in wonder. This magical woman saw my future and felt compelled to tell me about it. Miguel and I were meant to be. What an incredible story for our beautiful-eyed kids.

She let my hand drop and squinted. "You have to pay me now."

"Huh?"

"You must pay me for the fortune." Her voice carried a new forcefulness. I handed her a couple of bills.

"*Más*," she said, holding her hand out.

Flustered, I forked out a few more and finally snapped out of my trance. The other woman was pulling the same routine on Nat. I grabbed my mesmerized friend and dragged her away, yelling, "*¡No gracias!*"

Nat glared at me. "What the hell, Stef!?"

"It's a scam. She's going to ask you for money."

"Really?" Nat looked as disappointed as I was.

"I feel like a dumbass. I got all wrapped up in it and gave her six bucks for a few compliments and lucky guesses."

"What'd she say?" Nat asked.

"That I'm a beautiful, smart American who's going to come back in a year and marry a dark-haired man who loves me, and we'll have two kids."

Nat stopped in her tracks. "Shut the hell up." She gaped at me, eyes wide with the vision of me, Miguel, and our babies.

"Calm down. It's not gonna happen. Probably."

We continued our walk down to town. Sunlight filtered through the canopy of leaves, leaving splotches of light on the cobblestones. A gust of wind carried the spicy scent of cypress trees. At the base of the hill was a large square, covered in tables and chairs and terse waiters. "Should we get some snails?" I asked.

"Eff that shit. I'll eat some ham, though," Nat said, and everything made sense again.

Two days later, Nat was sleeping next to me on a bus—head cushioned on the window with a balled-up long sleeve Abercrombie T-shirt, lips ajar, leaking Darth Vader breaths. I sent Miguel a text.

Nat and I are having fun. I miss you.

And I did miss him during quiet moments with nothing to distract me. But mostly, I immersed myself in the experience too much to think about anything outside of that exact moment.

I glanced out the windshield and gasped. A yellow limestone cliff rose from a riverbank, topped by a cathedral and castle of the same color. Tightly packed square homes sat in their shadows and spilled down the hillside into a broad plain. A cloudless sky enhanced the gleaming whitewash of every house. Arcos de la Frontera was as beautiful and illogical as a Dalí painting.

The bus dropped us at the bottom of the ridge. Nat stretched, yawned, and scowled at the climb to the top. "Jesus, why would you put a town up there?"

"It was probably easy to defend."

"I didn't actually want you to tell me."

I made a face at her. "This will be my training for hiking in the Alps this summer," I said, tightening the straps on my stiff new orange-and-navy backpack.

The roads meandered and narrowed the higher we went, and the white buildings pressed right onto the sidewalk. Their perpetual shade kept the streets cool in the southern sun. With just a sliver of blue directly above, we were wandering a monochrome labyrinth. But sometimes, wooden doors hung open, revealing brightly tiled courtyards. Vibrant potted plants covered the interior walls, and on occasion, an orange tree grew in the center of the open space.

Most cars couldn't fit down the slender lanes, so aside from the growl of an occasional scooter, the streets were calm. Neighbors chatted on their doorsteps while kids ran around, their laughter echoing down the alleys. The little town and way of life enchanted me.

We stopped by a railing at the edge of the cliff, looking out over the countryside. The wind whipped our hair into knots. "Can you imagine living here?" I mused. "I want a house with an orange tree in it."

"I thought you didn't want to live in Spain."

I sighed. "I don't know what the hell I'm doing."

Nat rolled her eyes dramatically. "Pick a country and deal with it."

I scowled and playfully pushed her.

"Love you!" she said, throwing her arm around my shoulder while we walked back to the guesthouse.

After a nap, we were ready for a night out, but front doors were shut, cobblestone alleys empty. Flickering TVs illuminated small windows. Arcos was asleep. Just before we gave up, we spotted a couple guys our age talking by a compact car. "*Perdónenme*, are there places here to get a drink?" I asked.

"*Sí, hay un bar*," one said. "Get in. We will take you."

Without a second thought, we jumped in their car, and they dropped us at a bar at the base of the mount.

We stepped inside, and the room fell silent. The young women stared for a moment and resumed their conversations. The young men watched while we approached the bartender, ordered drinks, and sipped them on the patio.

"This is freaking weird," Nat whispered.

One of the curious guys approached. "*Hola, guapas. Me llamo José.* May I buy you a drink?"

Suddenly eight more surrounded us, nudging each other out of the way like tiger cubs fighting over fresh meat. "What the hell?" I mouthed to Nat as she attended to her admirers.

José and his friends spoiled us with attention and free drinks. Late that night, he walked us home. The hill seemed to have grown steeper and longer in the past few hours.

A young man pulled over on a scooter that sounded like a giant metal mosquito.

"*¡Oye, Cucaracha!*" José said with a nod.

Nat playfully touched Cockroach's arm and complimented his shitty Vespa.

"*Guapa*, want to ride it?" he offered.

"*¡Claro que sí!*" Nat jumped on the back and wrapped her arms around his waist.

"Nat, are you sure—"

She waved goodbye as they buzzed up the hill. I felt concerned for her safety but also jealous she'd flirted herself a ride up the mountain.

José and I resumed the hike.

"Do you have a boyfriend?" he asked.

"*Sí.*"

"Where is he?"

"Valladolid."

"Are you faithful?"

"*¡Sí!*" I scolded him and scolded myself for being so naive. And apparently not mentioning Miguel.

We arrived in a plaza by the cathedral. I plopped on a bench to catch my breath under the orange halo of a streetlight. José straddled me and leaned in for a kiss. I stood up, knocking him off my lap onto the cobblestones. He looked surprised to find himself on the ground and scrambled to his feet. I charged to the hotel. José followed.

"Dammit!" I muttered at the door to the guesthouse. Nat had our only key. I sat on the cool stone stoop, leaned my head on the wall, and tried not to fall asleep while José hovered nearby.

Nat appeared from around the corner, sans Cockroach, looking sheepish. She wordlessly pulled the key from her purse and fumbled at the door. It creaked open, and she stumbled up the stairs.

As I climbed the steps, José called after me. "Wait! I need something to remember you!"

"Huh? Why?" I pulled my Dr. Pepper Lip Smacker from my pocket, tossed it down to him, and continued up to the room.

"Wait!" José called again. "You need something to remember me!"

I reluctantly turned around. José was pulling up the waistband of his boxer shorts like he was giving himself a wedgie. He contorted himself to find the tag in the back, ripped it out, and ran up the stairs to present it to me with an earnest grin. "Don't forget me ever!"

"Okay," I mumbled and rounded the corner without looking back.

I woke up in my underwear around noon the next day. Nat lay awake but perfectly still.

"You okay?" I asked.

Nat moaned in response.

I reached for my glass of water. When I saw the clothing tag on the nightstand, I laughed, sending a throb through my brain. "Dammit, that Lip Smacker was my favorite," I muttered. Nat just moaned again.

CHAPTER 9
JAMES

'Fuckin 'ell!' It burned so much I grabbed my willy and squeezed it shut. Amanda knocked on the bathroom door. 'You OK in there, James?'

'I'm fine.' I loosened my grip and let out another trickle. Still stinging. I silent-screamed. My swollen bladder ached. I washed my hands and gathered my composure before going back into Amanda's bedroom.

'Come back to bed,' Amanda said in a tired voice.

'Sorry, love.' I gathered up my clothes. 'Work just called,' I lied, stumbling out of the room while putting my shoes on. I knocked on several doors in the long hallway before Dave answered.

'Alright, mate?' He leaned against the doorframe, arms folded.

'We're leaving. Now!'

'What? Why?' He picked up his shirt. Kate rolled over in bed behind him.

'I can't pee.'

The previous night, my mate Dave and I were watching a '90s cover band at the Three Wise Monkeys, an upscale bar on George St, the main thoroughfare in Sydney's Central Business District. Silver buildings stretched on and on, all the way to Harbour Bridge. Professionals around me rinsed away office stresses with beer and wine.

I'd been in town for two months, living in a hostel, but occasionally I ditched the backpacker dive bars in an attempt to feel classier. Infiltrating a world I used to belong to.

A cute girl walked up to me and introduced herself as Amanda and her friend as Kate. In her American accent, she told me she lived in a shared house with other students. We chatted over the loud music. Dave and Kate stood in awkward silence.

'You wanna come back to our place?' Amanda asked and played with her long hair.

I almost spat my drink out. 'Erm…yeah!'

'OK, but your friend's gotta come too to keep Kate company.'

'Wait a minute.' I turned to Dave. 'Amanda's invited me back to hers.'

'Good for you, mate,' Dave said, patting me on the shoulder.

'The thing is, you have to come to keep Kate company.'

He looked at Kate and frowned. 'Really?'

'Please, mate! For me.'

'Go on, then. I'll take one for the team.'

Amanda and I spent the night in the throes of drunken passion. I awoke the next morning needing to wee like I'd never needed to wee in my life and stood over the toilet in Amanda's fancy ensuite bathroom, ready for the sweet relief. It never came.

I explained my predicament to Dave on the slow walk to the train station. He burst out laughing, attracting disapproving looks from suited commuters. I sat in a subway car, hair dishevelled, shirt wrinkled. I held my belly, swaying back and forth with the rhythm of the train. At our stop, I rose to my feet with the caution of a pregnant woman and waddled up the stairs. My bladder pulsated with each step. Dave followed along behind me, chuckling.

'Shut up, Dave!'

Back at our hostel, I tried again. Each drop stabbed like I was passing broken glass. I banged on the bathroom wall. 'Fuuuuuuck!'

I entered the busy courtyard, and the conversation stopped. Dave smirked behind a mug of coffee. Laughter erupted.

'Nice one, Dave.' I gave him two fingers.

'You might have an STD, James,' said Laundry-Matt, a lad named for shagging a girl on top of the washing machine.

I shook my head, doubled over. 'I hope not.'

'There's a clinic across the street,' someone said.

I limped to it and paced the waiting room.

'Drop your pants.' The old doctor put on thick eyeglasses, bent down, held up my old chap and shined a small flashlight into it. 'Was there anything unusual about the sex you had last night?' he asked, deadpan.

'Unusual? No, I don't think so. Do I have an STD?'

I'd always had girlfriends in England and been in several years-long relationships. I'd found while travelling Australia that I not only enjoyed the freedom from a permanent job tying me down, but I also enjoyed being single. I was free to go and do as I pleased. I had zero interest in finding a girlfriend, but suddenly playing the field was less appealing.

'No. You have urethral trauma, young man.'

I looked down. 'What?'

He furrowed his bushy eyebrows. 'The tube is inflamed and swollen.'

'What should I do?'

'Urine is acidic, and it's irritating the lining. I'll give you alkaline powder. It will help neutralise the acid. If you haven't urinated in two hours, you'll have to come back for catheterization.'

I winced at the thought.

I went home and guzzled the alkaline solution. My bladder was at the breaking point. In the bathroom, I bit my fist, pushed through the pain, and exited with the proud grin of a newly potty-trained toddler.

A few weeks later, when I could pee without flinching, I organized to meet up with Amanda and Kate at a bar downtown.

Valerie laughed as I got ready in our dorm room. 'Is that the girl that broke your—'

'Yeah. I know, I know, it's hilarious.' I'd made the mistake of telling her when she moved into the hostel a few days ago.

'Well, have fun. Be careful,' she said with another laugh.

At the bar, Kate pulled me aside. 'You should be thanking me.'

'Oh yeah. Why's that?'

'I took one for the team, hooking up with your friend Dave.'

I concealed my amusement, but I couldn't wait to tell him.

At the end of the night, exhausted and suitably rat-arsed, I passed out face down on Amanda's bed.

The next morning, I awoke but refused to open my eyes and allow my hangover to begin. Though fully clothed, shoes included, and under a duvet, I was freezing. My jeans and shirt tangled as I rolled onto my side. As I reached down to fix them, I realised they were soaking wet. My jeans stuck to me like cling film. Amanda slept beside me, unaware she was lying in urine.

I'd have given me left nut to pee this much last time I was here.

I peeled back the covers and tiptoed across the room. Amanda stirred. I froze and assessed the damage. Wet from nipples to knees. I could leave before she woke up, but I risked bumping into Kate or another roommate. Needing to think, I walked out on her bedroom's balcony. The chilly morning sent a shiver through my wet body. Amanda yawned.

Fuck! Fuck! Fuck!

'James?'

I leapt over the railings. Bags of rubbish broke my fall and burst under my weight. I rolled onto the tarmac, surrounded by the smell of rotting food, and scurried to the end of the alley, wiping wilted lettuce and coffee grinds off my clothes. I hailed a taxi, jumped in the back, and hunched over to conceal my substantial wet patch. Though still cold, I wound the window down to let in some fresh air.

I made it to my hostel dorm room without being seen. Luckily my roommates, including Valerie, were still asleep. I wriggled one leg out of my jeans and pulled furiously on the other. Finally, it freed, and I fell back into some shelves.

'What are you doing, you eejit?' Valerie said, half asleep. "Whoa, you stink. Why are you wet?"

'Erm, I spilt pop all over meself at the 7-11.'

'Yeah, right!' she said, trying to stifle her laugh.

'Go back to sleep,' I whispered.

Shivering, I rummaged in my backpack for dry clothes. I needed a shower but craved the warmth of my bed. My hangover had been postponed but was arriving quickly. I turned off my phone and closed my eyes, waking a few hours later.

I'd slept in my contact lenses and had to force my eyes open. I turned on my phone and held the screen up to my face. Five voice mails.

Beep. 'Hi James, it's Amanda. Where are you?'

Beep. 'Hi James, it's Amanda again. Why's the bed all wet?'

Beep. 'It's me, again. I think I know what happened and—'

I couldn't bear to listen to the rest of the messages. I pulled my blanket over my head and went back to sleep.

CHAPTER 10
STEF

Miguel paced the train platform, his gaze fixed on the tiles under his feet. I sent goodbye texts to Seema, Erica, and Myah, and checked my purse for my ticket again, as if it could have disappeared in the two minutes since I last checked.

My chest felt hollow. "I can't believe it's already over."

Miguel didn't look up. "I don't want to talk about it. It is like saying *adiós* a thousand times."

The words hit me like a punch in the gut.

"Actually," he continued, still staring at the floor, "we said we should just be friends after you leave. But . . . I don't want that."

I'd been avoiding my sadness by focusing on the reunions we'd planned. I'd return to Valladolid for a weekend after camp. Miguel would visit me in Pittsburgh in August, and I'd come back in September for his sister's wedding. I hadn't thought past that.

Miguel finally looked up at me.

Tears stung my eyes. "I'm sorry, Miguel. I don't know—"

"Stef!" Nat appeared on the platform. "Hey, guys!"

Miguel gave a little wave and resumed staring at the floor.

"Hey!" Nat and I chatted for a couple minutes, making plans to meet up at home. Then the train whistled in the distance like an alarm signaling time was up. I instantly felt sick.

"Shit. Okay." I threw my colorful backpack over my shoulder. "Thanks for coming to say bye, Nat. Love you, girl. Keep in touch." I gave Nat a big hug, and she left.

The train squealed to a stop, smelling of metal and grease. Miguel stepped forward and wrapped his arms around me. He looked me in the eyes, studying them like he was trying to memorize every fleck of blue and gray. *"Te quiero."*

"I'll see you in August. *Te quiero."* I kissed him, grabbed my luggage, boarded the train, and hoisted my bags on the shelf. I looked out the window as we chugged away. He was already gone.

The moment I'd dreaded for months had come and gone in seconds. I cut through a group of rowdy frat boys and settled into a seat at the empty end of the car, resting my head against the glass. I'd barely slept the night before. We chugged into the countryside, and the warm, late-May sun coaxed me into a nap.

When I woke hours later, the world had changed. Gone were the vineyards, cows, and farmhouses crawling with ivy. Brilliant Spanish sun had disappeared behind battleship clouds. Raindrops smacked sideways against my window as the train dashed through the outskirts of a French city. Spray paint autographs claimed derelict buildings. Trash littered the tracks, and power lines split the sky.

I grabbed my portable CD player and put *The Beach* soundtrack in it. Moby's melancholy song "Play" matched my mood. Kissing Miguel at the Valladolid station that morning already felt like a faded memory.

Miguel was amazing. I allowed myself to fall for him, and worse, allowed him to fall for me. I tried to reassure myself I'd made the right choice by leaving. That I wasn't going to hold myself back from experiences I'd waited my whole life to have. But I felt like a heartless bitch.

I stared at my dismal surroundings, thankful to be alone. I had a twenty-four-hour journey to France. A full day to transition from the sadness of an ending to the excitement of a beginning.

As the train chugged closer to the station in Bourg St. Maurice, I felt flutters of anticipation in my chest, immediately followed by guilt. I decided it was okay to feel conflicting emotions and reminded myself I didn't come to France just to mope. I grabbed my bags, jumped off the train, and waved hello to Kenneth, whom I'd met on my last visit. Pete had decided to work at home with his family for the summer, so I was on my own.

A few days later, I found myself in a bucking rubber raft. Ginger Jack shouted over the thunder of the waves, his red hair soaking. "Okay, we gotta dig deep!"

I shoved my paddle into the rapids, pushing as hard as I could against the water. My shoulders strained, and my muscles burned. I wedged my feet tightly under the cross tube and braced for impact. The raft jolted up and down, and water splashed us from all directions. Then suddenly, calm.

We whooped in celebration. "You've got some arms on ya, Yankee," Angel Butt said with a smile.

I'd given him the nickname the day before, after his wet butt print on a bench looked like a pair of angel wings. I was the only female staff member and the only American at training, but luckily, the shared experience of being in a raft for hours at a time quickly turns strangers into friends.

We reached the takeout point and dragged the heavy rafts onto the shore. The Isère river glittered, and the Alps towered around me, piercing a cerulean sky. We packed up quickly, and I threw my shorts over my wet bathing suit, instantly regretting it when I climbed into the back of our van and squelched around on the vinyl seat. "Ugh. My fanny's all wet."

Every guy whipped around, eyes wide and eyebrows raised.

I shrank into my seat. "Whoa. What?"

They looked at each other and burst out laughing.

"What did you say?" Ginger Jack asked.

"I said my butt's all wet."

"That's *not* what you said," Angel Butt countered. "You said your *fanny's* all wet."

"Same thing!"

"No, in England, a fanny is, um . . ." Kenneth chuckled awkwardly. "Only women have one."

"Are you serious? Well. That is *not* what I meant!" I laughed, not surprised it had only taken a few days to embarrass myself.

We returned to the hotel, and I trudged up to my room, sunburned and weary, but exhilarated. I changed into dry clothes and then headed to the staff room. An envelope, postmarked from Spain, sat on the table. I took it up to my room and tore it open. Miguel had sent it the morning I left. He'd had a knot in his stomach since we said goodbye at the train station. He wanted me to finish my degree and come back to Spain to get married and have Spanish babies.

I sat on the edge of my bed and dialed his number.

"*Hola, mi niña.*"

My heart ached at the sound of his voice. "*Hola.*"

"*¿Qué tal?*"

"Really good. My coworkers are awesome. I'm the only girl right now, but the guys are hilarious. We went white water rafting today, and it's so beautiful up here."

"I'm glad you're happy."

I was happy. And instantly felt guilty for being so. "I got your letter. I'm sorry. I just, I don't know what to do. Can we just wait and see?"

"Claro, mi niña."

After a week of staff training, the first student group arrived for their seven days of summer fun. I spent days rafting, rock climbing, and mountain biking—a contrast from my five months in the city, but a lifestyle I enjoyed just as much. Though the guys hated hiking or "hillwalking," as they called it, I loved it. A simple activity meant time for talking. The English teens bombarded me with questions about prom, yellow school buses, and house parties with red plastic cups, as apparently all they knew about my country was from the movie *American Pie*.

A group of fourteen-year-olds from the Liverpool Boys' School arrived in mid-June, and I heard the guys grumbling a lot about the "Scousers."

Kenneth and I were assigned hiking. "Walking sucks arse," Kenneth mumbled as he led the group, and the kids filed like goslings behind him. We climbed up the mountain, past steep, lush fields scattered with mooing cows and their clanging bells. I spent a lot of time telling the boys to stay on the path and stop running, squirting water, and throwing rocks.

"Hang on a mo', yous!" a boy named Danny panted from the end of the line.

"If you weren't such a fat wap . . ." a tall kid said, triggering laughter from the rest.

Danny's eyes flashed with hurt. "Fuck off," he mumbled toward his shoes.

I waved the tall boy over. A wave of anxiety washed over me. I'd grown up in a conflict-free environment and wasn't used to confrontation. But if I wanted to be a teacher, I had to learn how to discipline. "That was really mean," I said. "Don't talk to him like that."

"Yes, miss."

I sent him back in line and breathed a sigh of relief.

I patted Danny on the back. "I know these hills are bigger than in Liverpool, huh?"

"Yes, miss."

I stayed by Danny's side. We stopped at a humble white chapel so high it looked like it dropped from the clouds. A reportedly miraculous spring bubbled beside the chapel. We cupped our hands and sipped the frigid, healing water. Danny splashed some on his face and gasped at the shock of cold, making us both laugh.

Mossy flowers covered the ground at the summit, smelling like Juicy Fruit gum when they crushed under my boot. Danny sat down on a rock to catch his breath. He looked across the wide valley at peaks that rose from green through gray to white. Tiny towns dotted the expanse, connected with narrow, zigzagging roads. Danny grinned. "That's boss."

I remembered being Danny's age. I remembered being Danny. Being the target.

A few of us from junior high were watching TV in a friend's sunroom one spring Saturday. I was wearing my favorite pink and orange Hypercolor T-shirt, and though my yearly perm was growing out, my bangs were still perfectly curled.

I came back from the bathroom to find everyone had disappeared. I roamed the yard, came back through the kitchen, climbed the stairs. Calling, listening. I went back downstairs and tried the basement door. It was locked. I heard giggling.

"Guys?"

Shhhhhhh! Shhh!

"Guys, come on!"

Silence.

I waited another minute before I walked back to the sunroom and watched TV on my own. A *Simpsons* short on a rerun of the *Tracey Ullman Show*. I didn't understand what was so different about me. Why *I* was always chosen. I debated calling my dad to come pick me up. After ten minutes or so, the girls filed back in as if nothing happened, so I let it go.

"Hey, Danny," I said, "I know it's hard, but try not to let those guys get to you."

He nodded silently.

"I used to get picked on, too."

He looked over at me, surprised. "Really?"

"Yeah."

"Huh." He seemed to mull this fact over. "Maybe I'll turn out nice like you."

At the end of the day, I flopped onto the ratty couch in the staff room.

"Have fun walking today, Stef?" Kenneth asked.

"Yeah, definitely."

Angel Butt grinned. "Not as much as rafting, though."

I shot him a look as everyone laughed. "Anyway, those kids are really tough."

"Yeah, they come from a rough part of Liverpool," Kenneth said. "Fair dues for trying to connect with them."

I'd always thought about teaching at an inner-city school. I wanted to help the kids who needed it most, but I didn't think I'd be strong enough. Still, I decided to consider it.

I called Miguel that evening, excited to tell him about my experience with Danny. I'd called him almost every night for the past three weeks, and I still looked forward to hearing his voice. We'd always comment on how we missed each other. But constantly being surrounded by people and activity meant that most of the time, I was too distracted to feel sad, just like what happened with Alex.

Sometimes I wondered why the hell I was attempting this long-distance relationship when I clearly wasn't cut out for it. Was there a chance that we'd make it through the summer, I'd go home to student teach and graduate, and then scrap all my plans and return to Spain? I had no idea.

After our phone call, I met up with everyone, and we roamed up the road to the Bar Mont Blanc.

I settled into a comfy loveseat next to Ginger Jack in the rustic, wood-filled tavern.

"I like that necklace," I said, pointing to the deep green carving dangling around his neck. It looked like an artistic fishhook.

"Oh, it's a *hei matau*." He ran his fingers over the smooth jade. "The Maori people in New Zealand wore them for good luck and protection while traveling over water."

"You've been to New Zealand?"

"Yeah, when I was eighteen, I traveled around the world for a year."

"Wow. I want to go to New Zealand. I'll have to get one."

Fascinated by the concept of a gap year, I pestered him with questions about his trip for the next hour or so.

Angel Butt plopped into an overstuffed chair across from us, foamy pint held high, singing.

> *I used to work in Chicago, in an old department store*
> *I used to work in Chicago, I don't work there anymore*

I grinned. "What are you singing?"

"An old rugby song. Come on, lads. And lass." He pointed at me. "I'll teach you."

> *A woman came in and asked for some cake*
> *I asked her what kind she'd adore*
> *Layer, she said*
> *So lay her I did*
> *I don't work there anymore.*

Angel Butt led us through several verses in which the employee sold liquor, screws, and a pearl necklace.

As we sang, I swelled with affection for my fellow wanderers, having trouble believing I'd only known them a few weeks. Living together, working together, and being foreigners together bonds people like nothing else.

A few weeks later, on my twenty-second birthday, I stood high atop a mountain, knees shaking slightly. A harness connected me to a man and connected to that man was a parachute laid out behind us on a grassy slope.

"On the count of three, we're gonna run, ay?" he said.

"Yup. Okay," I replied and blew out one long breath.

"One. Two. Three."

I ran. Wind filled the parachute, and suddenly, my feet left the ground. We were flying. Once aloft, fear left me, and I felt strangely serene. I looked down at my dirty tennis shoes, dangling in space, and then at the green expanse thousands of feet below, but it didn't scare me. I felt secure, like it was a totally normal place for me to be. Birds circled underneath me. I felt limitless.

CHAPTER 11
JAMES

On my first day working for George, we had to lift a piano up a flight of stairs. I bore the piano's full weight as George endeavoured to balance it. My muscles burned, and I held my breath. My sole focus became avoiding being crushed to death. My feet almost slipped entirely out of my cheap trainers. Lactic acid filled my muscles. At the top of the stairs, I finally exhaled.

'You alright, mate?' George said in his strong Aussie accent. He adjusted his ever-present baseball cap, which kept his complexion as white as his goatee was black.

'Yeah, sound,' I wheezed.

George and I became an effective work team, and I earned his respect through long hours of hard graft. He'd pick me up at the hostel in the morning, and I'd sleep while he drove. Then we'd work our bollocks off, sometimes for twelve hours. George knew every technique in the furniture removal business, from stacking, to tying, to manoeuvring sofa beds down three flights of narrow stairs. He was skinny with a beer belly, but that didn't stop him picking up pianos like they were pillows. At the end of the shift, I'd be dropped off with some cash in my pocket. It wasn't much, but I was making enough to pay my rent and keep me in Australia. Until my visa expired in three months anyway.

George regularly had me over for dinner and introduced me to his wife, daughter and parents. He asked if I wanted to live in Sydney permanently and brought up the possibility of sponsoring me.

Could I really leave my old life behind? Could I earn enough to pay off my debts eventually?

'Brian! It's James.' I knocked again. 'It's time for work, mate.' No answer.

George had expanded the business and hired Brian, a likeable local with floppy hair. I peered through his window. Beer cans littered the floor, outlining areas where a sofa and a bookshelf once stood. In the kitchen, dirty dishes rose high from the sink.

Brian rushed out the front door. "Sorry, mate. Been on the phone since early. My roommate's fucked off and sold all me bloody furniture. He's got a gambling problem. D'ya mind lending me a hundred bucks? I gotta pay all the rent now."

Without a second thought, I pulled two fifty-dollar notes from my pocket and handed them to him.

Hanging out with Brain and George made me feel like I was living a double life. I'd sit on the back of the truck with them after a long day, sharing a carton of VB. Sometimes I'd sit in the hostel courtyard playing cards with fellow travellers. Sometimes the worlds would overlap. I'd bring extra lads to work when we needed help, and I took George and Brian to O'Malley's Irish pub for a taste of backpacker life.

A few weeks after my sponsorship conversation with George, I sat on a train headed to work. The suburbs of Sydney were bathed in early morning sunshine. I'd been running for nearly a year, but now I dared to stop. I imagined loading a surfboard into my ute and driving to Bondi to catch some early morning waves. Beaches, downtown, mountains, great weather, people from all over the world. Sydney had it all, and I was going to live there.

On the walk from the train station to George's, I met up with Brian. He asked to borrow another fifty dollars. This time I had to refuse. I told him George owed me close to three grand. He wanted to buy another truck, so I'd let him slip further behind with my wages. I trusted George and believed in the sponsorship.

A few days later, George called to tell me he'd seen a doctor about pain he'd been having. The diagnosis was two broken ribs and a herniated disc in his back, caused by the wear and tear of our job. For the next month, Brian and I worked tirelessly while George recuperated. Sixteen-hour days, seven days a week.

Most days consisted of multiple removals. My arms ached, ribs bruised, knuckles peeled, skin scorched, legs tired, and back spasmed. I suffered numerous bouts of sunstroke and heat exhaustion. Always short on time, we shovelled thousands of fast-food calories into our mouths between jobs.

At the end of each day, I handed George the bag of cash we'd collected. Brian received his wages in full, and I accepted whatever George could spare. I had enough for rent at the hostel and food but not much else.

George entrusted me to work on his accounts, using his home as an office. I didn't like doing accounting work again, but I wanted to prove myself to George and help him through a tight spot. He and his family had been good to me, and I didn't want to let them down.

Large, dark bags formed under my eyes and the days blurred together. Most nights, I'd collapse on my bed in my stinking clothes and shoes, wake up, and go straight out the door and back to work.

One morning, George called me aside while Brian folded blankets in the truck.

'James, who collects the money from the customers? Is it you?'

'It's both of us, mate.'

He looked at me and back down at the paperwork in his hand. 'And you've been keeping all the money in the pouch, right?'

'Yeah, why?'

He rustled the papers. 'Well, I got behind on the paperwork. I reckoned it all up last night and came up short three grand.'

'Fuck!' I blurted. 'Really?'

George glared at me. I'd never seen him like this.

My palms felt sweaty. *He thinks I've nicked it. Shit! He thinks it's me.* 'I don't know where it could have—'

'Here's your list of jobs for today,' he cut me off and looked towards the truck. 'From now on, only you handle the cash.

CHAPTER 12
STEF

As the summer wore on, my skin tanned, my hair lightened, and my muscles strengthened. Being outside all day, every day, felt like home. I'd often ask the guys about their previous jobs—raft guide in Nepal or ski instructor in Canada—and I envied their adventurous, nomadic lifestyle.

Angel Butt and I sat in the open window of his bedroom on July 4th, legs hanging over the side of the building. Cool night air blew in. "Mountain biking was fun today," I recalled. "Nadine was pedalling hard, and Kenneth starts chanting, 'Go Nads! Go Nads!'"

Angel Butt cracked up. "Brilliant."

I nodded. "If you yell 'gonads' at a kid in America, you're gonna get fired."

Across the dark valley, a thunderstorm raged. White bursts illuminated mountaintops miles away.

"I guess these will be my fireworks this year." I longed for home and family, burnt hot dogs, and lightning bugs.

"We should go to the Mont Blanc," Angel Butt said. "I think a headslammer is in order."

"Oh, lord. Okay."

A crew of us walked up the hill as a sprinkle of rain fell. I silently brought up the rear, my pensive mood now extending to Miguel. Our relationship had started with a big glittering bang and then fizzled into nothing. We'd spoken less frequently over the past two weeks. He wouldn't pick up when I called and would text me late at night, telling me he'd been busy with work.

I couldn't stop thinking about Ginger Jack's round-the-world trip. That maybe I could postpone work after graduation and go to New Zealand. And suddenly, it became clear—my future wasn't holding me back from Miguel, but Miguel could hold me back from my future. I'd been hiding behind my graduation-and-job excuse because it hurt less than admitting I didn't want to be tied down to a man I still loved very much.

At the Mont Blanc, Angel Butt handed me a ski helmet. "Headslammer time!"

The guys held my body in a horizontal position, and I rested my helmeted head against the wooden bar. The bartender held two liquor bottles upside down in each hand and dumped their assorted contents into my gaping mouth. I shut my lips tight, and the guys hoisted me up and down. "One, two, three!" they shouted as my cranium whacked the bar.

I swallowed and stood up with crossed eyes and a burning throat. They cheered, "Happy Fourth of July, Yankee!"

"Thanks." I took the helmet off and plopped on a couch. "Happy Independence."

At the start of August, I squeezed my new friends tight, promising to keep in touch, and flew from Geneva to Barcelona—the cheapest flight I could find.

Miguel and I had communicated sporadically. We both knew it was over now, but I still wanted to see him before returning to America. I'd texted him to see if he was still picking me up at the airport or if I should take a train, and was surprised when he called me right away to reassure me he was coming.

I came out of the gate and saw him standing there, looking adorable as ever. He gave me two cheek kisses.

"*Hola, mi niña,*" he said and grabbed my backpack. "The car is outside. We're going stay with my aunt tonight."

I followed him to the car, and he stared straight out the windshield as I talked to him about my last days at camp and the flight over. "So, what's new with you?" I asked.

He shrugged, eyes never straying from the road. "*Nada mucho.*"

We went to the beach with his family and a festival that night. Miguel never touched me and rarely made eye contact. We slept in the same bed, but the inches between us felt like miles.

The next day, we drove to Valladolid. I looked out the window at the dry, red hills of Aragon, remembering how we used to be. Tears dripped down my cheeks.

"We have been apart almost long as we were together," Miguel said. "I don't think you thought about what that would feel like."

He was right.

He'd had the last two months to process what happened and get over me. But I felt like I'd pressed pause on Spain for two months and expected to pick up right where I left off. I was distracted and never dealt with the inevitable end. I never got over him. I never even started to.

We pulled up to the chalet. His extended family mingled on the lawn, having a picnic. I hugged and cheek-kissed and chatted with them. Miguel and I stepped inside the chalet. Same big table, same smoky smell. A tear dropped down Miguel's cheek. He took my hand and led me upstairs.

He sat on a narrow bed and patted the mattress. I sat beside him. He pulled me close, I buried my head into his chest, and his familiar touch broke me.

"I'm sorry. I'm so sorry," I said, crying on his shirt.

"I have been trying to stay strong all weekend," he said. "It was so hard the first time you left."

"I'm sorry. I never meant—"

He touched my cheek, and I looked up at him. The tension melted, and he kissed me. We no longer felt like strangers.

The next morning, he drove me to the airport and came inside. "Here." He gave me a plastic bag containing four magazines and some gummy candy. "You're going to have a long day, *amiga*," he said with the familiar twinkle in his eye.

I hugged him. "Thank you. For everything."

He gave me a sad half-smile. "*Tu vida está llena de despedidas.*" Your life is full of goodbyes. He gave me one last kiss, one last look, and walked out of the terminal.

I watched him walk away and considered that it might always be.

CHAPTER 13
JAMES

After hearing of the missing three grand, I struggled to focus. Brian cracked jokes and sang along to the radio as I drove in silence. My hands trembled on the train ride home that night. The Sydney streets outside the window were empty and cloaked in darkness.

I paced the floor of my tiny hostel bedroom, trying to recall the particulars of the last few weeks. I'd been so tired. Had I miscounted? Fucked up the paperwork? A few ATM receipts were at the bottom of my backpack, the most recent one showing a $250 balance. Rip. Rip. Rip.

Kneeling amongst the torn receipts, I couldn't remember the last time I'd had fun. Rare days off came during the week while my friends worked. I'd drink alone in a shitty pub while my mind carried me home. To my mum meeting up with my Nan and Auntie Dorothy in town. To the nieces and nephews I was missing seeing grow up. To my dad drinking his life away.

I texted Valerie. I missed her. She was my bunkmate for a while before heading up the East Coast in a camper van with some friends of ours. I'd given her my favourite rugby jersey as a leaving present. I filled her in about the money, and she told me to jump on a bus and join them. The photos in their emails made me jealous, and I often wished I'd gone with them. But even if I had the money, it wouldn't last long, and I'd be left with nothing but photos and hangovers.

I wanted a life here. Not a temporary fix. I'd sacrificed a lot by working with George, but finally, I saw a future. One that didn't frighten me. One that made me smile. If I got the sponsorship visa, it would all be worth it. *If not, it's home in two months.*

I picked up my mobile again. Its green screen glowed in the dimly lit room. My stomach flipped as I scrolled through my contacts, stopping on George's number. I sat on my bed and stared at his name for a few minutes before dialling.

'George, before you say anything, I know it looks bad. You owe me three grand, and that's the exact amount missing, but I promise it wasn't me,' I said in one breath.

'James—'

'Mate, I wouldn't do that to you. You've been really good to me, and I appreciate it.' I continued pacing the room.

'James, slow down.'

'Why would I risk the sponsorship? I kept your business going when you were sick, and I've given up a lot.' I drew in a large breath. 'I love working with you—'

'James, stop!' George shouted, followed by a long silence. I stood still. 'Listen to me. I trust you, mate. I don't think it was you.'

I ran my fingers through my hair and exhaled. 'I'm fuckin' gutted for you, mate. I'm relieved you don't think it was me, though.'

'No worries. I appreciate you calling and all the hard work you've done for me. I'll see you tomorrow.'

I sat back down on my bed and put my head in my hands. Tears of relief streamed down my face.

A few days later, in the middle of a removal, Brian complained of a sore back. He downed tools and sat in the truck with his feet up on the dashboard, making several phone calls. George drove Brian home before helping me finish the job, despite not being back to full fitness.

Later, Brian's phone went straight to voicemail, so we went to his house to check on him. We looked in through the window. No pizza boxes or beer cans. No dishes in the kitchen. Nothing. George looked at me and frowned. We went back to George's, where he called some other removal businesses in Sydney, to see if anyone else knew of Brian.

'Yeah, I know him. That fucker owes me money,' one owner said.

'Why? D'ya know where he is?' another asked. 'If I find him, I'm gonna break his fuckin' kneecaps!'

Three more calls bore similar results. I slumped onto George's sofa. 'I bet *he* had the gambling problem, not his roommate.'

'I always subbed him on his wages too,' George muttered.

My jaw dropped open. 'That twat tried to set me up! Bit of a coincidence three grand went missing, the exact same amount you owe me, right?'

'Looks that way, mate,' George said with a nod. 'I bet we'll never find him now. I'll get your money as soon as I can, James.'

How'd I not seen this? I'd been so gullible. My heart went out to George and his family, and I'd lost a friend.

I continued to run George's business for a few weeks, hiring backpackers from the hostel to work with me until George was fit. *I* was in charge now. *I* stacked the truck and tied things down. When George returned, we worked even harder. With my new skills, we finished quickly and took on more work than ever. George never complained about his health, but I would catch sight of him holding his back. Over the next month, he paid me the three grand, plus the money Brian owed me.

George suggested we meet with an immigration lawyer. Adrenaline rushed through me as we took our seats in a drab office. Opposite us sat the lawyer, a man with tufts of grey hair above his ears. He wore a beige suit, making him barely distinguishable from the off-white walls.

I beamed with pride as George explained what a good worker I'd been and how I'd kept him in business during his injuries. I thought of my dad, who'd worked long, hard hours in coal mines from an early age. I'd barely talked to him since I left. Our deteriorating relationship was another reason I didn't want to go home.

As George explained my role in the business, the lawyer studied a piece of paper through reading glasses balanced on the end of his nose. When George finished, he placed the form in front of him. 'Is his job on this list? This is a list of approved sponsor-worthy professions.'

I snatched the paper, scanning every word. Nurse, plumber, carpenter. I held my breath as the list went on. 'It's not on here,' I said in a low voice, without looking at either of them. My head dropped. 'It's not on here.'

'Is there anything we can do?' George asked.

The lawyer adjusted his glasses. 'I'm very sorry, but it has to be on the list.'

My future determined by a fucking list. My dream, wrapped up and choked by red tape in a few short minutes.

I gripped the paper hard, and it creased around my thumbs. I wanted to scrunch it into a ball, throw it at the lawyer and knock his fucking glasses off.

We left the office dejected. My stomach ached, and I couldn't eat. We spent the rest of the day working in silence.

All I could think about on the walk home was that my visa would expire in December, and I'd have to leave Australia and return to reality. *Nice try, James, but it's game fucking over.*

I remembered the letters I'd written to the bank and credit card companies. I pictured a stack of responses piled on my bed. Each one with more interest added and penalties and threats and fines and…fuck, I couldn't breathe. I pushed open a pub door.

Revellers from the hostels sang and danced around me. I pushed through them, sat at the bar and drank and drank until I felt nothing. Then I drank some more, pulled out my phone and texted George. I complained about the sacrifices I'd made and how I'd put my life on hold for nothing. I needed someone to blame. Someone to be angry at.

I awoke the following day with a sinking feeling. I read my sent text messages and the times—12:03, 1:15, 2:33. My phone beeped in the middle of typing a long apologetic text to George. His name flashed on the screen.

No worries, mate. I understand. I'm gutted too.
Take the day to recover, and I'll see you tomorrow.

CHAPTER 14
STEF

I sat behind my desk after dismissal on Day 1 and looked around the classroom. My classroom. My aunt, also a teacher, had sent me a "starter kit" with decorations and cut-out letters, and I'd enjoyed making my room warm and inviting. Colorful bulletin boards covered my walls, and large flags and fringed piñatas dangled from the ceiling.

After returning from France, I completed my student teaching in Pittsburgh and graduated from college summa cum laude. A perfect GPA to ensure a perfect career.

My friends all started jobs immediately after graduation. Under the influence of my parents and other normal people, a round-the-world trip like Ginger Jack's made less sense. I returned to my original, responsible plan. The school year was only 180 days. I'd have plenty of time to travel over breaks.

I'd given each class my First Day Pep Talk. They sat up straight, pencils poised above notebooks, eyes sparkling with the optimism of a fresh start at a new charter school. These inner-city students had dropped out, failed out, or been kicked out of Pittsburgh Public Schools. I'd just turned twenty-three, and while most of my eleventh grade students were seventeen, a few were nineteen, even twenty, years old. I arranged my materials for Day 2 with excitement, proud to make a difference so early in my career.

By October, my students' sparkly eyes had dulled. They now slept through class, rarely arrived with notebooks, ignored me, and gave me attitude if I asked them to work. Many had fallen back into the behaviors that pushed them out of public school.

During first period on Day 25, Latrisha and Nevaeh chatted loudly in the corner. They sneered when I asked them to stop and went back to their conversation. Jayson sat in the back row, head on his desk, wearing the same old green sweatshirt that stunk of weed. Only two students had finished their homework, and my fun game flopped because nobody knew the vocabulary. I returned tests marked with Ds and Fs in glittery purple gel pen. None of this was what I had envisioned.

The kids left. I locked the door and turned off the lights. It was my planning period, but my only plan was to breathe deep and not cry. I lay on the linoleum floor in the back of the classroom, an intruder in the domain of abandoned pencils and forgotten worksheets. The chill of the floor seeped through my ivory blouse. I stared up at the flags and piñatas, muted in the shadows of the dark room. The clock ticked away each second of my respite, and I wiped one defiant tear from my cheek before the students came back.

I impatiently waited for Day 45. We had a week-long break between each grading period, so I packed my car for a road trip south.

Dad sat me down before my departure. "You have your map, Steffie?"

I held up the TripTik I'd gotten from AAA.

"Did you check the air in your tires? The oil? You need some snacks?

I smiled. "Dad. I'm good, thanks."

I roamed that week, visiting college and summer camp friends in West Virginia, Mississippi, and South Carolina. A weight lifted. While I rafted the Gauley River, toured Elvis's birthplace, and drank sweet tea, the stress of my new career didn't exist.

Day 63. "Aja, I've asked you twice to take your headphones off."

She stared at me, leaking "Get Ur Freak On" into the atmosphere, and rolled her eyes.

My face flushed and sweat beaded on my forehead. "Okay, just go to the principal's office."

She snapped her gum and muttered as she passed me. "Bitch."

"Don't you ever call me that ever again!" I shouted after her.

My stomach turned, and my hands trembled. Nobody had ever talked to me like that. I'd never yelled at anyone before.

Day 95. "You're wasting your potential," I told Marquis. I'd spent hours rewriting notes to replace the ones he kept losing. I labored to stoke any spark of interest into a flame, like I did with all my students. After school, Marquis's cousin was shot in the street. Marquis never came to school again.

Students that hated school the most stayed after dismissal, possibly because they hated home more. I was happy to be there for them and enjoyed getting to know them in those relaxed moments. On Day 113, Tyree, Jamal, and Noelle sat on desktops by the bookshelf, heads bobbing to beats playing on the classroom stereo, weaving spontaneous lyrics about classmates and teachers.

It wasn't tough all day, every day, with every student. Jimmy asked me to be his prom date. DeTavion invited me to party in the graveyard with him and his friends. I liked my students, and I thought the students liked me, but I took it so personally when they made snide comments or ignored me when I asked them to pay attention or do classwork. And unfortunately, for me, that overshadowed the good times.

I never considered quitting mid-year. After June, I'd look for something new. I etched mini countdown numbers into the squares on my desk calendar. At every dismissal, I crossed off the day with a rush of relief. But every night, my ribcage tightened as I laid my clothes out and packed my lunch.

I traveled as much as possible with my old high school friends. We stood shivering early one February morning in Punxsutawney as a groundhog saw his shadow and predicted six more weeks of winter. We drank hurricanes in New Orleans over Mardi Gras and developed an irrational obsession with cheap plastic beads. We drove to Philadelphia where our friend Christina had gotten a job. I visited my English pal Pete when he flew over to see his brother, and I met up with Nat in Atlantic City.

The trips helped for the weekend or the week, but the stress always returned. I felt guilty for wanting to quit when my students had real problems I couldn't imagine. Some were hungry, neglected, raising themselves and their siblings. I knew, logically, why they behaved the way they did, but I couldn't relate because my parents had spoiled me with love, safety, and consistency. A fortunate start to life, but one that left me ill-equipped to understand the cruel realities that had always existed outside my bubble. And I was too sensitive to separate their anger at the world from disdain for me. I had to accept that I couldn't do this job and felt naive for ever thinking I was strong enough for it. After years of studying foreign cultures, I dropped into one I didn't understand, twenty minutes from home.

In my spare time, I watched the movie Blue Crush on repeat, envying the surfer girls riding waves at dawn before their hotel housekeeping shift. I wanted to live in the now and didn't give any more shits about a stable job with benefits.

I spent hours using the dial-up internet in my parents' basement, applying for outdoor jobs around the world. Some places told me I needed a visa, so I applied for working holiday visas for Australia and New Zealand. That would give me six months to work, support myself, and keep looking for extended employment. I'd leave at the end of October when flights were cheaper than in the summer.

Dad came downstairs as I searched "Sydney hostels" on Yahoo. "Are you sure you don't want to settle down somewhere? Get married someday?" He frowned, seemingly imagining my lonely life.

"Nah. I don't care about getting married. And I wouldn't want anyone to hold me back."

"Maybe you could find someone to travel with. It's nice to have a partner."

I patted him on the arm. "I'm okay, Dad, really. There's enough people that love me."

On Day 175, I thanked my principal for the job and told him I wouldn't be returning the following school year. I drove home, windows down and stereo up, blasting my Adventure Mix Tape, singing John Mayer's "No Such Thing" at the top of my lungs.

Day 180, my last, was spent just chatting with my students. It was relaxed and fun, though my heart sank when some of them looked disappointed to find out I wouldn't be back. I said goodbye and have a great summer and got a few hugs in return.

I packed up my classroom after school. I pulled a motivational poster off the wall after months of it mocking me. Never give up! Rolled into a tube, silenced with a rubber band. I took down the flags, piñatas, and Aunt Emily's cut-out letters. An optimistic facade, concealing the fact everyone in the room, including me, wanted out.

I disappointed myself, and I was sure I disappointed my parents, though they never said so. But the weight of my failure was lightened by my new freedom. I had to let my plan go and work on Stef's Future 2.0.

I looked over the empty desks, accepting I might never stand in front of a classroom again. Then I crossed out the last square on my calendar with a squeaky Sharpie, threw them both in a box, and left.

PART TWO:

FALLING DOWN UNDER

(2002 – 2003)

CHAPTER 15
JAMES

The drone of a Hoover in the hallway woke me from a deep sleep. I jumped out of bed, smashing my head on the top bunk. 'Motherfucker!' I rubbed my head, scooped my belongings off the floor and threw them in a heap on my bunk. On cleaning day, anything left on the floor was dumped in the Lost Property bin at reception.

I sat on my bed, rubbing crusty sleep from my eyes. In the middle of the night, two Swedish girls packed their shit for an early bus. The crinkling of bags and buzzing of zippers woke me, but I was too drunk to complain. Their old ticket stubs now littered the floor, and a wet towel they left overpowered the usual smell of feet.

The cleaner burst in. I got up and made my way through the dormant hostel, still dressed from the night before, poured a bowl of cereal in the kitchen and took it to the TV room.

The door only opened halfway. Behind it, two partially dressed people rolled around on a beat-up beanbag chair. I averted my eyes, stepped over them and found the TV remote. I retreated to the courtyard and changed the channel through the window to watch BBC News.

I'd been living at The Pink House hostel in Kings Cross, Sydney for six months, in direct violation of the sign in reception stating *Thirty Days Max Stay*. I chose not to go to university when all my friends did, so this was my uni experience. Sure, I put washing powder in the dryer and could only cook spaghetti Bolognese, but I was taking care of myself for once.

I headed out the door into a beautiful spring Tuesday in late October. An older woman slumped against some wheelie bins in an alleyway near the police station. She clenched and unclenched her fist, preparing a vein for the needle she held.

As I rounded the corner onto Darlinghurst Road, the bubbling from the fountain grew louder. Its chlorine barely noticeable over a rising wave of cheap floral perfume.

'Morning, honey,' said a woman with a grin outlined in faded lipstick. Mascara-clumped lashes surrounded her bloodshot eyes. With one hand on her hip and the other holding a cigarette, she struck an enticing pose.

Before I could decline, she recognized me, remembering I'd rejected all of her previous offers. She turned and strutted across the street towards another potential customer, her tatty high heels clicking on the concrete.

On my way to the subway station, I passed a plethora of strip clubs. Patrons exited, raising their hands to their eyes to lessen the sobering effects of the morning sun. I spotted a man entering one and wondered if he was beginning or ending his day.

A wide-eyed bloke with long, straggly hair stumbled past me. He shook his head from side to side, arguing with himself. A street cleaning truck beeped while washing away the evidence of last night's merriment in preparation for the cycle to continue.

Another day on the truck. Another hard day's yakka. Another day closer to the end. I hauled furniture with George under glorious sunshine in a land I'd never call home. Australia had come to symbolize freedom to me. Ironic, considering Australia's penal colony past.

'I'm still gutted, mate,' George said, stacking furniture in the back of the truck.

I shook my head. 'So am I, mate, so am I.'

'Whattaya gonna do now?'

'I've heard good things about Thailand from people in the hostel.' I handed him a rope, and we tied the pile in place. 'It's cheap, too. If I save up, I could probably stay there for a while.'

Work distracted me from thoughts of home during the day, and alcohol did the same in the evenings. Now that my return was imminent, I thought about my previous life a lot and questioned what I could've done differently.

With my old school mates at university, and a recent breakup, I'd begun hanging around with a colleague from work and his friends. I was so glad to have them that I never turned down a chance to hang out with them. But they all had better jobs than me. On top of all my bills, I spent money to keep up with their lifestyle.

Maybe I could have stayed in more. Maybe I could have spent less money, but I needed the escape from the house. Whenever I was around my dad, he found a way to argue with me and upset my mum. I needed to get out. I regretted the debt but, in a way, it saved me.

I trudged home after work. The Victorian mansion's flamingo-pink facade peeked through the trees in its front courtyard. The reek of weed wafted from under the closed door of the music room. I imagined the stoners in a cloud of smoke, slumped next to one another on faded sofas. The sounds of *The Simpsons* and laughter blasted from the TV room. Current tenants packed every seat, and party photos of previous tenants adorned the bright yellow walls. The beanbag housed an unsuspecting backpacker. I chuckled to myself as I walked to the kitchen and opened the fridge door.

'Wanker!' I shouted.

The bustling kitchen ground to a halt.

'Alright, mate?' asked Laundry-Matt.

'Some scumbag's stolen two of me beers,' I grumbled. At least they had the decency to leave me one.

I rustled up an Incredible Hulk-sized portion of spag bol and entered the courtyard carrying my plate and my remaining beer. I wanted nothing to do with the '70s-themed fancy-dress BBQ, but this was the only place to sit. Alone across the table, a lad buried his nose in the pristine pages of his Lonely Planet guidebook.

For fuck's sake. He's going to talk to me. All I want is to eat me tea in peace.

He glanced at me several times but said nothing. I remembered my time at the hostel in Melbourne before I met Valerie. I'd sat in the kitchen pretending to read my guidebook. Everyone in the clique cooked, chatted and laughed around me like I was invisible.

'Alright, mate?' I asked him.

His eyes lit up. 'I'm only here for a couple of nights and don't know which bars to go to.'

'Everyone's going to O'Malley's in a bit.' I twirled a massive knot of spaghetti around my fork. 'You should come.'

'Cheers, mate.' He grinned. 'I'll get changed.'

After eating, I relaxed in my dorm, lying on my bottom bunk next to the pile of clothes. I read the names of previous occupants, inked into the wooden slats of the bed above. 'Andrew loves Ann with an e' caught my eye.

I cleaned myself up, avoiding the designated 'sex shower,' and looked everywhere in my room for my favourite French Connection T-shirt. Instead, I found a phone card. Maybe a few precious minutes remained.

My stomach knotted with guilt. I pictured my mum ironing my dad's handkerchiefs into perfect squares before preparing his dinner. The dinner he expected to be on the table after another all-day session at Busby's, or

The White House, or The Pickled Egg. Or maybe he'd found a new shithole to drink in, full of deadhead day-drinkers that wasted their lives worse than him. People he used to justify his own behaviour.

I took comfort in knowing that at least my mum's life was more peaceful without me there. She didn't have to play the mediator for my dad and me. She didn't have to watch as my dad threatened to throw me out of the house for no reason. She didn't have to cry in the kitchen as she pleaded with *me* to back down. To keep the peace.

The phone rang once. 'Oh, hello, love.' Her thick northern accent transported me home, and I could hear the happiness in her voice. 'You alright? What time is it there? What's the weather like?'

'Well, it's—' I tried.

'I'm OK, tired today. I got up a bit ago and made some toast. I made two slices, but I only ate one. I didn't feel like the other one, so I gave it 'dog. He likes toast. I went shopping yesterday, but it took ages. They've moved them frozen tikka masalas again. Them ones your dad likes. I walked up and down. You know where I found 'em?' Her accent sounded even stronger now that I'd been away for a while.

'I don't know, Mum.' I scratched my head and smiled. *Classic mum.*

'Near th'ice cream. Now, why would you put 'em near the bloomin' ice cream?'

'I don't—'

'Well, I asked the young lad stackin' shelves, but he said he 'adn't a clue. I got a taxi home then. Remember that fella who used work at 'timber place? The one who's lad used knock about with that girl who went to your school?'

I held up my hands. 'No idea, mum.'

'You do. She used 'ave blonde hair but dyed it brown. I always see her at 'bus stop in a morning....'

'Honestly, mum, I've no idea. What about him anyway?'

'He drives taxis now.'

'Oh, OK.'

'Anyway, let me finish this ironing.'

'Alright, ta-ra mum.'

'Bye love...bye...bye love. Miss you. Bye...bye.' Her voice trailed off.

I put the phone down. *Never change, mum. Never change.*

A large Pink House contingent, with the new lad in tow, marched down Darlinghurst Road. Past strip club doors with flashing neon signs and busy bars with blaring speakers. Past internet cafes where travellers typed frenzied messages of adventures to loved ones.

Kings Cross pulsed twenty-four hours a day, an alternate Sydney governed by its own set of rules. They swept the dirt here, so the rest of the city stayed clean. A middle-aged man stood under the bright red glow of the Coca-Cola sign. He looked down at his hotel-issued map, then back up at the chaos before him. A woman approached in towering heels and a short, tight skirt, swinging a pink handbag. His jaw dropped, and he scurried away, his camera hanging around his neck. To him, the Cross was disgusting. To me, it was home.

'Nicer' areas of Sydney, such as Bondi or Manly, were havens for backpackers with their beach scenes. The Cross felt more real to me. Growing up on a council estate can have that effect on your way of thinking.

O'Malley's came alive on Sunday and Tuesday nights, filled with travellers from all over the world, united by the dulcet tones of Beau Smith, a big man with a big personality. A dark beard tinged with grey surrounded his broad, permanent grin, and thick red braces always held up his large black trousers.

We huddled, moving as one, singing "Country Roads" with Beau. Beer sloshed in my glass and sweat soaked my clothes.

I chatted to a cute Dutch girl during a break in the music. The hostel drunk walked up beside me.

'Hey, nice T-shirt, mate,' I asked him. 'Where'd ya get it?'

'Lost property.' He looked down at it. 'Nice innit?'

'Yeah, and it's fuckin' mine!'

'I told you, I got it from lost property, James.'

'I don't give a shit. I want it back tomorrow.'

He walked away, rolling his eyes. All was well with the world again.

I left O'Malley's with the Dutch girl. We propped each other up on our drunken walk home and tried several times to enter the code on the keypad to the hostel front door, giggling with each wrong entry. Someone let us in, and we stumbled to my room, where I tucked a beach towel under the top bunk's mattress, letting it hang down over my bed for privacy.

Later, she lay asleep next to me. She was nice enough, but I enjoyed my independence. Soon, she and this group of friends would move on, leaving me here to join the next wave. And in six weeks, my time here would be a memory. My face, lost in the crowd of photos in the TV room, and my name, written on my bunk, the only things remaining.

CHAPTER 16
STEF

"Room 9 is the best room in the Pink House." The girl at the front desk dangled two sets of keys from her fingertips. "Up the steps, on the left."
Three teal bunk beds lined lemon-yellow walls, and a tattered couch blocked a fireplace. Mugs and cardboard boxes of red wine littered the mantel. Six cubbies overflowed with clothes and half-empty toiletries.

"Nice," Christina said.

I dumped my big backpack on the floor and gingerly touched my sunburned shoulders. "All I want is my bed." I scaled the ladder to an unclaimed top bunk, slow as a koala in a eucalyptus tree, and spread my body face-down across the mattress. We'd just flown to Sydney from Magnetic Island, after a busy few days visiting the Great Barrier Reef.

"Hey," Christina said, "Get your ass up." She mock-glared at me with her big brown cow eyes and walked onto our balcony, baking under November's summer sun. "We need to meet people and have fun."

I mumbled into my pillow. "My ass is burnt from snorkeling. Let me lie here and enjoy the best room in the hostel."

"There are people in the courtyard," Christina said. "Let's go."

Christina had been my partner in crime through high school and even college, though we went to different schools. She'd just quit her job in Philly to come travel with me. I didn't know if that made me a bad influence or a good one.

It was Christina's idea when we pranked our guy friends with open casting-call letters from an imaginary porn producer in West Virginia, so the bad influencing went both ways. We even drove all the way to Wheeling to mail the envelopes, so the postmark matched the imaginary address because we were so detail oriented.

We walked into the courtyard as everyone was walking out. Christina's slim figure caught the eye of a sloppy-looking guy with wispy brown hair and two days' worth of scruff. "We're off to O'Malley's to watch the Melbourne Cup," he said in a London accent. "Coming?"

"Sure!" Christina answered for us.

As we followed the crowd down the street, I wondered what the Melbourne Cup was. We paraded down Darlinghurst Road toward an enormous, neon Coca-Cola sign, unofficially marking the confines of Kings Cross. Far down the hill, the golden Sydney Tower kept watch over the Central Business District, where actual grownups in suits were working in glass skyscrapers. Along with sex workers and drug addicts, Kings Cross swarmed with backpackers in wrinkled T-shirts, postponing real life under the guise of self-enrichment. I belonged up here.

"So, you two are mates from home?" our new friend Sam asked. "I bet you got into all sorts."

I feigned offense. "We never got in trouble!"

Sam winked at Christina. "That just means you never got caught."

We walked under a large green sign designating "O'Malley's Hotel" and straight up to the dark wooden bar. Sam looked at the bartender. "Carlton, darling," A Guinness sign glowed behind the bar, and a banner of Irish flags dangled from embossed ceiling tiles.

"So," Christina said, "what's the Melbourne Cup?"

"A horse race."

"Okay, and why is it important?"

"Aussies are like the Brits. They like horse racing. And it's important to *me* because I put a bet on."

I giggled. A short guy approached Christina and me. "Youse are new, yeah?" he said in an Irish accent. "I'm Declan. What room are you in?"

"I'm Stef. This is Christina." I touched her on the shoulder. "We're in Room 9."

"Ah, brilliant! That's my room. Best room in the hostel." Declan held up his pint glass. "*Sláinte.*"

Just before 3 p.m., the bar buzzed with anticipation. By 3:03, the race finished, and Sam celebrated.

"That seemed like a big to-do for a very short race," Christina said.

Sam scratched his scalp. "What sports do you watch, darling? American football?"

"What's wrong with football?" Christina argued.

"For starters, you call it football, but nobody uses their feet."

Christina's face hardened. "*Sometimes* they use their feet. I think *cricket* is ridiculous. What game has tea breaks?" She squinted. "Have you ever *watched* a football game?"

"No. But I enjoyed winding you up about it."

Christina smirked at him while Declan and I laughed.

"Let's head back to the Pink House courtyard," Sam continued. "I'll buy us a slab of beer with my winnings."

At the hostel, we sat for a few hours, drinking Sam's victory beer. The evening sky darkened to indigo, enhancing the orange glow of the lights in the house. The courtyard filled with backpackers relaxing after work, drinking and eating dinner at wooden picnic tables.

Framed by the open kitchen window stood a tall, beautiful man. The Sydney sunshine had bronzed his skin and bleached his short, messy hair. His red T-shirt showed off muscular biceps, and he wore black wire-rimmed glasses that made him look smart. He stirred a pot, sending the aroma of tomato and garlic into the courtyard. He laughed with someone in the kitchen, and his smile made me melt.

Christina and I followed our new tribe back to O'Malley's that night. I craned my neck, looking around the swarm to see if Hot Guy From the Kitchen was with us. The pub steamed with travelers, dancing and singing along with a performer named Beau. I belted the lyrics to "Leaving on a Jet Plane," confident nobody could hear my horrendous singing. When Beau stepped off his platform to take a break, I spotted Sam talking to Hot Guy.

"Christina." I pointed to the guys. "Let's go say hi to Sam."

She looked over and then grinned at me. "Sure."

"Shut up."

We approached the guys.

"Alright, darlings," Sam said, "have you two met this diamond geezer yet?"

"Y'alright? I'm James." James put his pint down to shake my hand. His English accent differed from Sam's, and he looked at me with eyes bluer than any sky in Britain.

"Stef. What's a diamond geezer?"

Sam patted James on the back. "It means he's a sound mate."

"That's so funny! In America, a geezer is an old man!" I said, chuckling.

Sam said, "Oh." James just looked at me, and Christina grimaced. Beau retook the stage and played "Under the Boardwalk," halting our conversation and saving me from further awkwardness.

Sometime in the early morning, Sam, James, Christina, and I sat back in the hostel courtyard, soaking up the booze in our bellies with burgers from Hungry Jacks. James peered into a greasy paper bag. "Do we have any more sachets of tomahto sauce?"

I giggled, and he looked up.

"Is that funny?"

I shook my head, flushing. "Um, no. It just sounded very British."

"What would you say?" Sam asked. He put on an exaggerated Southern drawl. "Uh paycket uh kaytchup?"

Christina frowned at him.

After we finished our food, James said he had to work in the morning, so we said good night and went our separate ways. As I lay in my top bunk, a flutter rose in my chest.

For the next few days, Christina and I applied for jobs and explored our new city. We hiked through the botanical gardens, where foot-long bats dangled from lush tree branches. We snapped photos of the Sydney Harbour Bridge and Opera House, sparkling under brilliant sunshine. And we wandered the cobbled streets of The Rocks, Sydney's oldest section and site of the original penal colony.

Christina and I sat on the bench on our balcony one afternoon after canvassing the town with resumes. Christina elbowed me in the side. "So, how about James?" She Groucho-wiggled her eyebrows.

"While you were shopping last night, I hung out in the TV room just because he was there. I watched two episodes of Baywatch."

"That's sad."

"I know."

"Stalker." Christina pulled her bare feet up onto the bench cushion. "At least we don't need to stealth-drive past his house like we did to the guys in high school."

"Remember when we thought Brandon Cleary spotted us, and you almost crashed into his mailbox?"

Christina cackled and shook her head in shame. "Did I ever tell you he had that porn audition letter framed on the wall of his apartment at Penn State?"

"No! That's awesome." I felt a burst of pride. "But seriously, I'm not enjoying this crush." I slumped in my seat and pulled a yellow pillow onto my lap. "After everything with Miguel, I should just stay away."

"Well, we're leaving in three months, but you could have fun while you're here," Christina said. "And *I'm* enjoying it because you act like an idiot around him."

I smirked and threw the pillow at her.

Christina and I took temp jobs as housekeepers at a hostel called the Globe. We arrived early Sunday morning to an eerily quiet building. The manager pointed us to a supply closet and rattled off our list of chores.

We gathered dozens of half-empty cans of Carlton and boxes of Stanley wine from the tables in the TV room and wiped away cigarette ash and a sticky layer of unknown origin. As Christina cleaned the party mess in the kitchen, I vacuumed the bedrooms with a backpack vacuum, sweeping around clothing piles while hungover people lay on their bunks, ignoring me.

I met Christina in the hallway to do the bathrooms, and she laughed. "Nice Proton Pack."

I followed her up the stairs and bumped into her after she stopped abruptly.

"Dude," she said flatly.

"Dude? Dude what?" I peeked around her. A large, chunky puddle on the floor stunk of booze and bile.

"Gross!" My shoulders heaved forward in an involuntary gag. I mummified my hand with paper towels and mopped up the mess, trying my best not to contribute to it.

I entered the courtyard that evening, hopeful I'd see James after work. I wore a striped American Eagle halter top and low-rise jeans—an outfit carefully chosen for its equal ratio of cuteness to nonchalance. Declan waved me over and patted the bench. "How was work?" he asked and poured me a mug of boxed wine.

I yanked my jeans up by the belt loops and sat down, adjusted my waistband so it stopped slicing into my belly, and pulled the back of my shirt down over my butt.

Declan watched the process. "Jaysus, you finished?

"These pants aren't designed for sitting."

Declan looked at me like that was the dumbest thing he'd ever heard.

I shrugged. "So, I touched a stranger's barf at work."

"Aye, it's been a tough day," he said.

"You're full of shit. You read books on your bunk, you lazy leprechaun."

"Feck off!" He grinned. "But I did, yeah." Declan had been laid off in Ireland and was living off his severance pay.

James dragged himself through the door, and my heart leaped into my throat. Over the past five days, we'd said hello a few times, and though I didn't want to care, my body tingled every time I saw him. He slumped onto a bench and closed his eyes. His nose and cheeks were sunburned.

"Hey," I said.

He opened his eyes. "Alright, Stef?"

"Yeah. Good! You going to watch Beau tonight?"

"Nah. I'm knackered." He took off his glasses to rub his eyes. "I'll probably take a shower and go to bed."

"I'm sorry you had a long day. But I think you should still come." I smiled.

"Maybe. I'm going to shower," he said and shuffled back inside.

"James doesn't like me," I told Christina later when we gathered to walk to O'Malley's.

"Why?" she said, rustling in her purse for her key and wallet.

"I don't know. It's fine. Better, actually."

Christina looked up, and a grin spread across her face. I glanced behind me, and my stomach somersaulted. James had showered and changed into a nice black T-shirt that showed off his tan skin and strong arms. He'd put contacts in and gelled his blond hair.

I looked back at Christina. "Dammit," I whispered.

"Oh, you're done for," she said with a grin.

At the pub, we gathered in front of the stage. Beau sang "Man in the Mirror," and I sang along and danced. James stood nearby. I leaned over toward him. "Not a dancer?"

He laughed. "No, if I'm dancing, I'm pissed and need to go home."

I pictured Kevin Bacon's angry warehouse dance in Footloose and hoped I had misunderstood. I just laughed anyway.

"Need a drink?" he asked and pointed toward the bar. I followed him over, and he bought me a bottle of Archer's Cranberry. It was quieter back there.

"The Steelers are on in the morning!" I said, knowing he liked sports.

He swallowed a sip of beer. "Who?"

"Um, the Steelers? Yeah, I guess you wouldn't know who they are. They're my city's football team."

"American football?"

"Yes, American football, where they never use their feet. I know, I know." I held up my palms, automatically conceding. "Anyway, Christina and I are getting up early to watch the game."

"I don't have to work. Maybe I should watch it with you," he suggested.

"Sweet, it's a plan."

We talked for hours. The world around us faded into indistinct colors and sounds. Everyone we knew left.

"Our mates have all ditched us," James said.

"I know! The nerve!"

"Eh, Sam's not as pretty as you are, anyway." He laughed nervously.

I looked up, riveted by his baby blue eyes. He caressed my cheek with his hand, and when his soft lips touched mine, my pulse raced. It felt like I'd waited a lifetime for this kiss.

He pulled back and smiled. "That was a long time coming, wasn't it?"

I nodded—breathless and surprised he felt the same way.

We walked to a twenty-four-hour bar called the Empire. "This trip's changed me a lot," he said. "Everyone at home does the same shit. Work five days, go to the pub at the weekends. There's so much more to life."

I held up my bottle. "Cheers to that. Where are you going next?"

I thought a look of sadness flashed across his face, but then he gave me a smile. "I had wanted to stay here in Australia, but that fell through, so I'm headed to Thailand in December. It's going to be fucking quality. How about you? Where next?"

"Christina and I have visas to work in New Zealand in January." I grinned. "And then in April, I have a second interview in California with a company that guides outdoor trips for teens in Peru."

"Peru?" James raised his eyebrows like he'd never considered going there.

"Yeah. It's a dream job! I applied ages ago, and of course, they contacted me right before we flew down here, so I did a phone interview. I think the visit is pretty much a formality."

"Well, good luck!"

We met Christina in the TV room at dawn, waiting for kick-off in her black and gold jersey. James watched ten seconds of the game and fell asleep on the beanbag chair. Christina looked at me and waved her Terrible Towel as soon as he passed out.

James and I picked up groceries the next day and walked home along Darlinghurst. He wore a white ringer T-shirt with the red St. George's Cross of England on the chest, paired with flat sneakers and short pants that flaunted his ankles.

"You look like a British Backpacker cliché. Nice capris."

"These are *three-quarter-length trousers*," he scoffed. "I'm a man, they're not capr—" He halted, moving his head and sniffing like a bloodhound picking up a scent. "That smells de-goddamn-licious." The aroma of warm waffle cones lured us into an ice cream shop on the corner.

"I want iiice creeaam!" he shouted in a deep voice.

"Sshh!" I scolded.

"Ssshhh," he mocked me. "Ssshhhish kabob." He cracked up at himself and added, "Ssshhhawshank Redemption."

"Ssshhhitake mushrooms?"

He laughed. "Nice one!"

The teenage girl standing on the other side of the counter snapped her gum and waited for our orders with crossed arms and a bored stare. James ordered a ridiculously monstrous waffle cone with whipped cream and chocolate sauce that was so big it smeared on his face as he ate it.

We carried our treats into the courtyard amid a rousing game of shithead. Playing cards lay scattered across the picnic table. "James, mate," Sam said.

Christina caught my eye and burst out laughing while I squeezed onto the end of the bench next to Declan and a guy called Laundry-Matt.

"Yes?" James said.

Sam just shook his head.

When James finally got down to the ice cream, he took one lick, and his scoop of vanilla plopped off the cone onto the wooden table. "Noooo!!!" he yelled.

Everyone else howled with laughter. I glanced across the table at James, realizing just how much I liked this goofy English guy with a sprinkle stuck to his cheek.

A couple weeks later, I woke up early while Christina, Declan, and my other roommates slept on in the glowing dawn light. I crept down from my bunk, grabbed my swimsuit and clothes from my cubby, and dressed in the bathroom down the hall.

I fueled up on muesli, alone in the courtyard. Signs of life gradually filled the Pink House. A clock alarm screeched. Newscasters' voices emanated from the TV room.

Christina and I had officially settled in. She got a job at Fossil watches, and I worked at an outdoor gear store called Kathmandu. I felt in my element, surrounded by outdoorsy people, selling tents and sleeping bags. I also found work putting up Christmas decorations overnight in local malls. A few times, I decorated all night, crashed at the hostel for a few hours, and went to work at Kathmandu—where sparkly snowflakes hung from the ceiling and "Let It Snow" played while shoppers in tank tops and shorts bought holiday presents.

James and I both had Mondays and Tuesdays off. We'd hung out our whole "weekend" and many weekday evenings at the bars, surrounded by backpacker friends. Exhausted and tipsy, he'd forget everything we talked about—setting us up to have the same conversation next time he was exhausted and tipsy. The only time I'd spent alone with him was behind the beach towel on his bunk.

I was thrilled when he asked me to go surfing. It could be an adorable, sober, actual date.

James peeked his head into the courtyard. "Alright, Stef, you ready?"

"Yeah! I'm excited."

"Okay. I just have to round up Declan and Dave."

I nodded. Talking would have betrayed my disappointment.

A few minutes later, the three guys and I headed up the street to catch the bus to world-famous Bondi Beach. The bus's doors squeaked closed behind us after we got off, and it pulled away in a puff of diesel. Hot air rose from the pavement, distorting the view into shimmering ripples: an amber crescent of sand, bookended by cliffs supporting million-dollar homes. The air smelled of salt and sunscreen, and the sun glistened off crashing swells and oiled sunbathers. A few surfers carved smooth curves into each wave.

We picked up boards and wetsuits from a rental store. I emerged from the changing room hesitantly, dressed in neck-to-toe rubber.

We dragged our boards to the sand. Declan and Dave headed straight into the waves.

"Okay, James." I put my hands on my hips. "How do I do this?"

"Just drag it out and ride it back," he said and dashed into the crystal surf.

I stared at my board for a second and hauled it into the sea. I gasped when the first ice-cold wave slammed against the board and shoved me backward to shore.

Again. By the time I lumbered out far enough, I'd already exhausted myself. I lay on my board and paddled furiously. The first wave rolled underneath me, and I hadn't moved an inch closer to shore. Again. Again. A wave lifted me up, rocketing the board forward. I hollered and popped up to my knees. The board lurched, I toppled into the foam, and I tumbled until I literally didn't know which way was up.

I ground to a halt in a tangled heap—sandy hair pasted to my cheeks, a stream of salty snot smeared under my nose. I beamed and charged back into the waves. Out and back, out and back—just like James had told me to. My muscles burned. My lungs heaved. I stood upright on the board for a few exhilarating seconds, forgetting about everything and everyone else.

On the bus back to Sydney, the four of us sat quietly in exhausted contentment. *This* was why I traveled. For new experiences. Not new guys.

James broke our silence as we got off at our stop. "Anyone fancy a steak for tea?"

I looked at him. "Steak for tea?"

"Supper. In Northern England, tea means supper."

"We call that dinner."

"Yeah, dinner means lunch."

I laughed. "Okay. Well, steak for tea sounds good." We agreed to regroup after we cleaned up.

A cold shower rinsed salt and a concerning amount of sand from my skin. I wondered where I'd been storing it all. I chose a short jean skirt and my favorite yellow sweater, did my hair and makeup, and added a spritz of Cucumber Melon body spray.

I sat next to James at the picnic table in the courtyard and smelled his fresh cologne. He wore his favorite French Connection UK shirt, with "FCUK Fashion" printed in tiny white letters. "You're knackered, aren't you?" He chuckled, showcasing his adorable smile.

"Yeah. But it was amazing."

We chatted a bit about how my first time surfing went. "So, I'm starving now," I added and waited a beat. "Are you still planning on going out to eat?" I asked, hating myself for being so fucking pathetic.

"Dave and Dec are tired. But I'll see if Sam wants to go."

"Okay. Christina should be home. I'll see if she wants to go, too."

Christina lay on her top bunk, reading. She held her page with her finger and looked up. "How was surfing!? Give me all the details."

I climbed up the ladder and plopped at the foot of her mattress. "Good. Declan and Dave had fun, too."

Christina grimaced. "That sucks. Sorry."

"It's okay. Want to come out to dinner? We're getting steaks."

"Who's going?" she asked.

"Me and James."

"I'm not going with just you two." She sat up and set her book on the bed. "Why don't you go by yourselves?"

"Because the thought of spending time alone with me repulses him."

"Clearly."

I made a face at her and added, "Sam might go."

"Maybe I'll go if Sam goes."

She followed me halfway downstairs. James stood at the bottom of the staircase and called up, "Sam's not coming."

"I guess it's just you two, then," Christina whispered in my ear. She went back upstairs singing, "Have fun!"

"Okay, let's go," James said and walked out to the road to hail a taxi.

I followed him out the door, wondering if his haste was indicative of his attitude toward our quasi-date. Was he just wanting to get it over with? But as we sat in the back of the taxi, we chatted comfortably, like we always did.

The hostess at Forrester's sat us at a table clothed in white, and my heart raced. I reminded myself he wasn't even alone with me by choice.

I picked up my glass of pink wine. "What's your family like?" I asked.

"Um, I spend a lot of time with my brother and his wife. I miss them and their kids. I had a rough childhood, so I want to be there for them as they grow up."

"Why was it rough?"

"I grew up on an estate—"

"What?" I interrupted, picturing Wuthering Heights.

"No," he laughed, realizing what I was thinking. "A council estate—

government housing. I used to get bullied a lot."

"That's horrible. I'm sorry."

"I took karate, and I used to watch the fight scene in *Karate Kid* every morning to help me face the bullies," he admitted with a sheepish look that made me want to smother him with hugs.

"Are you close to your parents, too?" I asked.

"Not as much. I love me mum… Let's just say, their relationship has definitely shown me why I never want to get married." He laughed awkwardly.

Fantastic. I'd managed to dredge up all his childhood baggage within ten minutes of sitting down to dinner.

"So, do you like being a mover?" I asked.

He smiled, hopefully wiping the previous conversation from memory. "Yeah, it's alright! I get along great with my boss. I'm always tired, but I need to save money for Thailand."

"When do you leave again?" I asked.

"December."

I sipped my wine, but a lump in my throat remained.

One month. But Christina and I would be heading to New Zealand in January, anyway. Then I'd fly to California in April for my interview, land a guiding job, and move to Peru. "Stef's Future 2.0" was set, and my romantic history was zero for two as far as changing my plans for any guy.

His departure would be a good thing. I could stop swooning over him and live my life.

We finished dinner, and James paid the bill, which was sweet because he hadn't actually asked me out. The sun had set, and the air had cooled. "It's lovely out. Shall we walk back to the Cross?" James said, throwing his arm around my shoulder. "Um. So I was pretty nervous to go out with you tonight."

I looked over at him, but he stared straight down Darlinghurst.

"I know I seem all loud and goofy, but I'm honestly quite shy. That's why I always chicken out and ask people to come out with us."

I beamed. "Is that why you abandoned me at the beach today?" I joked.

"Huh? Oh. No. That was because we only had the boards for two hours."

I cracked up. "And here I was waiting for a private lesson," I joked, but James didn't laugh.

"I like you!" he said suddenly. "And I'm sorry I was drunk all those times in the beginning, but I was upset about not getting sponsored."

"Hey," I said softly, "it's okay."

James smiled, looking relieved. "Sam told me I had to grow a pair and go out with you by myself tonight."

"Do you still wish he was here?"

"Nope." He stopped walking and turned toward me. He put his other arm around me, pulled me close, and kissed me. This kiss felt different. Sober. Real. We still had separate futures starting in a month, but for the moment, I couldn't have been happier.

CHAPTER 17
JAMES

I sat on a cheap rented surfboard, rocking in the Pacific Ocean. A breeze brushed over my hot skin and through my wet hair. The cold sea lapped against my waist and numbed my tired muscles. This might be the last time I'd get to do this.

Although Bondi Beach bustled with people, it often offered me an escape. Some time away from my moving job and money worries. I'd imagine what it would be like if I were the only one there. In my mind, I cleared the sand of locals and tourists along with their towels, chairs and suntan lotion. Then the shops and restaurants and finally the road faded away. All that remained was the pristine sandy beach, rocky cliffs being pummelled by waves, and me, bathing in glorious sunshine.

For the past few weeks, I'd been in immigration-rejection free fall. Partying and drowning my sorrows. Making up for all the nights out I'd declined due to work. During one of these nights in O'Malley's, Sam introduced me to Stef, an American girl from Pittsburgh. I was very drunk. The whole pub was singing along to Beau, and I couldn't hear much of what she said. Instead, I just stared into her beautiful blue eyes.

Every time I was out, Stef was there, and we'd always end up together. I'd be drunk and rambling, and she had an uncanny way of finishing my sentences as though inside my head. Hanging out with her was fun and funny, and she was easy to be around, though I don't remember many details of our first few weeks together.

I caught a wave and stood up on my surfboard, then glanced around, all proud, hoping Stef would see me before I fell face-first into the water. The swell spun me around multiple times, eventually letting me up and ever so gracefully dumping me onto the shore.

I took a deep breath and sucked in my belly as I walked towards Stef. The wetsuit was not flattering at all. I lay my board next to hers.

'How's it going?' I asked.

Stef put her hand above her eyes to block the sun. 'Surfing is hard.'

'Yeah, but it's fun, though, innit?'

'Definitely.'

I was glad she had fun. I'd been really excited to take her to Bondi Beach. Initially, it was just going to be the two of us, but that made me nervous. This would be the first significant amount of time I'd spend with her sober, so I'd recruited some hostel mates to come with us.

After the bus ride back to Kings Cross, I was starving and suggested to the group that we get steaks for tea, prompting an explanation of my northern English vernacular.

In the courtyard, Stef reminded me about the steaks. I went to ask Sam to come.

'Who's going?'

'Me and Stef.'

He laughed. 'Just grow a pair and go out with her by yourself.'

I crossed my arms. 'Why? We're not dating!'

I asked three more friends and received similar responses. I walked to reception, hoping Christina would come. But then I saw Stef. Even in her ugly yellow jumper, she looked pretty. Somehow her hair looked blonder now and her eyes even bluer. It was as if I saw her for the first time. She smiled when she saw me.

'Sam's not coming,' I said.

'Have fun!' Christina shouted as she made her way back upstairs.

Is this a date? Suddenly a nervous energy filled my body.

'OK, let's go,' I said.

At the restaurant, we chatted effortlessly, and she asked me questions about my parents, childhood and nieces and nephews. I told her my embarrassing *Karate Kid* story. No one knew my *Karate Kid* story. Then came *the* question.

'When do you leave again?'

'December.'

We both picked up our drinks and took long sips.

After dinner, I paid the bill and suggested we walk back to take advantage of the beautiful evening. But really, I needed time to think. Stef had been chipping away at my boundaries. She made me feel like I could tell her anything. She made me feel comfortable. She made me feel.

I could see the bright light of the Coca-Cola sign getting ever closer. Time was running out. I needed to do this now. I put my arm around her but wasn't brave enough to look at her.

'I was really nervous to go out with you tonight,' I said. Stef looked over at me.

'I know I seem outgoing, but I'm actually quite shy, and that's why I always chicken out and ask people to come out with us.'

Stef smiled. 'Is that why you abandoned me at the beach today?' she said.

I had no clue what she meant. 'Huh? Oh. No. That was because we only had the boards for two hours.'

'No time for a private lesson, then?'

Stop asking questions, I thought. I needed to say this now before I talked myself out of it.

'I really like you!' I blurted. 'I feel embarrassed about being so drunk all those times we hung out, but I was sad and pissed off about not getting sponsored.'

We stopped walking. Stef's gaze pulled me in. 'That's OK,' she said.

'Sam told me I had to grow a pair and go out with you by myself tonight.'

'Do you still wish he was here?' Stef asked.

'Nope.' I put my other arm around her and sealed the moment with a kiss. Stef squeezed me tight, and I could tell she felt the same.

CHAPTER 18
STEF

Christina put some change in the jukebox, and "Thriller" pumped through the sports bar. James leaned over a pool table, expertly sinking the eight ball into a corner pocket. Sam laughed and shook his head in defeat.

"Again?" James asked.

"Naw, mate. I can't take being battered four times in a row."

As Christina and I tried to replicate the zombie dance, the world spun slightly. My fruity Archer's schnapps drinks went down like Kool-Aid, and I lost track of how many times James asked me, "Ready for another?"

James and Sam had organized an "All Day Bender." A full day of drinking, hopping from bar to bar, like St. Patrick's Day. But Brits don't need a holiday—just a day.

"So, tell me about Stef," James asked Christina. "Some good old stories."

Christina laughed deviously.

"Oh, let's not," I said.

Christina ignored me. "I've got a stockpile of embarrassing Stef stories. This one time she went to wash her car . . ."

Sam and James leaned in. I groaned and looked down at my feet.

"And this lady—"

"Okay, if you're gonna tell it—" I interrupted. "I went to the change machine and then came back to the car to put the coins in to start the foaming brush thing. I started to wash my car, and a woman stopped by and just watched me wash my car. She's staring at me for a *long time*, and I'm just soaping up my car, scrubbing the tires, thinking, 'What the hell is she staring at?' And then she walks closer to me and says, kind of timidly,

'Excuse me, I think you're washing my car.'"

Everyone cracked up. "Were you drunk?" Sam asked.

"Of course not!"

"Was it the same car as yours?" James asked.

"It wasn't even the same color!" Christina howled.

"You guys suck." I stuck out my tongue and went to the bathroom as they all laughed.

That's the thing about old friends—they know everything. Nobody was better at embarrassing me than me, but my high school friends did pitch in to help a lot.

Christina was there when I got thrown in the lake and when I got my sweatpants pulled down at sleepovers. Or the time I got locked on the roof and had to moon my friends to be let back in. They secretly filmed it on a camcorder and tried to play the tape at a crowded after-prom party, but I stood in front of the TV, heart pounding, and covered the screen with a blanket while someone tried to pull it away.

Looking stupid had become part of my identity, but it did teach me not to take myself seriously. Now, when I did ridiculous things, I felt compelled to tell everyone about it so they could laugh at me because subconsciously, I had accepted that being the fool was my role in the world. I just owned it.

I sat down in the bar bathroom, feeling unstable. After I peed, I noticed just a bit of spotting. "Aw, maaaaan," I mumbled. Luckily, I had a light tampon in my purse. I sat on the toilet for a bit longer, just to catch my breath, and returned to the party.

"All! Day! Benderrrr!" I announced and threw my arms in the air.

"Oh, dear," James said. "Slow down, love. It's a marathon, not a sprint."

I stopped trying to keep up with the Brits and felt much better. James and I walked back to the Pink House that evening—arm in arm and very cheerful. I leaned on the wall outside Room 5, giggling while I watched James's unsuccessful attempts to get his key in the door.

"You, you be quiet. This is tricky," he said as he fumbled.

The door clicked open, and we cheered. His roommates were out for the night. We sat on his bunk and fumbled in the dark, a mix of impatient passion and impaired motor skills. In my fog of schnapps, I forgot about the tampon I'd put in when I was hammered.

"Stop! Ohhhh, stopstopstop! Shit!" I pushed him off and reached in to find the tampon, panicking that he'd punched it up into my uterus.

He froze against the wall, eyes bugging out of his head. I realized I had not yet informed him of what I was doing.

"I have a tampon in. I can't find the string."

He stayed back, tense and unsure of what to do.

"Your fingers are longer. Can you try to find it?"

He obliged, too bewildered to protest. "Um. Uh, I can't. I can't find it," he said.

"Okay." I wrapped myself in his beach towel, hustled to the bathroom, and corrected the situation with some laborious pushing. And possibly some grunting.

When I returned, he was sitting motionless, with the vacant eyes of someone making sense of an unspeakable horror.

I crawled onto the mattress next to him. "Sorr-eeeey," I sang.

"You fuckwit."

We burst into laughter. I sighed and buried my head in my hands. "I know."

James leaned back against his pillow and pulled me close. "Only you, Stef. Only you."

CHAPTER 19
JAMES

I rummaged under my bunk for my only dress shirt and headed up to the third-floor storage closet to grab the rusty ironing board. Tingles of anxiety pulsed through my hands as I steered the crusty iron. Stef and I were going to a Spanish restaurant downtown. A proper date, since apparently, I'd fucked up a first date I didn't know was happening. The iron hissed and spat water all over my shirt. "Son of a bitch!"

Why was I even doing this? My visa would expire in three weeks, and I'd booked a trip to Thailand, so there was no point getting involved with someone. I liked Stef, but I tried to keep my emotional distance.

Friends in the courtyard greeted me with wolf whistles and clapping. 'It's about time, mate!' Sam shouted.

I felt my face flush. I sat on a bench next to Christina.

'You look nice,' she said, nudging my arm. 'Are you excited for your *actual* date?'

'Yeah, but what the fuck is Spanish food? Is it stinky fish and dodgy wine with fruit in it?'

Christina laughed. 'It's tapas. Like, lots of appetizers. You'll like it.'

What are appetizers? I'd been raised on bacon butties and mum's lamb hotpot.

I couldn't sit still and walked to reception to wait for Stef. Her hair bounced as she made her way down the stairs. Her ugly yellow jumper was replaced by a tight pink and white top that tied around her neck. She waved nonchalantly with one hand and brushed her blonde hair behind her ear with the other. Her freckled cheeks glowed, and her eyes sparkled.

I opened the door for her with sweaty hands, and our friends waved us off.

Once seated at the restaurant, Stef immediately picked up the menu. 'Chorizo is a cured sausage. It's delicious. Jamon Serrano is thinly sliced ham. You'll love that. Tortilla is a thick omelette with onions and potatoes.'

I watched her smile grow wider and her eyes brighten with every new dish. Who *was* this beautiful, passionate girl from Pittsburgh?

When our waiter came to take our order, he and Stef chatted in Spanish for a minute. She spoke fluently and rolled her r's like an expert. She ordered our food and a pitcher of sangria. I asked for a large beer.

Plates of sausage and ham arrived. I discreetly sniffed the cured meats while Stef poured herself a glass of wine. They didn't *smell* weird. I took a small bite of the red chorizo, and the intense flavour flooded my mouth. "Wow! That's good!" I said, relieved.

With contagious enthusiasm, Stef told me about her time studying in Spain. The scenery, the architecture, her language mishaps. A plate of Spanish omelette came next. 'Spuds and eggs, you say? I think I can handle this.' I revelled in my newfound culinary confidence. 'I never ate any of this stuff when I went on holiday to Spain.'

She shook her head in disappointment. 'That's a shame.'

'Magaluf was full of British pubs with English breakfasts and *Only Fools and Horses*.'

'Fools and what?'

'Never mind.'

She poured some more wine. 'We should go someday. I'll show you real Spain.'

'I'd like that,' I said. And meant it. The thought of us in Spain, eating tapas in the sunshine, excited me.

Our waiter reappeared and nodded in approval as Stef rattled off something in Spanish.

'Erm, what did you just order?'

'Octopus.'

'Oh, OK.' I took a long sip of beer.

Fuck.

The plate arrived. 'That's paprika sprinkled on top,' Stef informed me.

I didn't know what the hell paprika was, but the purple tentacles underneath it worried me more.

Stef dove in, closed her eyes and let out an audible 'Mmmm!' I could see her travelling to Spain in her mind. She opened her eyes and waited for me to try. I pushed the appendage around the plate before stabbing a suction cup with my fork. I couldn't smell it first without looking like a twat, so I readied my beer and shoved the fork into my mouth. It was squishy, slimy, rubbery and delicious. I chewed on it, looking Stef in the eyes with a smug grin on my face, and went straight back for another piece.

After dinner, I suggested we watch a live band at the Three Wise Monkeys, where we flirted and kissed amidst the trendy crowd.

I considered asking Stef if she wanted to watch Manchester United play Liverpool, which would mean heading to a shitty sports bar in the Cross. I raised my arm, pulled back my shirt cuff and ever-so-subtly glanced at my watch.

'Everything OK?' she asked.

'Yeah, great. It's just that me football team's playing a big match at two.' I pictured myself fast asleep in the TV room when the Steelers played and instantly regretted telling her.

'We can go watch them if you want.'

'Are you sure?' I touched her on the shoulder. 'Cos I'm fine here, really.'

'Yeah. Let's go,' she said and gestured towards the door. It took restraint not to celebrate.

A short taxi ride later, we arrived in Kings Cross outside the sports bar, its big-screen TVs visible through the windows.

'Wow! There's a line,' Stef said.

'It's a massive match. These are our big rivals.'

'Oh, cool. So why are you a Manchester United fan?'

I was impressed she asked. In the queue, Stef listened intently as I filled her in on the last fifty years of Man U history. 'Sorry if I'm boring you.'

She shot me a surprised look and then smiled. 'You're not.'

I rambled on about how I'd supported them because of my childhood adoration of George Best, and that growing up in the '80s meant having to endure Liverpool winning everything.

The crowd's singing grew louder as we inched closer to the entrance. Just before kick-off, we squeezed through the throngs of sweaty football fans in shorts and T-shirts. Stef's smile disappeared. It returned when she spotted a group from The Pink House. Sam asked about the date, but it would have to wait.

United scored, and beer spilt on our glad rags, but Stef kept smiling. She jumped up and down with me and laughed as strangers hugged us.

How am I going to leave this in a month?

I needed to find a way for us to spend more time together.

CHAPTER 20
STEF

"Hey Stef, I want to talk to you for a sec," James said. He left for Thailand in two weeks, and though I'd known from the start that this was how it would end, I still braced myself.

"Okay."

We sat on the top step of the back staircase. The freshly vacuumed carpet smelled like corn chips and feet. Fake pine garland wound up the bannister, and a glittery Rudolph had been stuck to the wall near posters advertising pub crawls and day trips to the Blue Mountains. A large world map just behind James's head had yellowed and curled with age.

James smiled nervously and touched my hand with his. "You know I'm leaving in two weeks . . ." I noticed the lamination on the corner of the map had frayed into three layers. ". . . so I was wondering if it might be okay with you if I push my flight back."

I looked at him, my breath stopping short.

"I'm just having a lot of fun. With you," he continued, "so I thought I'd stay until you leave for New—"

I cut him off with a bear hug. "Yes. Yes! It's okay with me!" I let go so I could see his adorable face, and he looked relieved. He'd been looking forward to Thailand so much. And he wanted to postpone it. For me.

"I'm going to have to switch flights and—"

"Shhhh. We'll plan later." I squeezed him again. We had six more weeks.

Since James's Australian work visa expired, he had to leave the country to get a new one. He flew to New Zealand for a couple of days and returned to Australia on a tourist visa.

He found me in the teeming courtyard on Christmas Eve. "I've got you something," he said and pulled me by the hand toward Room 5.

"Oh, wait! I got you something, too!" I ran upstairs to grab his present from my cubby, and we sat on his bunk bed in his empty room. "For my Manly Mover." I handed him my gift—a silver frame holding his favorite photo of us—dressed up for a night out downtown, arms wrapped around each other.

"That's quality. Cheers, love." He pulled a small package wrapped in white paper from his bunk shelf. "I knew you always wanted one of these, and someone told me it's bad luck to get one for yourself."

I pulled back the paper and revealed a jade *hei matau* pendant—the Maori fishhook carving like the one I'd seen around Ginger Jack's neck in France. "Thank you! It's beautiful."

He leaned close to put it around my neck. "I love you," I blurted, surprising myself with the news as much as James.

James sat back, and his eyes widened. "Did I hear you right?"

"Yes?" I whispered.

He smiled. "I love you, too."

I grinned, relieved and blissful. But in an instant, I remembered loving him was a stupid fucking mistake, and I felt pissed off with myself for allowing this to happen again. My smile faded. I looked at him quietly, absorbing him. Fixing him in my memory, since soon that's all he would be.

"Chin up, love. No moping." He touched my cheek and gave me a sweet kiss, then looked into my eyes. "Okay?"

"Okay."

James went to the courtyard, but I zipped back up to Room 9 first. Christina, Declan, and our other roommates sat on the couch drinking. "Cute necklace," Christina said. She opened a care package from her parents, and I spotted a large clear bag filled with tiny fake snowflakes.

"Aw! They sent winter!"

"Yeah, I told my mom how weird summertime Christmas is."

"Guys." I grabbed the bag of flakes. "We should make it snow!" I shook the bag and wiggled excitedly, making Declan laugh.

We gathered discreetly on our balcony and sprinkled the snow onto our housemates' heads, snickering at their confused faces. They looked to the sky in disbelief, and when they noticed us delivering the wintery weather, they cheered.

"Nice one, Stef," Declan said, tossing a fistful of flakes into the warm air.

I caught James's eye, and he looked up and gave me a big grin.

Sam craned his neck back and held his can of Carlton high. "I'm dreaming of a White Christmas," he belted, and the rest of our housemates joined in. I sang in loud, unapologetic disharmony. Our fellow backpackers from the northern hemisphere threw their arms around each other, swaying and caroling, a testament to the quick and strong bond travelers feel.

Our whole crew then took taxis to the Coogee Beach Hotel pub. We drank on the patio as the ocean crashed behind us, knowing we'd all soon move on in different directions.

James and I walked down to the beach at midnight, after everyone else went home. The ocean was a bottomless black. In the distance, the moon's reflection shattered into glitter.

We sat on the sand, and I buried my toes in the cool grains. "This Christmas has felt weird. Nice, but weird."

"On the beach in summer?" James nodded.

"Yeah . . . but also this is the first one I've spent without my family."

"You miss them?"

"Yeah. I love Christmas morning. My dad lights a fire, and we eat breakfast casserole on the good plates. Then we put *A Christmas Story* on TV and spend forever opening presents and drinking eggnog." I looked down and ran my fingers through the sand.

"Sounds nice. Christmas wasn't a big deal for us. A few years, my parents went on holiday."

"Wait—without you?" I looked up at him. "They left you at Christmas?"

"Yeah. I was a teenager. I thought it was great." He shrugged. "My dad's kind of an arsehole."

"Wow. I'm sorry." I reached over and squeezed his hand as he stared out to sea. I suddenly wanted to take him home, show him what Christmas should be. What a family should be.

For two months, I'd been telling myself this couldn't last. I probably had a job in Peru. But thinking of us together far in the future felt natural. I didn't question it, and it didn't scare me.

The moon coaxed the water closer while the rolling waves shushed us. I pulled my toes back from the silver froth, and we sat quietly for a moment.

James glanced at his watch and looked over at me. He patted my hand. "You ready?"

I looked at his handsome face, softly reflecting the moonlight, and smiled. "Yeah. I'm ready."

Rust-red dirt stretched to the horizon in all directions. Parched plants in muted greens dotted the earth under an enormous blue sky. The region had magical names that hinted at the emptiness: The Outback, The Red Center, The Never-Never, Back of Beyond. Christina and I had booked this trip months ago. Though sad to lose five precious days with James, I really looked forward to road-tripping the Northern Territory, a place unlike anything I'd ever seen.

Christina crunched on a handful of crackers called Chicken Crimpies and glanced at our map as I drove our rental car. "A town called Barrow Creek is ahead. We should get gas."

The Stuart Highway's two barren lanes ran perfectly straight for miles. Once in a while, a road train would approach, the huge Mack truck growing larger and louder until it thundered past with its five trailers rattling. In an instant, it was a memory in the rearview mirror, and we were on our own again.

Thirty minutes later, we arrived. "I guess a gas station and bar equal a town out here?" Christina said as we approached a dusty saloon. Two equally dusty men sat on rickety chairs under the shade of a corrugated metal roof.

"No power," one man grumbled.

"Why?" I asked.

"'Cause there's no power." He never glanced up from his stubby of Victoria Bitter.

We stepped into the dark, stuffy tavern and sat at a graffiti-covered bar. Leather ranchers' hats hung around the small room, and liquor bottles and knickknacks cluttered the shelves. Signed global currencies fringed the walls, guaranteeing travelers money for a beer the next time they passed through. Some of the yellowed bills in the "bush bank" had been waiting for decades. The bartender served us two lukewarm cans of Coke. Not expecting scintillating conversation from the locals, we guzzled the drinks and left.

Christina pumped the gas while I drew a smiley face in the orange powder caking the car. The painted numbers on the pump clicked round and round. I snapped a photo of some black chickens pecking the dirt by the sun-bleached saloon, and when my shutter clicked, they stopped pecking and stared me down. The herd charged me, furry feet flying. Christina started the car, and I jumped in and slammed the door. Christina rolled with laughter. "Are you afraid of chickens?" she squealed.

I ignored her and spotted the flock in the side mirror, chasing our car out of town.

"Okay, you'll have to navigate for me," Christina said.

"According to the map, we drive north for . . . a million miles."

"Got it, thanks."

"I read that Aboriginal people navigated by singing songs that described the terrain they passed. They call the routes Songlines."

"Huh. That's interesting. No way I'd travel anywhere with you, then." I frowned at her.

She grinned. "Hand me some Crimpies?"

We pulled into Kings Canyon at dusk, pitched our tent under a lavender sky, and walked to the campsite bar for one drink. Hours of driving in the Red Monotony had made us sleepy, and we planned on waking early to hike. We'd just ordered two mango Bacardi Breezers when a young Australian man approached. "Hello ladies, how're you going this lovely evening?" he chirped.

"Fine, thanks. How are you?"

"Ace! Would you like to join me in the pool tournament tonight?"

I shook my head. "Oh, thanks, but I'm not that great at pool."

"Well, you have to come do karaoke later, then," he insisted.

We gave him a "Maybe!" that meant "No," took our drinks outside, and sat on an empty porch in the cooling desert air. We reminisced about our Aussie adventure so far and planned our Kiwi adventure yet to come.

"I can't believe we only have three days left in Sydney after this," I said.

"Three days with James," Christina clarified for me.

I sighed. "Why do I fall for guys in impossible situations?"

"'Cause you're a pain in the ass who likes to make things difficult."

"True. I feel different about James, though. I feel like he's someone I might want to be in my life . . . for a while."

Christina raised her eyebrows. "Shit, Stef. Like, no Peru?"

"Maybe. I'm annoyed at myself for even thinking it."

The bar door opened. The same guy peeked out and announced, "I think you left something inside—your smiles."

We couldn't help laughing.

"I won the pool comp!" he continued. "I can't drink fifty dollars' worth of grog on my own."

"Okay. Twist our arms," Christina said.

"Excellent!" He held the door open for us. We stepped back into the dim bar just as the karaoke DJ called, "Luke? Luke?"

"Oh, I better get up there." He rubbed his hands together and grabbed the mic. Christina and I exchanged amused glances.

Another Aussie our age approached. "I know he's a bit aloof, but he'll warm up when he gets to know ya." He stuck his hand out. "I'm Ed."

Luke spoke the intro to his selected reggae-rap, "Boombastic," in a convincing Jamaican accent.

I looked back at Ed, who shrugged. "Luke's shout—same?" he asked, pointing to our bottles. We nodded. "Sign me up for a song," he said as he

102

walked to the bar to get our drinks. "Surprise me."

"Oh, you're gonna regret that," Christina teased.

When Luke finished, the twenty other people in the bar clapped, and he took a slight bow. Ed came back with our drinks as the DJ called his name and the song we chose flashed on the screen. Christina and I snickered, but Ed didn't flinch. He grabbed the mic and sang "Bootylicious" with unanticipated sincerity.

Luke and Ed's enthusiasm infected the others in the bar. Two dozen strangers sang, cheered, and bonded. Ed dragged Christina up to the mic, leaving Luke and me at the table. "You having a good time?" Luke asked. "You looked kinda serious out there."

"Ah. Yeah, next week we're going to New Zealand, and I don't know what's going to happen with my boyfriend and me."

"Long-distance is tough. But don't worry. If it's meant to be, you'll find a way." He gave me an encouraging pat on the shoulder.

Unfortunately for everyone in the bar, I sang a lot. I sang with Christina, I sang with Luke and Ed, and I sang with Joe—a short, middle-aged Chinese dude wearing a T-shirt with *Chicks Dig It* printed across the chest. He clapped and cheered after every song, including those he sang himself.

After a soulful rendition of "Moon River," Joe sat down next to me. "Let me see, Stefanie." He took my hand and traced the creases of my palm with his finger. "You love to travel. You're like Marco Polo!" He tapped one spot. "This one says you always do what you want. You make your own path." He looked up at me for confirmation.

"Yeah, I guess so."

"You have a boyfriend?"

"Yes."

"What are your birthdays?" Joe frowned when I told him. "Both Year of Horse. You'll fight a lot. But maybe it will be okay."

I nodded, unconcerned. And then Joe taught me some Kung Fu moves while Christina and Luke sang "You Shook Me All Night Long."

At last call, Christina and I brought the house down with "The Devil Went Down to Georgia," complete with square dancing. Everyone in the steamy bar belted the words out and swung around, linked at the elbows.

We walked outside with Luke, Ed, and Joe as the lights flicked on and bartenders stacked chairs on tabletops. "Thanks for forcing us to hang out with you, Luke," I said.

He gave me a wink. "No worries."

Christina and I hugged our new besties. Joe looked genuinely sad to see us go. As we headed toward our tent, Luke called out after us, "You girls rock!"

A few hours later, my watch alarm beeped.

"No. It is not morning already," Christina whined.

Though exhausted, we forced ourselves to get up and hike the canyon. I took postcard-perfect pictures of sheer red cliffs, flawless blue sky, scorched black trees, and a hidden green oasis—but still, when I think of Kings Canyon, I think of karaoke.

The myths of the Dreamtime explain the creation of the Aboriginal world. Near Karlu Karlu, the Devil Man twirled strings of hair to make a belt. He dropped some clusters on the ground, seen today as round boulders strewn about the crimson sand.

The Indigenous Australians are the world's oldest civilization. The original inhabitants of the Outback thrived in a land most would consider barren. They dug for witchetty grubs with a knowledge of the land and hunted kangaroos with the flick of a boomerang. Teenage boys completed a rite of passage known as Walkabout, where they roamed the land, surviving alone for months. Then colonists deliberately destroyed 50,000 years of skill and culture in just a couple centuries.

Christina parked our car near the historical site, and we meandered respectfully among red rocks twice our height. Some perched in precarious piles, others were cleaved perfectly in half. I ran my fingers over rough granite glowing in late afternoon light, until low clouds rolled in and filled the sky, smooth and rounded as the boulders beneath them.

We walked back to the parking lot, covered in red dust and indefatigable flies. "Fuck off!" I shouted as they buzzed into every facial orifice.

"I feel like I ate chalk," Christina said, taking a long swig from her water bottle.

"Did you know the Aborigines used to squeeze water from the skin of a frog?"

Christina frowned. "Nope."

When a fly plunged into my ear canal, I yelped and jumped into the car, thankful I'd never had to live in a place so desolate and difficult.

From Karlu Karlu, we drove south to Alice Springs, the Outback's largest town. Reminders of its remoteness were pervasive. We visited The Royal Flying Doctor Service, a hub that sends out ambulance planes while doctors on radios talk distant patients through self-treatment. At the School of the Air, we toured a broadcast station where teachers gave lessons to children isolated hundreds of miles away at cattle stations or aboriginal communities.

At the Aboriginal Art and Culture Center, Christina and I met Wayne. "Didgeridoo sounds are based on nature," he said in his strong Aboriginal accent, showing us a long instrument made from a termite-hollowed tree trunk. "Kangaroo, emu, dingo, frog. Even the wind. Sometimes I'll go into the bush and try to capture the spirit of an animal in the music."

"Why?" I asked.

"It's just the Aboriginal way. Sometimes we'll play for days. It's a way of being close to nature and thanking the spirits of the animals."

Wayne placed his lips on the waxed top of his didgeridoo and blew a deep, vibrating tone.

After a brief lesson, I blew into my didge. Spit flew everywhere, and a fart sound squeaked out.

Christina cracked up.

I stuck my tongue out at her. "How do you make it look so easy, Wayne?"

"I play every day. At night, I play at a dinner show for tourists," Wayne said with a weak smile.

"That's nice," Christina said.

"Well, the Big Men say they're trying to help us, but they're really just making a profit. It's draining our spirits." He looked down at his dirty sneakers.

Wayne was forced to perform his culture when all he wanted to do was live it. But Aboriginal people could no longer survive the same way in their own land. Aboriginal society is mobile. Modern life depends on settlement. They're forced to exist in two incompatible cultures simultaneously.

Walking back to our hostel, we passed a group of Aboriginal girls sitting on the sidewalk. They had wavy chestnut hair streaked with sunny highlights. Not so long ago, they might have been sent to a boarding school to eradicate their language, culture, and skin color.

These girls joked and giggled, showing off big white smiles. One girl, about eight years old, in a pair of pink shorts and bare feet, approached me. "I like your blond hair. It's pretty."

She took me by surprise. I smiled and said, "Aw, thank you!" as we kept walking. I instantly regretted not stopping. Then I worried it would be weird to go back. I wanted to ask them about their lives. School. Dreams for the future. I wished I had told them their hair was pretty, too.

On our last night in the Outback, Christina and I watched the sun set over the desert and admired Uluru as the monolith faded through tones of red, orange, violet, and purple.

Walkabout. Songlines. Dreamtime. The poetry of the words haunted me just like the beauty of the stark terrain and I began to understand the pull of the land. Fluorescent pink clouds streaked across the expansive sky as a flaming sun dropped from view, ending our day and starting another one somewhere far away, just like it has, every night, for millennia.

CHAPTER 21
JAMES

On a typical sunny Sydney day, Stef and I sat on the sand at Bondi Beach. But the situation was anything but typical. Even though we'd only been together for three months, we were getting serious. She only had two days left before her trip to New Zealand, and I was starting to let myself envision a future that included her.

Before I could contemplate that future, she needed to know about my money troubles. I had no idea what would happen, but I did know that my debt could drastically impact any future plans. Plus, I felt like I was hiding a big secret from her. I'd given this a lot of thought while Stef was visiting the Outback with Christina, and I wanted to do it in person before she left.

We people-watched for hours as the waves crashed in front of us. I looked for a segue in our conversations, but it wasn't easy.

'James, can you pass me my water bottle?'

'Here you go, love. Oh, by the way, I'm secretly a fucking loser with shit tons of debt waiting for me back home that's making me nervous about planning any kind of future with you. Fancy a swim?'

My heart was pounding, but I'd waited long enough. 'Stef, love. There's something I need to tell you.'

She swivelled her head to face me. 'O . . . K.'

'There's something you deserve to know about me.'

'What is it, James?'

I put on my sunglasses. 'The thing is, I've got a LOT of debt back home. I had a lot of expenses I had to pay to my parents, and I worked a low-paid job for years instead of going to uni, and then I made some friends that I really liked, but we went out all the time, and I thought I could maybe earn enough in Australia to pay it back, but that was impossible. Anyway, I'm really not sure what's gonna happen when I get home.'

I looked towards the sea. It was embarrassing enough that my family knew this about me, but I hadn't told anyone else until now.

'Thank God for that,' Stef said, moving her hand to her chest.

'Wait, what?'

'I was worried you were gonna tell me you'd murdered someone or something.'

I turned to face her. 'Shit! Sorry. No, nothing like that.'

'That happened to a friend of mine. I know how it spirals.'

'Really?'

Stef put her arm on my shoulder. 'Don't worry, I don't think any less of you.'

'Thanks, love. I just thought I should tell you.'

I wrapped my arms around her.

'It'll be OK,' Stef said reassuringly.

CHAPTER 22
STEF

On our last night in Australia, Beau stood on stage, wearing his usual red suspenders, grinning his usual grin. James had a beer; I had an Archer's. People laughed and sang, but I felt hollow. I looked around O'Malley's for the last time.

"So, I have a request," Beau announced. "For Stef, from James."

I looked over to James, and he smiled. He put his arm around my shoulder as Beau began to sing, "Leaving on a Jet Plane."

My face crumpled into an ugly mess, and I buried it in my hands and sobbed until I couldn't breathe. I wiped under my nose with my finger to quell the flow of snot.

James's face fell, and he hugged me tightly. "Oh, no. I'm sorry, love. It was supposed to be nice."

I felt awful for ruining his sweet send-off, but hearing "Leaving on a Jet Plane" at O'Malley's, where it all began three months before, overwhelmed me with sadness.

James and I stayed up the whole night, sitting in the hostel hallway.

"I probably wouldn't be so upset if I knew I'd see you again," I said. But people get distracted, people move on. People being me. I couldn't let that happen with James.

"I can come visit you in America. I'd like to see New York. I can come after Thailand, in May. Maybe we can squeeze it in before you leave for Peru?"

I smiled. "I'd love that."

Early next morning, James quietly waited for the airport shuttle in front of the hostel with Christina and me. When the van pulled up to the sidewalk, my stomach flipped over. James and I hugged and kissed for the hundredth time, and I got in the van. The driver shut the door with an unsympathetic slam.

I looked back. James stood alone on the sidewalk, weakly waving goodbye until we turned the corner.

"Sorry I'm being so depressing," I said to Christina. "I'm ruining this for you."

"It's okay," she said. "And it'll *be* okay." She gave me a side hug in the van. "You'll see him again."

"Yeah. I hope so."

Our plane descended through damp clouds over jade fields dotted with New Zealand sheep. We bussed to Queenstown, checked into our hostel, found our room, and dropped our bags. "Come on, let's go check it out," Christina said with an encouraging smile.

Tourists and locals in rain jackets bustled down the damp, brick-paved pedestrian mall, past locally-owned restaurants and cozy pubs. Souvenir stores displayed pearly abalone jewelry and sweatshirts printed with "Aotearoa," the Maori word for New Zealand—Land of the Long White Cloud.

Christina nudged me with her elbow. "This is so cute!"

On one side of town lay a still lake. A patch of sun broke through the clouds and streaked across its silver waters. Posh hotels and homes climbed a verdant hill on the other side. Majestic mountains ruled over Queenstown, their summits crowned in mist. It was everything I'd always hoped for, but I felt numb.

Christina took a nap after returning to the hostel, and I called James from the common area payphone.

"I felt like I'd been kicked in the gut when you left," he said. "It's weird being here without you. I'm just ready to head to Thailand now."

"I know. But soon you'll start your new adventure, too."

We didn't have much else to report, but hearing his voice helped. After we reluctantly hung up, I sat on a computer in the hostel lobby, trying to figure out my life.

Since landing *one* position for the guiding company in Peru was like winning the lottery, there was no way they'd hire both of us and let two newbies run trips together.

Maybe James could come to America, or I could go to England. An internet search revealed that our countries didn't offer working holiday visas like those for Australia and New Zealand. We couldn't just show up and find a job—one of us would have to have an employer willing to sponsor us from the start. After an hour, I'd found no way other than through an international corporation—a nearly impossible task. James's accounting qualifications meant nothing in the US, and I had literally no skills other than teaching. Frustrated, I shut the computer down and went to the room for a long nap.

CHAPTER 23
JAMES

I sat shirtless with the windows down. Hot air whirled around us, transforming the truck's cab into a tumble dryer. I could barely hear my own voice over the wind and engine groan. George and I were moving furniture 660 miles up the east coast of Australia, from Sydney to Noosa, in our 'new' truck. New to the business, as the truck itself was older than Caesar's whip.

Caesar's pluses: it carried furniture, and it drove. Minuses: it lacked power steering, air brakes, air conditioning, a radio, a first gear, engine-noise reduction technology, any technology at all, comfy seats, a hydraulic lift, legroom and almost all of its original horsepower.

The long drive up the Gold Coast gave me plenty of time to think about the last few months with Stef. We'd walked in the Blue Mountains, watched kangaroos boxing on the beach in Apollo Bay and driven the Great Ocean Road, where jagged rock formations offshore baked in the sun.

I'd managed to make Stef cry her eyes out after requesting that Beau sing "Leaving on a Jet Plane" in O'Malleys on her last night. I stood in silence the following day as she and Christina loaded their backpacks into an airport shuttle. I wrapped my arms around Stef for one more hug, and nausea filled my stomach when she waved at me from the backseat.

The latest group of friends had moved on from The Pink House. Goodbye notes dotted the bulletin board by reception, filled with email addresses and promises to keep in touch. It wasn't home anymore. Enthusiasm for making new friends was at an all-time low. George kindly offered me the spare room in his flat for the next couple of months. I pinned a scrap of paper with my email address to the board, and though grateful to George, I still left the Pink House with a heavy heart.

George's whole family was extremely kind to me. For the first time in months, I had my own room and home-cooked meals most nights. One Saturday, he invited a few friends over. We drank VB stubbies and stayed up all night building a model Millennium Falcon. George's place was out in the Sydney suburbs, and on quiet evenings, I craved the city. I craved the backpacker scene. I craved Stef. Our relationship had been stripped down to emails and phone calls, and the thought of losing her in the distance saddened me. With not much else to do, I threw myself into work and focused on saving for Thailand.

After sixteen hours, we pulled into a car park in Noosa. I turned off the ignition, and Caesar shuddered and stopped.

'Shall we check into our hotel and then get some dinner?' I asked George.

'Hotel? You're in it, mate,' he replied.

'We're sleeping in Caesar?'

'Aw, yeah.'

I glared at him. 'You're having a fuckin' laugh, aren't ya?'

'Well, I figure we got two options, mate. Option One, I pay for a hotel, and we eat fast food, or Option Two, I buy us steaks and beers, and we sleep in the truck.'

'Option Two it is, then.'

Before we ate, I called Stef in New Zealand.

'Hi!' Stef said enthusiastically.

'Hiya, love. I'm in a place called Noosa. Been driving all day, and George is making us sleep in the truck.'

'That's kinda shitty,' Stef said.

She laughed when I told her why.

'So, I've made proper plans to meet Keith and Rick in Thailand, and I'll look into flights to Pittsburgh soon,' I said. 'I'd better earn some more money.'

'Talk soon.'

'Ta-ra, love.'

George and I feasted and drank the night away before checking into Hotel Caesar. George pulled his cap over his eyes and passed out. I contorted my sweaty body into all manner of positions but couldn't fall asleep.

'Fuck you, George!' I shouted in a vain attempt to disturb him and climbed onto Caesar's roof.

Itching forced me awake, and I squinted in the early morning light. I winced from a stiff back as I inspected and scratched my legs. Gingerly, I climbed down into the cab.

'Get up, George!' I shouted.

George woke, startled. 'Fuck me drunk. Whattaya want?'

'Look at the fuckin' state of me. I've got twenty-five mozzie bites. *Twenty-five!'*

He shrugged. 'You shoulda slept in the cab.'

The last rays of sunshine gleamed over the hive of activity on Khao San Road, Bangkok. It was the first day of my two-month trip to Thailand and Malaysia. A chance to unwind after months of hard work in Australia. A chance to enjoy myself. The previous weeks had been hard with Stef in New Zealand.

I slouched on a chair in a restaurant called Central Cafe where the completely open front allowed me to immerse myself in the street. On a table in front of me sat a bowl with the remnants of a Thai green curry. I picked up my ice-cold bottle of Chang beer and took a well-earned swig.

'Orange juice ten Baaaaaaaaaaht!' a Thai lady called out, her soft voice trailing off. She meandered down the street, weaving her cart through the throngs of travellers, dodging their large backpacks as she went. Street-side proprietors closed their eclectic stalls, neatly packing watches, handbags, T-shirts, copied DVDs and all manner of trinkets into large plastic laundry bags.

Street vendors flooded the air with the aroma of peanuts from their sizzling woks of Pad Thai. Hungry customers waited patiently around them on plastic stools.

'Where should we go tonight, James?' Keith asked.

I looked at him. 'Dunno, my mate. You lot 'ave been here before. You tell me.'

Keith and Rick had led me around all day, and I was fine with letting them continue. I enjoyed not being in charge. Keith was of Iranian descent—short, with spiky jet-black hair, and Rick was pale, tall and lanky. Both spoke with London accents. They chatted with some of Keith's friends from home, who were also in Bangkok, about our evening plans.

I grabbed my camera from my pocket and placed it on the table, eager to finish the roll of film and have it developed. I smiled as I remembered Mum's photos from back home. Each packet ended on some random images she had taken to finish the roll. A wall, the floor, my dad's startled face.

Keith, Rick and I had spent the day exploring the Grand Palace—a complex of majestic temples and palatial buildings. Structures adorned in gold and jewels shimmered against a clear blue sky. On arrival, we were handed old, wrinkled trousers to put on over our shorts. No explanation given, but the stern faces of staff members implied it was necessary. I cringed at the thought of who might have worn them before me.

We walked the grounds, filling my camera with their beauty. I noticed the locals leaving their shoes at the entrances to the temples and we followed suit. At temples containing statues of Buddha, they sat crouched down with their feet behind them, so we did, too.

One of the temples, Wat Pho, housed a 150-foot-long reclining Buddha. He lay on his side, his right arm supporting a head of tight curls. The soles of his feet were inlaid with mother-of-pearl, and his elegant body was covered in gold leaf.

Stef would love this. I imagined bringing her here one day. Seeing the joy on her face as she immersed herself in another culture. Communication would be scarce until my visit to America. I called her from an internet cafe, and the few seconds of voicemail I left on her mobile cost more than a night's accommodation.

I knew that after Asia and my visit to the US, I'd have to return to England. Tanned, blond and broke again. So, I promised myself I'd try and make the most of my time and not think about returning home and starting from scratch at twenty-four.

I read through some pages of my guidebook at Central, intrigued by the etiquette shown at the temples. It was all about respect. Especially the way people sat. In Thai culture, the feet, being the lowest part of the body, are dirty. Therefore, it's considered disrespectful to point them towards someone.

'Drink up, James, we're leaving,' Keith announced, pulling me out of my reverie.

'Where are we going?' I grabbed my camera.

'To see a show at Patpong.'

We headed to the end of Khao San to hail a tuk-tuk, a three-wheeled motorbike with a canopy above and a bench in the back. Two speakers were screwed to the sides, and a string of half-dead flowers dangled from the rear-view mirror.

I snapped a quick photo of Keith and Rick in the seat before wedging myself beside them.

'Tuk-tuk Number One,' the driver said, revving the engine.

I gripped the metal framework of the canopy as he careened down a busy highway, zigzagging between buses and trucks and blasting dance music, which drowned out my shrieks. Our driver laughed and looked at us in his rear-view mirror with each near-death encounter.

To distract myself from my fear, I turned my attention to my surroundings. Thick exhaust fumes hung in the humidity. Run-down housing lined littered streets. My thoughts turned to the Grand Palace and the unfairness of the disparity within the same city.

We stopped abruptly a couple of feet from the car in front. Tyres squealed, and the smell of burning rubber filled the air. Traffic stood still. The engine sputtered amidst the symphony of horns. Our driver turned to us with a mischievous grin on his face.

'Tuk-tuk Number One.'

'Yeah, we know,' Rick said.

The driver pointed to the sky. 'Tuk-tuk like helicopter.'

'What the fuck does that mean?' I asked.

He yanked the throttle, shooting us up onto the two rear wheels. Canopy lights flashed in time with the loud music as we grabbed onto each other.

'Fuckin' 'ell!' I shouted.

We jerked forward and back down on all three wheels with an inch to spare. Silence. Cue maniacal laughter from our driver, followed by nervous laughter from his passengers.

I jumped out of the tuk-tuk in Patpong. Around us, a night market buzzed with activity. Well-dressed tourists perused stalls of counterfeit designer watches and handbags, followed closely by haggling salesmen.

'Is this a real Prada purse?' a middle-aged woman asked.

'Yes, yes,' a local salesman answered, nodding. 'Same same. Same same but different.'

Deeper into the market, music pumped from the neon-lit bars, each one vying for our attention. No Pad Thai here, just the smell of vomit-infused alcohol.

'Where you go? Where you go?' A local shouted and shoved a menu in my face.

'I'm not hungry, mate,' I replied, swatting it away. 'Why have we come here again?' I asked the group. No one replied.

In the bars, overweight European men ogled half-naked women with half-smiles gyrating against metal poles. Each one had a numbered badge pinned to her thong.

'You look. You look.' Another menu appeared in my face.

'For fuck's sake.' I snatched it. This was no food menu unless darts and ping-pong balls were a Thai delicacy.

I studied the menu until the man grew impatient. He took it back and walked away. 'Ping-pong show! Banana show!' he shouted at other passers-by.

I jogged to catch up with my group. They headed up a dark staircase underneath a red-and-blue neon sign in the shape of the Superman emblem. I hesitated for a moment. Another menu man approached. I ran up the stairs.

Inside the club, long mirrors hung from every wall, making it hard to find my bearings or the group. My sandals stuck to the threadbare black carpet. Flashing pink lights illuminated a stage with a wraparound bar. Older men filled the booths, surrounded by scantily clad Thai women and clouds of cigarette smoke.

I found my group at the bar and sat on a stool, arms by my side to avoid touching anything.

'What's up, mate?' Rick said, smiling.

'Why have you brought me to a strip club? This place is fuckin' well mingin'.'

The barman arrived with a round of beers. 'No pointing. Tell me number,' he explained, nodding back towards the numbered dancers flooding the stage.

'Cheers!' Keith said. We clinked bottles, and I wiped the top of mine with my T-shirt before taking a sip.

After the dancing, the stage cleared, silence fell and the club descended into darkness. A lone spotlight illuminated the middle of the stage. A naked Thai lady appeared holding a trumpet. She lay on her back and played a catchy tune with her 'lips'.

I'd heard about ping-pong shows but never really believed they existed. This was even more creative and seeing it in person felt surreal. Like those of the rest of the group, my eyes were glued on her. She manoeuvred her body around, ensuring a good view for all.

'Holy shit!' I said and nudged Keith in the ribs.

Bang! Bang! Bang! The next woman pulled an endless string of toy-gun caps from her special bits in rapid-fire succession. I looked at Keith and Rick, my eyes bulging.

I didn't have time to process what I'd seen because immediately, a giant Martini glass descended from the ceiling. In it, a naked woman writhed around in soap suds to the theme song to *Titanic*. Our faces bore the same quizzical expression. *What the actual fuck?*

The strong Chang beers flowed freely, and more Thai women showcased their gynaecological talents, including shooting the well-advertised ping-pong balls and blowing out candles on a birthday cake.

The dancers returned to advertise themselves. 'It's my mate's birthday,' Keith shouted to them while pointing at his friend, Patrick. Two of the women pulled on Patrick's arms, dragging him reluctantly up to the stage. The crowd cheered. Patrick smiled and showed off some dance moves. The women surrounded him, yanking off his shirt and pulling down his shorts. Patrick stopped smiling.

He stood motionless in his boxers as the women danced around him.

Keith laughed so hard he almost fell off his bar stool. I reached into my pocket for my camera. A click and bright flash captured Patrick's predicament.

For the grand finale, a woman dressed only in shiny high-heeled shoes lay on her back. She inserted a peeled banana, pushed her body up towards the ceiling, shot the banana straight up into the air and caught it with one hand. The defiance of gravity and physics perplexed me.

She repeated the trick for all four sides of the room. We waited inquisitively as our turn neared, huddled together and leaning forward on the bar in unison. The banana shot straight out towards us with great force and military-like precision. Time slowed down as it flew across the stage, over the bar and into Rick's face. The used banana crumbled on impact and rolled down his cheek. Slimy yellow chunks dotted his black shirt.

'Fuuuuuuuck!' Rick grimaced in horror. He gingerly made his way to the toilet, careful to avoid getting any morsels on his shorts too.

My ribcage hurt, and my cheeks ached from laughing. Out of the corner of my eye, I noticed her reload and aim towards me. I leapt off my stool and ran as the bright yellow projectile barrelled my way. I ducked, and it flew over my head. 'Fuckin' 'ell!' I screamed.

The woman gracefully exited the stage, smiling at me.

A scowling Rick came back from the toilet, dabbing his shirt with a wet paper towel. 'I've had enough now,' he said.

We paid the bill and headed for the exit. A tall bouncer in a black suit and pristine white shirt blocked the doorway. His large, muscular arms folded across his chest.

'Give me camera.' He held out his hand.

'What?' I asked.

'No photos. Give me camera.' Four of his large bouncer friends joined him.

The effects of the beer wore off instantly. Then it really hit me. The seediness of it all. Why did they not want anyone to document this? My heart sank at the thought that these women might not have chosen to be here.

'Give him the film, James,' Chris suggested.

'I wanna keep the photos of the temples, though.'

The bouncer's nostrils flared, and he scowled at me.

'Please let us go,' Keith said.

'Camera, NOW!' he shouted. He stepped towards me. The music stopped, and I felt everyone's eyes on me.

I pictured the palace. Memories of my day spent wandering the ornate complex could be lost.

I studied the camera in my hand for a moment and punched it. Then again and again. The plastic creaked and shattered, sending splintered shards into the air. My knuckles bled. The film lay hidden amongst broken debris. The bouncer surveyed the damage in the dim light. He moved aside. 'OK, you can go.'

We ran down the stairs and didn't stop until we reached the tuk-tuk drivers at the end of the street.

CHAPTER 24
STEF

Over the first few weeks in New Zealand, Christina got a job waiting tables at night, and I cleaned rooms at the four-star St. Moritz hotel in the morning. I spent boring evenings in our hostel lobby, hogging the computer as unfamiliar tourists streamed in and out. No new friends. No games of shithead or boxes of wine.

Two nineteen-year-olds named Manaia and Nicola cleaned with me at the St. Moritz, and they offered to rent the extra bedroom at their apartment to Christina and me. The modest room had naked walls painted Rental White and a bare twin mattress on the floor.

Manaia and Nicola were often out with friends all night. Christina usually had a few drinks after work and would crash on the carpet at 4 a.m., rolling onto the warm mattress after I got up at seven. I spent most of my spare time alone.

Manaia waved goodbye on her way out one evening, her almond eyes mascaraed, dark hair straightened, coppery skin glowing.

"Have fun!" I waved from the couch, ready for another night of TV and pizza-flavored two-minute noodles.

Nicola stood three feet away, making tea in the kitchen. "I still feel rancid from last night. I just want to watch *Kath and Kim* in my pajamas." She pulled her hair into a messy pony and joined me. "You don't like to go out?"

"No, I do. I did a lot in Sydney. Just, not lately." I didn't like to do anything lately. I should have been running and mountain biking in the hills every day. I should have been living my *Blue Crush* fantasy—work as a housekeeper, sleep on the floor, play hard outside—but I didn't have it in me.

"Everything okay?" Nicola asked.

I chuckled. "Hmm, where to start?"

Nicola pulled her feet up onto the couch and pulled a crocheted blanket over us. She held her warm mug of tea with both hands and looked sincerely at me. "From the beginning."

I recounted meeting James my first night in the Pink House, seeing him every day, and falling in love. I described how incomplete I felt without him. How when he called, the sound of his voice fixed everything.

"Wow, you've got it bad." Nicola teased. "Maybe if you come out with us more, it would take your mind off of him."

"That's what I'm afraid of," I said.

Nicola looked at me quizzically.

"I guess that wasn't really the beginning." I told her how I chose an adventure over Alex. And Miguel. And I didn't miss them enough to come back. "I'm a big jerk, and I don't want that to happen again."

Nicola shook her head. "It's not your fault for wanting to live your life. And if your feelings change, that's not your fault either. It wasn't meant to be with the other guys. Don't let that stop you having fun here." She walked the two steps from the living room to the kitchen and clicked the electric kettle back on. "Fancy a cuppa before *Kath and Kim*?"

"No, but thanks for listening."

I walked down the hill after work one March afternoon, wrapped in a sweater to block the early fall air. Mountain trees showed the first tinges of red. I entered an internet café and sat at a computer. I hated that I was considering changing my plans for a guy. I used to judge girls who did that. But now I understood. Jobs come and go, but I had one shot to see where it went with James. And I didn't want to spend my life wondering what could have happened. I typed "Work visa for Britain." I paused and added "teaching" to my search. *Click.*

TEACH IN LONDON

I hit the link and skimmed the page. Teacher shortage in London. Year work visa. Possible extension.

It would be awesome to live in England, and all of Europe would be at our doorstep. I knew I could live in London, but I didn't know if I could get in front of a classroom again.

James called me that night from Thailand. "Hiya, love!"

"Hi. I don't want to go to Peru." I blabbed as soon as he picked up.

"Whoa, what?"

"Yeah. I could get a job and a visa through a program called Teach London. And we can live together in England."

"Love, are you sure? You were really excited about the guiding job."

"I know, but—I just want to be together."

"And you're okay with teaching again?"

"Yeah. I mean, I don't know." My chest tightened. "But I'll do it."

I knocked twice on the door. "Housekeeping?"

Nicola opened the room and went straight to the clock radio to turn it on. A popular hip-hop song by a group called Nesian Mystik filled the room, and we both danced and rapped along.

Nicola stripped the bedsheets while I wiped down the bathroom. When I stepped into the shower to scrub the glass door, an Avril Lavigne song came on, one I'd heard repeatedly in Sydney, about going somewhere new with someone she doesn't know. The lyrics slammed into me. I knelt on the tiles in my frumpy housekeeping dress and cried. I'd known James for three months and was about to give up a fantastic opportunity for him.

"Stef, you done?" Nicola called.

I wiped my eyes and hoped they weren't red. "Yup! Coming!" I tried to act normal but felt anything but. My excitement about our new plan had suddenly turned into fear that I was making a massive mistake.

My cell rang that night, and I opened it immediately. "James?"

"Alright, love? How's it going?"

"Ummm . . ." my voice wavered, and I started to cry.

"Hey, it's okay," he said softly, reading my mind. "We're making some big decisions based on each other, aren't we?"

I wiped my runny nose. "Yeah."

"But you know what," he continued, "If it doesn't work in Pittsburgh over the summer, I'll fly home. Same for you in London. I think things will work out great, but if not, it will be okay. I know you'd be offered another guiding job."

I took a deep breath. "I'm sorry. Everything kind of hit me, and I got overwhelmed."

"Don't apologize, love."

I smiled as we hung up, confident we were doing the right thing.

I called Dad the next day.

"Hi, honey. What's new down there?"

I updated him on my new plan. "The woman from Teach London said I should apply in May, and they can have me placed by September. So, I'm going to cancel my interview for Peru."

Dad went silent for a second. "Wow, Steffie. I didn't know it was that serious."

"Well, I told you James wants to visit this spring. Is that still okay?"

"Yeah, of course. I just don't want you to move to England forever. . .

. But it's better than the Peruvian wilderness, I guess."

I still missed James, but having a definite plan to reunite relaxed me, and I tried to enjoy New Zealand. Christina still worked all night, but I went out with Manaia and Nicola a few times. I started running up Queenstown Hill after work every day. A gorgeous wrought iron door marked the trailhead, so every time I stepped through, I felt like I was entering a magical forest.

Christina and I took a few days off work so we could explore the country I'd dreamt of seeing for years. We collected purple and green stones from the shore of Lake Te Anau. We climbed Franz Josef glacier, gripping the inclines with axes, crampons crunching in teal blue ice, chilled air from serac walls prickling our cheeks. Then we'd slide back down tunnels—like a giant game of chutes and ladders.

We pushed a tandem kayak into Milford Sound on a rare clear day. Calm water made paddling easy. Lush, triangular peaks shot straight from the crystal fiord and thin waterfalls dropped from mountaintops. A seal swam alongside us, bobbing in and out of the frigid water.

"Look!" Christina pointed with her paddle. A stout crested penguin waddled on some rocks. Two strips of yellow feathers splayed out from the sides of his head.

I giggled. "He looks like Danny DeVito." I leaned back in the kayak, letting the sun's rays warm my face, feeling like I could float out there forever.

"Happy?" Christina asked.

"Very." From this idyllic spot, the world, and the future, looked beautiful.

But black clouds blew in on our paddle back. Wind picked up, whipping past our faces. Cold raindrops battered hard and fast, stinging my skin like needles. I dug deep, the muscles in my arms and shoulders burning, but it seemed we got pushed back a foot for every two feet we paddled forward. What had been easy and fun became hard, painful work. But we were already out there and couldn't give up now.

CHAPTER 25
JAMES

Keith, Rick and I boarded a boat off the Thai island of Koh Phi Phi. New camera in hand, I snapped photos of giant limestone cliffs rising from the turquoise sea. The boat motored between some of the cliffs into a horseshoe-shaped lagoon. Palm trees stood tall behind a white sandy stretch made famous by the movie *The Beach*.

I put on my mask and snorkel, and my breaths became shallow and rapid.

'You're alright, mate,' Keith said, nodding. 'We'll stay right with you.'

I sucked in a large amount of air and slipped into the water. A black and white sea snake looked suspended in midair, its twisted body backlit by the clear, shimmering water. I stayed at the surface while Keith dove down towards the vivid colours of a coral reef. His presence drew out a moray eel from the vegetation, close enough for me to see its sharp teeth. Keith and I gave each other the thumbs up.

As the afternoon wore on, I ventured farther from the lads and wandered from a reef into open water. An ominous silhouette with a pointy nose and a dorsal fin came into view. I stopped breathing. I wanted to lift my head above the water but didn't want to lose track of the four-foot shark. It turned towards me, its silver body catching the sun's rays. It flicked its tail slightly and shot off into the blue. I lifted my head and yanked off my mask, grinning and tingling from adrenaline.

A celebratory drink was in order. Our night started at Apache Beach Bar, a low-key place nestled amidst the trees, away from the main street, where we sat on stools listening to the ocean and chill music. 'We should share a bucket tonight, James,' Keith said. 'For your first time snorkelling.'

I shook my head. 'Not this, again.' I'd been warned about the buckets of Thai rum, Coca-Cola and potent Thai Red Bull. 'Remember I told you about Dave? He drank some buckets in Bangkok and woke up in his hotel room with blood in his undies and no idea what happened.'

Rick made a disgusted face, and Keith rolled his eyes. 'You'll be fine, James. We'll look after you, mate.'

Still buzzing from my snorkelling adventure, I caved. I figured if Keith and Rick had kept me safe at sea, they could do the same on land. 'Go on then,' I said.

They beamed and rubbed their hands together when the bucket arrived. We each took a straw and gulped the sweet mixture.

When only partially melted ice and bent straws remained in the bucket, we moved on to Phi Phi Reggae Bar, loud and teeming with travellers. Two skinny men in long, shiny shorts squared off in a boxing ring at the centre of the bar. Cheering erupted when the one in blue kicked the one in red in the face, sending him to the canvas. Rick set down another bucket on a table beside me. I grabbed a straw.

My sleep-encrusted eyelids made it hard to open my eyes. My head pounded. I sat up in bed for a few seconds before my sour stomach forced me back down. I wore a T-shirt but was naked from the waist down. A thin sheet had been draped over my bits and bobs.

The only sound came from the pathetic blades of an old fan. I lifted my wrist to check the time and noticed my bruised and bloody knuckles.

Dehydration forced me to scan our bungalow for a water bottle. That's when the smell of vomit hit me. Three splatterings of it covered the white tile floor. My mouth tasted like the room smelled.

Rick lay on his back, awake but not ready for words. His hands covered his face.

Keith rolled over in his bed. 'How you feelin', mate?' he asked in a chirpy voice.

'Fuckin' shockin',' I replied in a gravelly voice. 'Is it five in the morning or five in the afternoon?'

He pulled back the curtain. 'It's five in the afternoon, James.'

I squinted in the sunlight. Rick moaned.

'What the fuck happened last night? I remember getting to that reggae place, and that's it.' I rubbed my eyes while Keith laughed out loud. 'Also, why don't you look as rough as us?'

'Yeah,' Rick mumbled.

'I stopped drinking so I could look after you two muppets. Especially you, James,' Keith said.

'Why are my bollocks out?'

Keith laughed again. Rick sat up and immediately lay back down, muttering and grunting.

'OK, here's what happened. After the Thai boxing finished, you got into the ring—'

'What?' I blurted.

Rick chuckled. Keith frowned. 'Do you wanna know what happened or what?'

'Sorry, mate. Continue.'

'You ran around shadow boxing like you were Muhammed Ali, shouting into the crowd. "Who wants to fight me? Come on!"'

My mouth dropped open

'Then you did some karate kicks for about ten minutes until you wore yourself out. You hugged one of the corner posts for a bit, and then you lay down and fell asleep wrapped around it.'

'What did you do?' I asked.

'Left you there. At least you were quiet.'

I took a long swig of water, and my throat burned. 'Wow!'

'When you came to, you weren't making any sense, just babbling. I propped you up for the walk home.'

Being that Keith was considerably smaller than me, this was no easy task.

'Where was I?' Rick chimed in.

'Zigzagging down the street, bouncing off shop shutters like a bloody pinball,' Keith explained. 'Then James, you decided you hated the advertising banners hanging from the restaurants. You tried to rip them down.'

'Oh, for fuck's sake,' I muttered.

'So, I pointed Rick straight down the middle of the street and let him go. I ran back to you, and you were stabbing all the buttons on an ATM with your fingers. Then you punched it.'

I looked down at my hands.

'A security guard came over to talk to you, but you scowled at him and screamed "Fuck off!" right in his face, and he legged it. Then, a gang of Thai lads showed up and made a circle around you. I gave them all the money I had on me so they wouldn't beat you up.'

'No! I'm really sorry.' I felt sick again.

Rick piped up. 'Had I gone home?'

'No, you'd just stopped trying. I found you leaning against a shop window with your eyes closed.'

I burst out laughing and grimaced at the jolt it sent through my throbbing brain. 'So, my shorts?'

'Right. We were nearly home, but you stopped at the entrance to our bungalows. You carefully removed your sandals, shorts and undies but left your T-shirt on. You folded your clothes neatly and tucked 'em under your arm and started walking with your free arm up in the air, singing, "Sign on, sign on and you'll never get a job."'

'Fuckin' 'ell!' I said.

'Your T-shirt kept riding up, flashing your knob to everyone.'

'Everyone? Who saw me?'

'I'm 'aving you on, mate. Apart from us, just our security guard. But his face was priceless. I got you inside, you puked everywhere and passed out.'

'Rick, do you remember any of this?' I asked.

'Vaguely,' he said, smiling.

I pulled my hands up over my face and shook my head in disbelief. 'I'm so, so sorry, my mate. I've never done anything like that before. I didn't do any damage, did I?'

'No, you couldn't quite reach the signs, so you just shouted at them.'

I rubbed my knuckles. 'And the ATM?'

'It was fine.'

'I'm embarrassed on behalf of meself and me family.'

Keith laughed. 'It's OK. I think you had a bad reaction to them buckets, though.'

'I feel like such an arsehole!' I said. 'I told you the buckets were a bad idea!'

CHAPTER 26
STEF

Christina and I said goodbye to Nicola and Manaia after a couple months in Queenstown and took the bus to the coastal town of Kaikoura, where we'd arranged to do odd jobs for a cattle farmer in exchange for room and board. In the chilly autumn mornings, I watered the family garden. Brown cows milled about on steep, misty hills behind the house. I imagined they enjoyed their view of the wild black sand beach a couple miles away. In the afternoons, I'd collect pinecones for the fireplace while low-angled sun cut through the turning leaves, gilding every half-naked limb.

I methodically paced the farm in the evenings for a signal, watching my phone for the appearance of a bar—like a metal detectorist searching for an invisible treasure. The end of the long gravel driveway was often the only good spot. In our last emails, we'd planned on a time James would call me from an island satellite phone, if he could get to one.

For a few nights in a row, I sat on the ground near the country road, snuggled in my sleeping bag, holding my phone in the air. The first night, he didn't call. The second night, I went inside fifteen minutes before he called, evidenced by the voicemail that finally buzzed through on night three.

Night four. The world was still. A faint scent of seawater breezed inland, and once in a while, the cows would moo. Cars rarely drove this road, especially after dark. In the distance, the farmhouse windows glowed golden, and directly above, galaxies twinkled in an obsidian sky. I pressed a button on my phone, and the screen glowed green. No bars. I switched hands and moved my arm bit by bit, like an old bunny-ear antenna, until I got a signal again.

My breath turned to fog, so I went inside to warm up. Twenty minutes later, Professor, the tabby cat, followed me back down the driveway and rubbed against my legs with a low rumble. I settled in my spot.

I knew James was hopping around Thai islands, so his emails were sporadic, and satellite phones were hard to find and expensive. But I wondered what adventures he was getting into. Was he meeting new people, seeing new things, and forgetting about me?

My phone vibrated with an announcement of a voice mail, left when I was inside the house. "Hey love, sorry I missed you again," James had said on a buzzy line. My frustration welled up and trickled from my eyes.

"Come on, Professor," I said, stroking his smooth head. "Let's go in."

After a couple weeks of garden watering and pinecone picking, the days blended together. A visit from Declan pleasantly broke the routine. Christina and I met our old friend from the Pink House at a restaurant down the street from the farm." "It's weird having you here, Declan," I said, scooping meat out of a lobster-sized crayfish.

"Cheers, you gobshite! Glad I came."

I laughed and wiped my fingers on a napkin. "No! Just like, out of context. It's good to see you. Are you enjoying New Zealand?"

"Yeah, I've been traveling all over. Today, I went to the seal colony," Declan said.

Christina cracked up. "They scared the shit out of Stef."

"Okay, first of all, they're enormous." I held my hands wide for emphasis. "And they kept popping their heads up from behind the rocks, like whack-a-mole. And they make weird noises, like someone blowing their nose really hard."

"Sounds terrifying," Declan said, making Christina laugh harder. "So I heard about James's drunken night in Koh Phi Phi," he said, apparently assuming I had, too.

My heart sank. What drunken night? "Oh, I haven't heard from him lately." I grabbed some fries and shoved them into my mouth.

"Oh." Declan looked awkward. "Um, I got an email from Keith. He said James climbed into a Thai boxing ring and then took his trousers off and sang football songs on the beach with his bollocks dangling under his T-shirt."

"Like a wasted Winnie the Pooh. Sounds about right." I forced a chuckle. Keith had time to email Declan, but James didn't have time to email me. I felt left behind and forgotten—like Alex and Miguel must have felt. And I knew I deserved it.

"Well, Declan, I'm glad you wanted to try the crayfish. Kaikoura actually means 'eat crayfish' in Maori!" I stated while Christina gave me a sympathetic pat on the knee under the table.

Nine days passed without a word. I took an evening walk down the country road, dragging my heavy limbs. An hour later, I found myself at the black sand beach. I sat on a volcanic rock and looked across the ocean in the direction of home, running my fingers over the smooth jade of my *hei matau* pendant. Christmas Eve seemed like a long time ago.

I wondered if it was over. If I'd ever see him again. If I'd made the wrong decision to cancel my interview. I'd spent my time in New Zealand under a Long Dark Cloud.

I returned to the house as the sun set behind the hills. I checked my phone, and an envelope icon on the screen made my heart skip. And the brief sound of James's deep voice and northern English accent soothed me once again.

CHAPTER 27
JAMES

After recovering from the buckets in Phi Phi, the lads and I spent the next few weeks island-hopping, looking for different experiences. We found laidback bars, rustic, electricity-free bungalows, packed tourist clubs, half-moon and full-moon parties and judgmental scuba divers. Fellow travellers had spun tales of a tourist-free paradise off the backpacker trail, with crystal-clear waters and white sand beaches. The Perhentian Islands, Malaysia. We booked tickets to the border with a vague itinerary and figured we'd piece the rest together when we got there.

The journey began like many before it: hungover. Keith, Rick, and I barely made our dawn pickup on the island of Ko Tao. A local man approached us, pressed a small, bright green, circular sticker on each of our T-shirts and ushered us onto the back of a pickup truck. We sat under a canopy on bare wooden benches, feeling every bump on the dirt road to the ferry port. I looked down at my green dot. 'Just go with it, James,' Keith said and shrugged.

I chose a piece of unclaimed floor on the ferry, surrounded by tired revellers and backpacks. I thought of my dad. I'd listened to him talk about Malaysia, or Malaya, as it was once known. He'd fought in the jungles there during the '60s with the Welsh Borders. Though he didn't mention the violence much, he would, on occasion, divulge details of his escapades and adventures. During a phone call home from Australia, I told him I'd be going, and he joked I might run into some brothers or sisters. The thought weirded me out, but I was excited we might share stories of Malaysia someday.

The journey continued with a bus to a car park, a taxi to a bus terminal, then another pickup truck to a travel agency. It was situated on a back street, flanked on both sides by scooter repair shops. The posters hanging on the walls were all in Thai, and there were no other westerners around. Staff informed us, 'Border closed on weekends. Need hotel here.' They gave us some recommendations for pricey lodging. 'Have to buy Malaysian money here, good exchange rate,' they added. By this point, we recognized a scam. We ignored them and waited outside.

Soon, an overcrowded people-carrier pulled up. The driver pointed to our stickers and beckoned us aboard. This had happened at every stop we'd made, so we boarded. I safeguarded my dot with my life, fearing I would be abandoned without it. Inside, we sat on hot leather seats, surrounded by locals, shopping bags and a few chickens.

Keith, Rick and I said few words to each other all day. We exchanged grunts every now and then to confirm we were still alive. I rested my throbbing head against the window and watched busy streets give way to endless miles of countryside. Grabbing some paracetamol from my backpack, I noticed the framed picture Stef had given me for Christmas. Her face brought a smile to mine.

We'd only spoken a few times since I left Australia. She'd be heading back to Pittsburgh soon, and my trip to see her was still weeks away. She sounded excited about it in our emails, but what if that wore off? Maybe being back in the real world would make her forget our holiday romance.

As the sun faded, the people-carrier emptied. Soon, only three bright green stickers remained.

'You alright back there, James?' Rick asked. Keith dozed next to him.

'Yeah, mate. Gonna get me head down, I'm knackered.' I took my seatbelt off and lay down on the back seat. After the heat, clucking and twelve modes of transport, my hangover devoured me, forcing my eyes closed.

My body hit the seat in front of me, jarring me awake. The brakes squealed. I lay staring at the floor for a moment before climbing back onto my seat. The side door flung open, allowing humid night air to rush in. A bright light blinded me, and I raised my hand to block it. The beam surveyed inside, allowing my pupils to adjust. A stern man in military uniform waved a torch around, shouting in Thai. He moved his free hand towards his waist, bringing his machine gun into view. I sat upright and slid slowly to the far side of the seat without blinking.

After a final sweep of the soldier's torch, he slammed the door shut and disappeared back into the night. We slowly drove past several armed soldiers at a checkpoint before resuming our journey. My jaw clenched and sweat poured down my forehead and chest. *Where the fuck are we?*

We sat in silence. No more naps.

After fourteen hours of traveling, we arrived on the edge of a small town called Sungai Kolok, on the Thai side of the border. There were no streetlights, shops were shuttered and rubbish swirled in the breeze. Our driver ordered us to get out. He pointed down the road and muttered in Thai before speeding off in the direction we'd come from.

We needed food, sleep and possibly new underpants. I removed my dirty, crinkled green dot and put it in my pocket. 'Let's get out of here,' Keith said.

We walked briskly down the empty street until we reached welcomed signs of life: neon and loud music. The usual crowd of backpackers and night markets had been replaced with businessmen gawking at scantily clad girls dancing in open-front bars. Our presence temporarily distracted the men. Our eyes met, and for a moment, we caught a glimpse into each other's worlds. The girls reached out and touched their faces, winning back their attention.

A multi-storey hotel beckoned, its large doors and tank of colourful fish in the window drawing us in. A woman at the front desk sold us a cheap room and seemed surprised that we wanted it for the whole night. 'Restaurant closed,' she said, handing us our room key.

'D'ya know anywhere we can get some food?' Keith asked.

The woman brought the owner to the desk, a tall Middle Eastern man with a dark beard.

'D'ya know anywhere we can—'

'Where are you from? England?'

'Yeah, mate,' Keith said.

'I'm Omar.' He smiled. 'I'm from Kuwait. During Desert Storm, I was rescued by the British Army. I have much love for the British.' He shouted instructions in Thai to his staff. They scurried to the kitchen and dining room, and suddenly, the restaurant was open.

He sat with us at a small wooden table. The smell of cooking rice emanated from the kitchen. Without even asking, beers arrived.

He barked more instructions, and his hustling staff transformed the quiet restaurant into a karaoke bar. A microphone squeaked to life, and a disco ball spun thin rays of light around the room. His reluctant employees trudged to the stage. Thai script flashed on a projector screen while they belted out a whiny pop song. We clapped and politely smiled.

'They should sing an English song for you,' Omar said. More orders.

The lead singer frowned and held his arms out in disbelief. He consulted their book of song choices, settling on 'I Believe I Can Fly' by R. Kelly, and the endearing band did their best.

Craving our beds, but not wanting to offend our gracious host, we feasted and calmed our nerves with more beer. Much to everyone's relief, we eventually called it a night. We shook Omar's hand, thanked him and the staff, and the karaoke club returned to being a dimly lit, closed restaurant.

The next morning, I clung to the thin waist of a scooter-taxi driver as he swerved in and out of traffic on the road to the Malaysian border. Across the Golok River, a large, blue, arched sign decorated with the Islamic star and crescent read: *Welcome to Malaysia.* We filled out the necessary paperwork in a hut while immigration officers stared at us.

I walked towards the bridge with my overstuffed backpack weighing heavy on my shoulders. Although convenient, arriving in a new place by plane isn't nearly as rewarding. With chests puffed out, we crossed proudly over the bridge and under the sign into Malaysia like intrepid explorers.

In the town of Rantau Panjang, locals haggled for food and textiles from the market instead of beer and girls from the bars. Women wore headscarves instead of miniskirts.

We hailed a taxi to take us to the ferry port. After ten yards or so, a Malaysian soldier stepped in front of the car, halting our progress. He waved one arm around and pointed his machine gun towards us with the other.

'Fuck me, not again,' I said.

'What should we do?' Rick asked our driver. He got out and gestured for us to do the same. We stood by the car as more soldiers with guns arrived, drawing a crowd of locals. A soldier shouted at our driver, who opened the boot and threw our backpacks onto the ground. With no hangover to subdue my fear, I watched anxiously as a soldier yanked open zips and began ransacking.

My brother's lecture before Bali came to mind. Though I wasn't carrying anything illegal, what if someone had planted something on me and I didn't know? I could see the headline in the newspapers back home, 'British Backpacker Rots in Malaysian Jail!'

He littered the ground with our clothes and toiletries. Stef's photo, in the silver frame, lay on the road. I was too scared to be mad. Finally, he muttered something in Malay to the others, and they all walked away, leaving our belongings scattered in the dirt.

We repacked in a hurry. 'Let's go,' Rick said to the driver.

I slid into the backseat. 'These islands better be fuckin' worth it!'

CHAPTER 28
STEF

I hoisted my backpack from the trunk of Christina's parents' car and shut the lid. My parents' gravel driveway crunched under my feet; I'd be staying with them in Pittsburgh over the summer until I left for London. "Thanks for the ride!" I called as they pulled away.

Christina smiled and waved goodbye through the rear window, looking as exhausted and bewildered as I felt.

Our white screen door creaked with a pull. The wooden door behind it sat wide open, letting in golden, mid-morning light and warm spring breeze. Cupcake, our elderly, half-blind Pekingese, sunbathed in the front hall. She thumped her tail twice with weary recognition.

I entered a living room frozen in 1988. Lace curtains. Tan carpet. Stone fireplace topped with a decorative mirror. A timeline of school pictures hung on wood-paneled walls.

Dad was out, and Mom was at my grandma's. Cassie lay on the plaid living room couch watching a *Dawson's Creek* rerun before her shift at Hollywood Video. I dropped my pack, still tinged with Outback dust and stuck with airport tags. CHC - LAX - PIT. An abbreviated archive of my last two days and the only physical evidence that my trip had actually happened. I gave Cassie a hug, grabbed a pop from the fridge, and plopped onto the end of the couch. Cass stretched her legs out across my lap.

"It's good to see you," she said.

"Yeah, you, too!" I patted her foot. "I always liked Joey with Pacey better."

"Yeah, me, too."

Being plopped right back into home as I'd left it felt surreal. Nothing

135

around me had changed, though I knew nothing in my life would ever be the same.

A couple weeks later, I set out at dawn to pick James up at JFK airport in New York City. I'd been so worried he would change his mind, but then he'd called with his flight details. He was on his way.

I stretched and wiggled my fingers, stiff from strangling my steering wheel. Placid Pennsylvania hills shimmered with dew, and morning mist swirled. I barely noticed, preoccupied with the thought that our reunion would be awkward and horrible. I pushed it away and visualized a romantic reunion instead. A long, sweet kiss. A tight embrace. Maybe he'd pick me up and spin me around like they do in the movies.

The large *Welcome to Ohio* sign startled me

"Fuck! Oh, shit, shit, shit! Fuuuuck!" In my nervous fog, I'd driven the wrong way on the Pennsylvania Turnpike *for an hour*. I looped around, going back the way I came, floored it to New York, and made it to James's gate ten minutes before he emerged.

"Oh my gosh, I'm so glad I made it," I blabbered immediately. "I sped here because I drove the wrong way for an hour, and I was so worried I wouldn't make it on time." I wiped sweat from my brow.

James looked down at me. "You plank. You didn't have to be here for the minute I arrived. I'd have just sat somewhere."

My tension finally cracked. "You wouldn't have wandered aimlessly toward the city?"

"Nope. Just sat."

I threw my arms around him. "Hi," I mumbled into his shirt.

"Hi." James smoothed my hair, and I looked up at him. Handsome, blond, and tan. He gave me a kiss.

"So when I filled in my arrival card, I asked the air hostess what state New York is in, and she looked at me like I was an idiot," James said while we walked through the terminal.

I laughed. "You dumbass. Didn't you ever hear that song 'New York, New York?"

James shrugged. "I thought they were just singing it twice."

We toured New York, Niagara Falls, and Washington DC. I showed off the best of Pittsburgh. We met up with Christina and my old high school friends, and James charmed them with goofy jokes and words like "bollocks." We spent time with my family. Cass seemed to like James and so did Mom, of course, but I wasn't sure about Dad. He didn't say much.

Often, James and I simply hung out in my parents' living room. I loved that room, so comfortable, woodsy, and warm—like being hugged by a tree.

My whole family used to read or watch TV together there every night. Dad had albums full of photographs taken in that room. Christmas action shots and dance recital poses in spangly costumes. Stiff portraits holding Easter baskets or diplomas. I grew up in that room.

While watching TV one day, James said, "Hang on," and ran downstairs. He returned holding a CD. "Keith got me into these in Thailand. They're called Oasis."

"Yeah, 'Wonderwall.' I like that song."

"Yeah, but they've got so many other good songs. This one always made me think of you." He put the CD in the stereo and pressed play. He sat on the edge of the coffee table and gestured for me to come over. I sat down, put my arm around his back, and listened to "Songbird," about a man who had never felt so much love from anyone before.

My uncertainty, accumulating for months, finally spilled out. Each teardrop held a worry. Did James forget about me? Was I crazy to move to London? Was I ready to teach again? What the hell were we doing?

I rested my head on his shoulder, and he wrapped his arms around me tight.

My home was a time capsule of my youth, and I thought it might be strange to have James there. My future colliding with my past. But it felt like he belonged.

CHAPTER 29
JAMES

Stef and I stood by the bar in a crowded TGI Fridays in New York City. The bright, flashing lights of Times Square leaked in through the windows. Car horns and sirens played in the background. Over the past few days, I'd taken two ferries, two taxis, two buses, three trains and three planes across three continents, from Ko Pha-ngan to Bangkok to London to New York.

'That'll be twenty-seven dollars, please,' said the barman in a thick New York accent.

'What?'

'That'll be—'

'I heard ya, mate.'

I used to get a place on the beach, three meals and a couple of beers for that.

I paid, grabbed my beer and handed Stef her bottle of Smirnoff Ice. 'Cheers, love!'

Over the next two days, Stef showed me the highlights of NYC. We walked down packed streets filled with loud chatter. Billows of steam emanated up through the street grates as though the subway was ablaze. Tall buildings blocked out the sky. After two months of spacious beaches, I felt claustrophobic. But I was with Stef. From the moment I saw her at JFK, the chasm of the last four months disappeared, and it felt natural to be around her.

We roamed endless blocks. To the base of the Brooklyn Bridge, through Central Park, by Chinatown, into Little Italy. We sat at a tiny table covered in a checked vinyl tablecloth, right on the sidewalk, and enjoyed a considerable portion of lasagne for $5. After rice and vegetables for the past two months, I couldn't even finish it.

When I looked down from the top of the Empire State Building, I saw an endless ocean of skyscrapers of all shapes, colours, styles and sizes, occasionally diverging and converging around old churches and historical buildings.

When rode the free Staten Island ferry across New York Harbor, I stood on the windy deck and shivered under a thin Thailand tracksuit top. Across the water stood the Statue of Liberty. That's when it really hit me that I was in New York.

Two days later, I awoke from a nap in the passenger seat of Stef's dad's Honda wagon and sat upright. We exited a tunnel on the highway.

'Oh, hi!' Stef said. 'We're getting close now.'

We rounded a big bend among the hills. 'Hey, there's a city over there!' I blurted.

'That's Pittsburgh.' Stef looked at me like I was an idiot.

I didn't expect skyscrapers. Especially a glass one with points on the top like a villain's lair.

'That's the PPG Building,' Stef said as though reading my mind. The skyline of New York was iconic, but the beauty of Pittsburgh's hills, rivers and bridges surprised me, upending my vision of steel mills, factories and smog. An impression garnered only from the name of the city's American football team, the Steelers.

Stef's family lived in a quiet neighbourhood just north of the city. Each house looked completely different, but they all had a large front garden. Most had American flags flying in them and many driveways held large SUVs and pickup trucks. Before going through her parents' unlocked front door, Stef left her keys in the car on purpose, along with her wallet. What kind of alternate universe was this?

Over the next few days, Stef introduced me to friends and family, all of whom were extremely nice. But I couldn't help feeling like I was on show. *So, this is the guy you're changing your plans for*, I imagined them thinking. The pressure to live up to expectations and worthiness weighed heavy.

At a Memorial Day picnic at her nan's house, aunts, uncles and seemingly a hundred cousins surrounded me. Dozens of dishes and platters covered the table. One of Stef's uncles approached. 'What do you think of America, James?'

'It's good. Different.'

He took a swig from his can of Iron City beer. 'Like how?'

'Well, people keep asking me, "What's up?" and I don't know what to say.'

'Stiff dicks and airplanes,' he said, matter of fact. 'That's what you should say.'

I almost choked on my beer. At least he'd cracked some of my tension.

Stef's parents, Frank and Evelyn, were good people, and they welcomed me warmly, always making time for me and asking questions about my trip.

They gave Stef some early birthday money and suggested she take me to Washington DC for a couple of days, unaware their act of kindness pained me. I hated taking money from them. I'd worked hard for every penny in Australia, but now I was broke. I had $400 left to my name when I arrived in the US and spent half of it in two days in New York.

Aside from the humidity being higher than Southeast Asia, I enjoyed DC. I had no expectations, as I knew very little about it. The atmosphere was relaxed compared to New York, and the absence of skyscrapers gave it a wide-open feel. We walked for an entire day, sweating in the heat. I was struck by the beauty of the architecture. Many buildings were made from huge white stone blocks decorated with columns and domes.

We visited all the presidential memorials and the rolling hills of Arlington Cemetery. The Korean War Memorial stopped me in my tracks. Rows and rows of ghostly figures adorned with long rain ponchos, machine guns and radios, frozen in time right there in a modern city. I'll never forget the haunting expressions on their faces.

After DC, Stef went into full-blown Pittsburgh tour guide mode. We whizzed around the city past a huge, illuminated Heinz ketchup bottle and the sports stadiums, over to Point Park, flanked on either side by two rivers coming together to form a third.

We ate at a popular restaurant called Primanti Bros, nestled in a plaza. The waitress set down two small silver trays covered in wax paper. What looked like a pound of meat, cheese, coleslaw and, surprisingly, French fries overflowed out of two little slices of bread. They were embarrassingly awkward to eat but delicious.

In the evenings, we watched VHS movies rented from Iggle Video. The 'Iggle' was supposed to be 'Eagle' but was named for how Pittsburghers pronounced it. We'd curl up on the sofa under a blanket crocheted by Stef's mum, their small dog snoring by our feet.

At night, Stef would go upstairs to sleep. I would go downstairs to be awake. I'd lay back on the sofa bed and stare at the random patterns on the ceiling tiles. The chronic jet lag kept me up while infomercials played on a small TV in the corner. This time was mostly spent contemplating the end of my adventure. I couldn't shake the feeling of failure. Travelling had become my identity and going home signalled the loss of it.

My anxiety ran rampant at the thought of returning to England. Finding a job, making money and a life for Stef and me. She'd be going back to teaching, but my stomach churned at the idea of being an accountant again. My lack of other qualifications meant I'd have to start from scratch. And that was only *if* I could resolve my debt problems.

A few days before leaving Pittsburgh, on a wooden bridge in a community park, words spilt out of me. 'Stef, love. I'm not sure about you coming to England. What if I can't sort out my money issues? What if you don't like it? What if we don't work out?' I hated saying them, but they had to be said.

Her eyebrows furled in horror, and her eyes glossed over. She turned away from me, looking at the ground. I exhaled slowly, and I resisted the urge to throw my arms around her. I had to stay firm. The guilt I felt now was far less than the guilt I'd feel if she came to London and we failed.

'You don't want me to come?' she said.

'I do! It's—it's just that I feel responsible for you. If you hate it, it'll be my fault.'

She shook her head vigorously. 'No, it won't. I've worked in other countries before. Remember?'

'I know, but you'd be teaching again…' What if we had to break up because I couldn't support us? Doing this now took the blame off me and my potential failings. 'You're coming because of me and…'

'So? I'm going even if you don't want me to. To live in London for a year will be a great experience, no matter what. You're not responsible for me, James.'

I teared up. I loved her confidence, her drive, her ambition and, most of all, her independence. I grinned. 'Fuck it, then. Send your application in. Let's do it!'

'Hiya, love!' My mum threw her arms around me at Liverpool Lime St Train Station. She squeezed me tightly and craned her neck to look up at me. 'Welcome home,' she said with tears in her eyes.

A pang of guilt washed over me. I'd been back in England for almost a month. But I needed to acclimate.

Arriving in London prompted a visit to Keith and Rick for a couple of days, which turned into a couple of weeks. They were already back in the swing of real life. I moped around during the day, watching anything on TV while they worked. My big adventure had ended. It took all my strength to leave the sofa most days.

I always knew I'd have to face the debt sometime, but I didn't know how. One day, I went into the Citizens Advice Bureau and explained my situation to a consultant.

'Bankruptcy,' he said without hesitation.

I frowned. 'Erm, what?'

'You don't own any property, right?'

'No.'

'Then it's your best option. With the amount you owe, and the interest incurred since you left, you'd be crippled by this debt for decades.'

'Wow. That sounds drastic, though,' I said.

'It's more common than you think. You'd be free of the debt,' he said.

I put my hands on my head. '*Free?* Just like that?'

'You won't be able to get a loan or a credit card for a long time, and things like renting a flat will be difficult, but you'd be able to start fresh.'

The words echoed in my mind as I thanked the man and left the office. *Start fresh.* A phrase that summed up my longing for the past eighteen months. Even better, I could start fresh with Stef.

To ease back into my old life, I spent the last of my money on a train ticket to Cardiff and stayed with my sister and her family for a week in Wales. It felt good to see them. They asked questions about my experiences and were genuinely interested in my journey. The kids didn't allow me to sit much. We kicked around a football and played games. It felt nice to be an uncle again.

My sister and I talked about home. She knew all too well how my dad could be but helped me focus on the positives. Soon, Stef would be here. Acceptance and hope began to dominate my thoughts. I was ready for the last leg of my trip.

As the lush, green Welsh countryside whizzed by my train window, I wrote down all the places I'd been. My whole trip was summarized on one small page that didn't do it justice. My experiences were far more significant than the places. Experiences I looked forward to sharing with my parents. *Will Dad respect me now? Why do I even care?*

When my mum finally let go at the train station, to my surprise, my dad leaned in for a brief and awkward hug.

'You look good,' he said. 'Come on then, let's get a drink.' We walked down the platform at the train station, across the road and into a dingy pub with toilets I could smell from outside. Two grey-haired pensioners sat by themselves. I hated that my dad brought my mum into places like this. I sat with her at a corner table while my dad went to the bar. She'd lost weight and had a new hairstyle that had taken years off her.

My dad joined us with two pints of bitter and an orange juice for Mum. I launched into tales about Malaysia, the beaches of the Perhentian Islands and the metropolis of Kuala Lumpur.

Dad ran his fingers over his pint glass, pushing the condensation downwards, his eyes studying it, assessing its richness. He glanced at me occasionally and nodded. 'Not a bad drop, that,' he said, after taking a sip. One of the pensioners interrupted us and said he fought in Malaysia during the '60s. My dad turned to face him. They talked for a while.

My heart sank, and I felt foolish for thinking he'd care. Mum listened to my stories gladly, occasionally interjecting to tell me which shops she'd been to and what she had for breakfast.

Eager to reconnect with friends, I called Nigel, a good mate and former coworker I'd been close to before my trip.

'Alright mate, it's James.'

'Alright. You back, then?' Nigel said in a calm voice.

'Yeah, mate. Fancy a pint?'

'Well, I'm off out with Phil in a bit.'

'OK.' A long pause followed while I waited for an invite that never came. 'Can I come and meet you?'

Another pause. 'Yeah,' he finally answered.

I went. Not one question about my trip. 'I can't believe that bird you shacked up with last night,' Nigel said to Phil. This night out, that night out, this girl, that girl. The two of them talked around me like I wasn't there. I didn't exist here anymore. All the more reason to move to London.

I completed the necessary paperwork to file for bankruptcy and was summoned for an interview at a local government office to discuss my case. Once again, I found my life in the hands of a suited man with reading glasses in a stuffy office. My heart didn't know how to feel. Excited, nervous, hopeful, embarrassed, guilty, ashamed.

Start fresh.

He asked me how I became so much in debt. The facts felt cold and hollow, devoid of the emotions behind them.

He quickly moved on to studying the large loan I had taken out to pay other debts. 'Quite frankly, they should never have given you this loan,' he said.

'OK,' I said, my eyes a little wider now.

After seeing that I had zero collateral, he stamped my paperwork. There it was, APPROVED in big red letters. I left the building and stood motionless for a long moment. It took some time to process that I'd never felt so grateful to be so worthless.

With my dad spending seven days a week in the pub, I knew I had to spend time with him on his terms. I walked into a half-empty, low-lit bar off the high street. Men with walking sticks sat at small tables while my dad stood at the bar.

I stood next to him. 'Alright, Dad?'

'Alright, Son. Pint of John Smiths,' he said to the barmaid while pointing at me.

He pulled out some coins from his pocket, and I fished around in his palm for the correct amount.

I took a sip of my pint. 'This place is new for you, right, Dad?'

'Aye. I like it, though. They do a good pint.'

We stood in silence for a while, sinking our beers. After a few rounds, he brought up his time spent in the British Army in the '60s. He fought to protect Malaysia, a British colony, from Indonesian invasion. He'd only told me snippets over the years.

I spotted some Tiger beer behind the bar, a popular drink in Malaysia. I bought two bottles while my dad was in the toilet. He smiled when he returned. I tried again to tell him about my trip, and he mostly listened. He told me the story of how he and his dad fell out when he was younger and how they'd patched things up before he joined the army. My grandfather was killed while my dad was in Malaysia.

He rarely talked about his dad, but this was a story he'd told me many times in the past. The first time, it actually sounded sad, but subsequent times, it felt like a threat, as if I should let him get away with being an arsehole because I'd feel guilty when he died.

'Did Grandad drink half pints?' I asked. I pictured the one photo of him in existence.

'No, that's a pint glass in the photo.'

'Wow! His hands must have been huge.' I said, holding my hand up next to my glass.

'He had miner's hands,' Dad said, raising his pint.

We both smiled. 'Do you think he would've liked me?' I asked.

My dad's smile quickly dissipated. 'He'd be turning in his grave over this bankruptcy.'

Two more pints were ordered and we sipped them in silence.

I called Stef to discuss our plans. She'd accepted a teaching job at Queensmead High School in the town of Enfield in North London and would fly over in August. I'd found a minimum wage job as a stock controller at a warehouse. Plans were developing fast, and they helped stave off feelings of sadness about the end of my trip.

Money would be tight, but Stef was all in. 'I can't wait to get our own place,' she said. I could hear the excitement in her voice.

'Our own place?'

'Yeah, why not?' Her voice became serious.

'I won't be able to get a lease because of the bankruptcy.'

'But I could get one, right? I have a good job.'

'I don't know, maybe. But what if we lose our jobs, and then we can't afford the rent?' I hated dampening her spirits, but I needed to be realistic.

'People get jobs, and they rent apartments,' she said, exasperated at my pessimism. I knew she viewed this as a lack of commitment, but I wanted to be cautious.

'OK, love. I'll look for one.'

The day I hunted for a flat in London happened to be the hottest day in living memory. I scoured the local newspaper before taking to the streets. From a sweltering telephone box, I scheduled showings with an agent. He picked me up in his car and showed me several massively overpriced flats before dropping me off in Enfield Town.

I stood sweating, dehydrated and deflated, outside a newsagent's on the high street. Leaning against the window, I chugged some water and poured the rest over my head. As I turned to throw the bottle in the bin, I spotted a card in the window. 'Room in shared house £275 per month.'

I called the number on the card and walked for twenty minutes. A German girl let me inside an old pebble-dashed house on the edge of town and led me to a tiny attic loft. The sunshine barely passed through the foggy double-glazed windows. The floorboards creaked as I manoeuvred under the slanted roof.

'You can take my place in the house by paying my £275 deposit,' the girl said.

'How many people live here?'

'Six.'

'And it's OK if me girlfriend moves in, too?'

'Just make sure she's not home when the landlord comes over. Only six people allowed.'

'I'll take it.'

PART THREE:

ACROSS THE POND

(2003 – 2005)

CHAPTER 30
STEF

I couldn't sleep and looked through my materials again while other passengers slept. Posh-looking English teens in pleated navy skirts and striped neckties smiled at me from the pages of my Teach London info packet. I'd been assigned to Queensmead School, a name out of a Harry Potter novel. Maybe this year would magically go well.

I turned off the reading light above my head and put the brochure back into my carry-on. A screen in the front of the dim, quiet plane glowed with a map of our location. A white dotted line arced up from NYC and culminated in a small airplane icon blinking near Iceland. I pulled up my window screen and peeked out. Amid the murky darkness, beyond the blinking red wing light, a green glow illuminated the sky. A transparent haze, like someone had dropped a piece of chartreuse tulle atop black velvet. The aurora changed shape so gradually and effortlessly, I didn't notice the evolution as it was happening. Rather, every few moments, I'd realize how different it was from before.

As I watched the sky, the horizon lightened, and a scarlet sliver of sunlight traced the curve of the Earth. The plane continued east toward a new day.

CHAPTER 31
JAMES

I stuffed the boot of my brother's car with clothes, donated cutlery, a duvet and a TV. It looked like I was going to university. Instead, I was an almost twenty-five-year-old with empty pockets and a head full of memories, setting off to start a life with my American girl in a loft in London.

My teenage nephew, Kevin, joined my brother and me for the six-hour journey. In the time I'd been gone, he'd grown taller, his voice had broken and his hair had grown long. I thought of him like a younger brother, and I feared he wouldn't think I was cool anymore, so I was thankful he chose to ride in the car with us all day. Archie and Kevin helped me move my few belongings in and headed home that same night.

Early the next morning, I sat on an Underground train hurtling towards Heathrow airport, hopped up on caffeine and excitement. I stood by Arrivals while a battle raged internally. My brain fixated on money and jobs while my heart overflowed with love and longing. Then there she was. The best souvenir from my trip.

Her wavy hair swished as she walked. She wore her orange backpack and dragged two old suitcases. She scoured the crowd, blue eyes glistening under the fluorescent lights. We locked eyes, and a huge smile spread across her face. She scurried over, threw down her backpack and flung her arms around me. It wasn't a nice to see you hug. It wasn't even a love hug. I knew right then and there it was a forever hug.

After a long ride on the Tube, we boarded a red double-decker bus for the last leg of our journey home. I paid the driver, and Stef ran upstairs, squealing with excitement.

'I'll sort the bags, then,' I said. I wanted a seat downstairs, but I heaved all the luggage onto a rack and trudged up the steps. 'Stef, why do we have to—'

I stopped when I saw the wonder on her face. She sat right at the front with her face inches from the window. It reminded me of taking the bus to the swimming baths in junior school. We all wanted to sit upstairs at the front.

Stef couldn't sit still. She marvelled at every house, school and pub. I noticed our reflection in the window. We looked comfortable. It was always so easy with Stef, no matter how long we spent apart. She caught my eye in the window, and I stuck my tongue out at her, making her laugh.

The bus dropped us a couple of minutes from the house. Stef looked around at the newsagent's, chippy and Indian takeaway while I stood with her ancient suitcases. One had a broken handle, and the other was held together with a bungee cord.

'Stef, where did you get these suitcases?'

'The thrift store. I've never had to pack this much before. They're fine!' She pulled one by the strap, and it tipped over. She ignored me laughing and got behind the case, pushing it down the street like a bobsled.

'You look like a moron,' I said but followed her lead.

She picked up the pace. '*You* look like a moron,' she called behind her. We raced to the front door, laughing and breathless.

'What is that?' Stef asked, pointing to the front wall of the house.

'It's called pebble-dash.'

Stef's eyes went wide. 'What?'

'Pebble-dash. They cover the bricks with cement and stick pebbles to them. It's kind of old-fashioned.' I raised an antique-looking key to unlock the cobalt blue door.

'That looks like a jail cell key from the Wild West,' Stef said.

I enjoyed her enthusiasm for everything, and I hoped the loft wouldn't disappoint her. We hauled the bags up a narrow, windy staircase. Stef saw the photos of us I'd put on the wall, and her eyes filled with tears. She peered through the window, looking over rooftops to the distant Canary Wharf skyscrapers. 'It's perfect.'

CHAPTER 32
STEF

A few days before I started teacher planning week at Queensmead, we drove up to Warrington, arriving around 11 p.m. James parked our rental car in front of a teeny lawn, and we walked past a tidy row of flowers into Eileen and Harry's government-issued duplex. Peach wallpaper covered the walls, and the laminate floor shined. Each knick-knack on every side table was dust-free and arranged intentionally. The room smelled of furniture polish.

Harry sat in a high-backed mauve chair two feet from a blaring TV, watching highlights of cricket matches.

"Alright, Dad?" James said.

No movement from Harry.

James stepped up and put his hand on Harry's shoulder. "Alright, Dad?" he repeated, louder.

Harry looked back and grinned. "Oh!" He held the remote out, and we all patiently waited for the volume to decrease.

"Alright, Son," Harry said when we could hear each other. He stood up, quite tall, with dark but silvering hair. He looked at me. "You must be the Yankee Doodle Dandy."

I shook his enormous hand. "I'm Stef. Nice to meet you," I said, even though it wasn't.

Eileen shuffled from the kitchen where she'd been watching TV. She was petite, with short platinum hair in curls. "Hello, love." She gave me and James hugs and presented me with a stuffed clown she'd knitted. He held a champagne bottle and wore a top hat that said *Stef*.

I grinned. "I love it. My mom crochets. Mostly blankets and baby clothes. Thank you!"

Eileen smiled shyly. "I'll put kettle on."

"Oh, no, thank you," I shook my head.

"We've got hot chocolate? Tea?" she suggested.

"No thanks, I don't really like hot drinks."

She looked perplexed, like I'd said I didn't really like breathing. "Hot water, maybe?"

"Mum, leave it!" James scolded delicately. "But I'll have a coffee, ta."

Eileen brought in three steaming mugs, and we chatted with James's parents for about an hour before heading upstairs to bed.

A square of white morning sunshine brightened the aquamarine wallpaper in James's little childhood bedroom. James gave a big yawn and stretch as he woke. He squinted in the sun, flipped onto his stomach and shoved his face back into his pillow.

"Last night, I didn't really appreciate the . . . turquoiseness of this room," I teased.

"You could barely see the walls when I lived here. I had my DJ turntables in the corner over there, TV set up here," he said, pointing. "I hardly left this room."

"Cass and I rarely spent time *in* our bedroom. Anyway . . ." I grinned excitedly. "What are we doing today?"

"Me and me dad are going to the pub. I don't know what you're doing."

I stared at him for a long second. "Are you serious?"

He sat up in bed, looking apologetic. "Yeah. You and me mum will probably run some errands and meet us at Wetherspoon's for tea. You'll be fine."

Our afternoon of gender-segregated fun started at the bank. Eileen entered her PIN at an ATM incorrectly. Twice. She dug a scrap of paper from her pink leather wallet, which she called a purse, and studied it through gold-framed eyeglasses.

"Ahh. Two-three-*six*-one." She entered it successfully and was rewarded with bills of various colors and sizes bearing the Queen's face. "Come on, love," Eileen said, and we shuffled slowly down the pedestrian mall. Eileen wasn't in perfect health—she'd had three surgeries, one bladder, two heart, and took numerous pills each day for myriad afflictions.

Everyday storefronts like Boots pharmacy or McDonald's lined the pavement, housed in beautiful stone buildings. I gazed at the elegance of a red brick facade with narrow, lead-paned windows. Wrought iron cresting and carved stone finials lined the roof. At street level—a discount bakery with a plain black sign. "Tasty Baking at Tasty Prices." We nipped into a mini-mart-newsstand-candy store, where she was able to pay her gas bill for some reason.

Throughout our chore tour, Eileen monologued about grandkids' birthday cards, redecorating the living room, and how they moved the bread aisle at Morrison's again.

"Shall we stop for a drink?" Eileen asked, leading us to a café in the town center. She ordered a hot chocolate and looked incredulous when I requested a Diet Coke.

"Hmm. I can't find me mobile," she mumbled while rummaging through the seventeen compartments in her handbag. "I've got me purse, me cigs . . ." She pulled out one item after another, identifying each one as if she were narrating the scene for a blind person. ". . . a spare pair of knickers in case I wee meself, me hairbrush . . ."

She continued her inventory, unaware she'd shared anything noteworthy with her son's new girlfriend. But it made me feel like we'd known each other forever. "Ah! Here it is." She pulled a pearly pink flip phone from her Mary Poppins bag and checked the time. "Shall we go meet the gentlemen?" She smiled.

James had been right. I was fine.

CHAPTER 33
JAMES

Beep! Beep! Beep! I smashed my hand down onto the alarm clock. 'Stef, we've gotta get up, love.'

'What's that smell?' Stef asked, rubbing her eyes.

'I don't know, why?'

'It's onions. I think Mark's making Spanish omelette!' Stef said, jumping out of bed.

We got dressed and ran downstairs, regaining composure in the hall and nonchalantly strolling into the kitchen, a large room with bright yellow walls, two refrigerators and an old wooden table and chairs in the centre.

'Dudes!' Mark said. He fist-bumped us both and returned his attention to the cooker. Mark was a tall, stocky man in his thirties from Trinidad. He had shoulder-length dreadlocks and a thin moustache that sat above his perpetual smile. 'Happy Friday! I'm making omelette. Do you want some?'

'OK, but only if there's enough,' I said, smiling at Stef.

Our house consisted of seven people, six nationalities, six bedrooms, two bathrooms, a kitchen, a living room being used as a storage room, an old-fashioned pulley clothes airer and a rubber ducky. It felt like an international halfway house for us. Not quite a backpacker hostel, but not real life either.

We cleaned Mark's dishes before leaving the house. It was Stef's last day of preparation before school started on Monday. I sensed her growing anxiety.

'It's gonna be fine, love,' I said with a reassuring hug at the corner of our street. I waved goodbye and headed past the condensation-covered cars that lined the road. En route to the train station, I stopped at the newsagent's for a copy of the Daily Star and a packet of prawn cocktail Skips. Commuters clutching steaming coffee cups filled the bright platform. I boarded the train and buried my head in my newspaper.

Months before, I'd imagined a life in sunny Sydney outside the train window. Now it was dreary London. In my Sydney life, I had a surfboard, but in my London life, I had Stef. After putting my money issues behind me, we could begin a new life together. We'd talked of travelling around Europe when we had enough money. It felt good to think about the future without dreading it.

Half an hour later, I sat at my desk in a warehouse where I worked as a stock controller. My morning consisted of receiving deliveries of computer equipment which I stacked and stored. In the afternoon, a few members of the IT team stopped by to collect new equipment. I helped them load their cars before challenging them to a race around the warehouse on pallet trucks. We whizzed up and down aisles of keyboards and monitors, grinning from ear to ear, something I couldn't even imagine doing as an accountant.

After work, I threw my newspaper on the kitchen table, grabbed a frozen garlic bread from the freezer and popped it in the oven to go with our frozen tikka masalas.

'Hey, James,' Stef said, joining me.

'Hello, love.'

'Good day?' Stef remarked, turning on the radio on the windowsill.

'Yeah, I won the pallet truck race,' I said proudly.

'You won what?'

'Never mind, it was fun.'

'Whoa!' Stef looked at me wide-eyed, holding the newspaper. 'There are boobs in here!'

'That's a Page 3 Girl.'

Our housemate, Bill, walked into the kitchen. 'Evening!' he said in his cockney accent. He flicked back his shaggy hair and adjusted his thick-rimmed glasses. 'Garlic bread with curry?'

'Yep,' Stef said. Garlic bread accompanied every meal, regardless of the main course.

'I'm off to Tesco if you need a lift. You'll have to sit on my tools in the back of the work van, though.' Bill offered.

'Do you mind going, love? I'm knackered,' I said to Stef.

'From all that racing?' Stef said, smirking.

'Ta, love.'

The real reason I wanted her to go was so that I could fix up the living room. It'd been used as a storage room, resulting in our home life revolving around our bedroom and the kitchen. I wanted to make this house feel like a home for Stef.

I stacked some old boxes and removed the sheets covering the furniture. Under them sat an old green velvet settee with thick cushions. I brushed off years of lint and dust, and the room looked semi-respectable. The only thing left to do was hoover the '70s floral carpet.

The only person in the house with a Hoover was Daphne, a twenty-something German girl with long brown hair and a no-nonsense attitude. I called her, but she didn't answer her phone. Stef would be home soon, and I wanted to have the room ready. I stood by Daphne's half-open bedroom door and spotted the Hoover. I ran in, grabbed it, used it and returned it.

Minutes later, Daphne came home.

'Wow! We have a living room?' she said in her thick German accent.

'Yeah, it took ages to fix up,' I said. 'I hope you don't mind, but I borrowed your Hoover.'

'You went in my room?' Her face was always stern, making her difficult to read.

'Sorry?' I said, gritting my teeth.

'You saw my rubber ducky then?'

'I didn't look around.'

'It's my vibrator,' she said. She turned around and walked to her room. We never spoke of it again.

Stef and Bill came home from Tesco. 'I saw cans labelled "spotted dick" and "saucy bangers." Brits are pervs!' Stef announced on her way in the door. She stopped in her tracks at the sight of the living room.

'Wait! We have a living room?' Stef said, setting the shopping bags on the floor.

'We do now,' I said.

'Thanks, James,' she said, wrapping her arms around me. 'I love it.'

CHAPTER 34
STEF

I woke in the dark before the alarm went off. I climbed over James, fumbled on the dress pants and black blouse I'd laid out, and crept downstairs to one of the shared bathrooms. The bright light above the mirror buzzed loudly in the house's silence. Shadows circled my eyes.

I'd been so certain, fifteen months ago, that I'd stood in front of a classroom for the last time. But I had to teach to live in London. To be with James. I ignored the reasons I quit and buried them deep, but in the past few days, the memories and accompanying dread had clawed their way to the surface.

During planning week, I'd met new coworkers and prepared lessons. I learned foreign procedures the other teachers took for granted, having gone through school in England themselves. Policies like uniform checks and homework notebooks the kids had to place in a container to be graded. At the last minute, the administrators changed all my classes to French. I'd never taught French, but I replaced posters of the Sagrada Familia and Machu Picchu with the Eiffel Tower and the Louvre and crossed my fingers.

At a staff meeting, our headmaster emphasized the importance of discipline. I'd be teaching secondary students, fifteen and sixteen years old. I convinced myself I could handle these British children in their plaid skirts and navy slacks. But Friday afternoon, with just a weekend separating me and my biggest fear, I had a gut feeling I'd made a colossal mistake.

I didn't eat breakfast. I peeked in the bedroom and whispered goodbye to James, still buried under the comforter. "Good luck, love," he said.

"You'll do great."

"K. Thanks." I tiptoed out the door and caught the bus to school. Commuters sat serenely reading the Star newspaper or looking out the window at the dreary sky. I wanted to throw up.

The bus pulled up to the campus filled with boxy, '70s-style architecture. A tall, black metal fence enclosed the brick buildings, cement courtyards, and parking lot. Teachers shuffled inside, loaded with bags and steaming travel mugs of coffee.

I stood by my open classroom door, savoring the stillness. Within minutes, dozens of kids swarmed the hall. They wore the same clothes as the kids in the brochure, but their expressions weren't the same. Their uniforms said "prep school" but their faces said, "fuck you." Many tied their neckties four inches long in a trendy act of rebellion. I greeted them warmly as they entered the classroom. No smiles, no responses. Just thinly veiled disdain.

The seats filled with rowdy kids chattering about their summers. I cleared my throat. "*Bonjour, classe.*" Nobody looked at me. "Excuse me. We're starting now."

One freckled, redheaded student in the front row opened a notebook.

I wiped my sweaty palms on my pants. "Please. I need you to quiet down." My wavering voice betrayed my authority.

"Shut up!" Freckles shouted at his classmates.

They ignored him, too.

I plowed on. "*Je m'appelle Madame Caroll.* I just want to go over—"

"You American, Miss?" a boy in the back called out.

I smiled, happy someone else had noticed me. "Yes, I am."

A sour-looking girl with frizzy hair mimicked me in a high, whiny voice. "Yes, I am."

The kids laughed, and I felt a flush rising up my neck. "What's your name?" I asked her.

"Margarita." With her strong London accent, it sounded like "Mah-gah-ree-ah."

"Margarita?" I verified.

The high voice again. "Margarita?" she mocked, heavy on the Yankee articulation. "No," she continued, condescendingly, "Mah-gah-ree-ah."

"Anyway, I wanted to go over some procedures. When you come into class, you can put your homework in the bin."

The class roared with laughter. My breath quickened, and my mouth dried up. I had no idea what was funny.

Freckles, my only ally, pointed toward the trash can. "The bin."

No. No no no. It couldn't continue like this. I had to take control.

Margarita stood up. "All right, now." The class quieted and watched her. "It's not her fault she's dim. She's American."

I marched to my desk, grabbed a referral form, and silently filled it out. The students discussed the scene. Is she serious? On the first day? A hush fell as I crossed the room and handed the yellow slip to Margarita. She glared at me and took the paper. Without a word and without breaking eye contact, she ripped the sheet into four pieces. The class gasped and erupted into chaotic squeals and howls.

Sweat beaded on my brow, and my silky blouse clung like saran wrap. I never dreamed it could go this wrong this quickly. The students in Pittsburgh often ignored me and gave me attitude, but never the whole class at once. And they never laughed at me. If the kids didn't respect me, and I couldn't control the class, I couldn't teach them.

I don't know what I said next. I don't know what I did. I've blocked out the rest of that day. I only remember by the last class, I gave up, sat behind my desk, and let the kids talk until dismissal.

"Aren't you going to teach, Miss?" that class's front-row nerd asked. I stared at the floor and shook my head no, fearing I'd cry if I spoke.

I took the bus home in a daze. I climbed the skinny stairs to our attic bedroom and collapsed on the bed tucked by the wall. The slanted ceiling provided a claustrophobic comfort during my all-encompassing, body-shaking, gasping-for-breath breakdown.

James pushed the door open when he got home from work. "Hey, love! How'd it—" His smile disappeared when he saw me curled up like a potato bug. "What happened?"

"I can't go back there, James. I just can't."

The look on his face as I recounted my day made me feel even worse. He sat next to me on our bed and calmly put his arm around my back. "Maybe the headmaster can help?"

"I. CAN'T." I put my head in my hands and sobbed. He probably thought I was overreacting, but it wasn't about being teased. They'd made it clear where the power lay, and it wasn't with me. I had no idea how to rein them in, and that meant I wouldn't be able to do my job.

"Okay. Well, you have a teaching visa. Maybe you could find a job at another school. Let's go up to the newsagent's and grab a local paper."

The possibility of a solution made me feel fractionally better. We walked to the shop, and I picked up the paper, scanning the ads. "Teacher Needed for Nursery," I read aloud and looked hopefully at James.

"Call 'em."

We stopped at the payphone, and I dialed the number. "Enfield Kindergartens," a chipper voice answered.

"Hi, I'm calling about the job?"

"Yes, of course. Can you come in for an interview tomorrow? At five?"

"Uh, sure." I glanced at James, eyes wide. "I can be there at five."

"Brill! See you then."

I hung up the phone. James rubbed my back soothingly. "See, it'll be okay."

I entered school on Tuesday less willing than a dead man walking. Classes continued in the same vein. Kids talked over me, ignored me, and mocked me. During my planning period, the headmaster stopped by the room. "So, you wrote a referral for Margarita yesterday?" he asked.

"She was being really disrespectful."

He sat on a table, looking concerned. "Well, it's unusual to write students a disciplinary referral on the first day."

I looked at him. "These kids don't respect me, and I can't get control of them."

The headmaster shut his eyes and rubbed his forehead. "What if I sat in a few classes? I could have a couple of other teachers help, too."

I looked down in embarrassment. "Okay."

I rushed home that afternoon and took another bus to my interview. I rang the doorbell at an entrance behind a brick building. Leaves in shades of orange and red had been painted on the windows. A perky blond answered the door. "Hiya! I'm Suzie. You must be here for the interview."

I followed her down the hall to soft sounds of laughter and Barney songs. "You'd be in here, with the two-year-olds." I peeked through the window in the door. Three children pushed plastic trucks on a colorful carpet, and a girl with pigtails scribbled on a paper with a fat crayon. One teacher sat on a chair in the corner, reading a book with exaggerated inflection. Four captivated kids sat cross-legged on the floor, craning their necks up to look at the illustrations.

"Here's the kitchen. We normally take turns preparing lunch," Suzie continued. She never asked me any questions. "So, what do you think? Are you interested?"

Relief spread through my chest. "Yes! Definitely!"

She clasped her hands. "Great, can you start Monday?"

"Absolutely! Thank you!"

Suzie shook my hand. "Brilliant! Just come in at six, yeah?"

I headed for the door and paused. "And you can definitely get my work visa transferred, right?"

"Of course. Cheers!"

I went home beaming. I just had three more days.

On Wednesday, I told the headmaster I'd finish out the week. He asked me to reconsider. He told me teachers would keep coming in to help, but they just sat in the back grading papers while the kids acted up. I couldn't blame them for resenting they had to babysit me.

Knowing it would be over soon made it bearable, but I didn't like quitting. Again. For how brave I felt in some situations, I was still so afraid of others. I fell apart under any kind of interpersonal conflict or tension. I'd already done this job for a year and didn't grow any stronger from it. If anything, it left me more phobic than before. My instant failure humiliated me, but sometimes you have to accept that what you want to do and what you can do aren't the same thing.

I ate my lunch in the concrete courtyard on Friday. A few brown leaves swirled in a brisk breeze. The headmaster caught my eye and came over. "So . . . your last day already."

I nodded sheepishly. "Yeah. I'm really sorry it didn't work out."

He sat down on the bench next to me. "Are you just going to go back to America?"

"No, I found a job at a local preschool. They're going to transfer my work visa."

"Oh, that's good," he said, looking at a tree. "Well, good luck to you," he muttered before walking away.

At the end of the day, I packed up my decorations and spent a couple hours writing extensive plans for whomever was taking over after the weekend—as if that absolved me from the guilt I felt for quitting after five days. I walked out late onto an empty and quiet lot. The gate was locked. I walked the circumference of the metal fence around campus and found no other exit.

I hurled my poster tube and school bag over the fence onto the sidewalk, prepared to climb out. Footsteps echoed across the concrete. A teacher pushed a red button on a pole. The gate mechanically rolled aside, and he walked out. I followed behind, snatching my belongings from the ground. I was free.

A week and a half later, I was lying on a squeaky vinyl mat, looking up at block letters decorating the walls. Next to me in the quiet darkness, his body curled into a ball, lay Oliver, my new two-year-old buddy. I looked at his baby face while he sighed in his sleep.

After Friday afternoon nap, we ate Friday afternoon snack—veggies and dip. I sat in a child-sized plastic chair, knees bent up under my chest. Oliver held out his plate and asked, "Stef, more tomahtoes?" in the cutest baby London accent ever.

Justine, the bookkeeper, peeked her head in and called me down to her office. She handed me a paycheck.

"I don't have my new work visa yet," I said. "I can't get paid until it comes through."

"Oh. Yes. Of course." She took back the check, looking embarrassed.

"I told you guys that when I was hired. Did anybody apply for my visa yet?"

She paused a beat. "No. I apologize. We'll do that shortly."

Suzie had hired me on the spot, assuring me they could get a visa. An inspection had taken place on my second day, checking for safety issues like the proper staff-to-child ratio. They'd needed me to take the job immediately.

"Well, I just can't accept this paycheck. I'll keep working, though, and you can back-pay me when it comes through."

Justine nodded. "Thank you. I'll talk to the owner, and we'll file straight away."

So, I kept calm and carried on. I looked forward to work—the kids' adorable comments and affection filled me with joy. A month in, during a competitive game of Duck, Duck, Goose, Justine peeked into our classroom. "Stefanie." She gestured, and I followed her down the hall, past low rows of hooks holding tiny coats.

We walked into her office, and she stepped behind her desk, looking uneasy. "We've just received a letter in the post. Immigration has rejected your application for a visa."

"What?" I stood dumbly, unsure of what to do. "Why?"

"I'm terribly sorry. It appears preschools aren't on the 'most needed teachers' list, so your visa doesn't transfer." Justine offered an awkward, apologetic pout. She picked up the letter from her wooden desk and skimmed it. "Hmm . . . hold on."

She held up a gold-ringed finger for an excruciating amount of time while she finished reading. "It states here we can appeal if we can prove no other qualified person in the UK would take the job."

"How in the world would we do that?" I asked, my volume and hands shooting up in frustration. "Sorry. I'm just—"

"It's okay, dear. We need to show proof of a national posting for the position. Maybe our internet advert would suffice. I'll start the reapplication. Don't worry, darling." She smiled and waved me back to the classroom.

Though we were broke, and our future uncertain, James and I carpe diemed the shit out of London. One rainy Saturday, we visited St. Paul's cathedral. I rustled my damp hair and looked down a long, echoing aisle lined with robust white arches. Black-and-white checkered tiles stretched across the floor, where tourists shifted like chess pieces. Above the altar, saints gazed down from a ceiling gleaming with gold.

We hiked the 528 steps between the church's stone walls, spiraling up and around the dome, and squeezed onto a cramped walkway at the very top. I leaned on the railing to catch my breath. James stood beside me and wrapped his arm around my waist.

"We live in London now," James said.

"That's crazy. How did we get here?"

James shook his head. "Fuck knows. But I'm happy we're here."

"I'm happy we're here, too." I snuggled into him as the wind whipped our hair and raindrops dotted our fleece jackets.

We ended our day in Covent Garden, emerging from an Underground station lined in grimy tiles and smelling of dirty concrete. Out on the street, the world opened into magical chaos. Tourists gathered in front of historic pubs and restaurants, forming wonky rings around jugglers or puppeteers. At the end of the street, an ornate stone terminal housed posh shops where visitors purchased lilac-perfumed soaps wrapped in pretty paper or jams made from whimsical fruits like gooseberries and brambleberries. We grabbed a pint in the old brick Punch and Judy pub, whose name called upon the earliest of Covent Garden's street entertainment, and took the last train home.

We caught the bus north a few times to visit James's parents. They brought us to Liverpool, and we ambled down a drab street, under a drab sky, to Harry's favorite Liverpudlian pub. He called it The Lamb, though the name had changed three times since that one.

A scattering of men and women sat at wooden tables or leaned against the bar. The worn carpet bore swirling patterns designed to camouflage spilled beer, and it stunk of stale cigarettes.

We sat at a table near the door. James looked at me. "Cider and blackcurrant?"

"And some cheese and onion crisps."

"So, are you liking the nursery?" Eileen asked as the men went to the bar. "Been there a month, now?"

I beamed. "Yes! I love it! The kids are so cute." I chatted with Eileen about the preschool until James and his dad returned with our drinks.

The front door opened, and a skinny man in an Adidas tracksuit stepped inside, carrying a plastic shopping bag. He brazenly approached our table, arms and legs swishing in striped nylon.

He held the bag toward me. "'Ave a look," he said, swiveling his head around to scan the premises. I peeked inside and saw several boxes of bottled perfume, still wrapped in plastic. I looked at James, confused.

Harry peered in the bag. "Get in there, love! He's got some nice ones."

I realized this guy was selling perfume he'd just shoplifted. "No. No thanks."

Tracksuit pushed the bag closer. "Cheap," he added.

I leaned back as if the bag would bite me and vigorously shook my head. Tracksuit shrugged and swished over to another table.

"Welcome to Liverpool!" James said, laughing. "Me dad brings crap home from the pub all the time. Huge cans of coffee, posters, meat . . ."

"Meat?" I wrinkled my nose.

"Yeah. A freezer truck will pull up outside and open the back. The old men buy something for their wives to cook later and tuck it under their chairs while they play dominos."

Harry looked unfazed. He sipped from his pint glass and added, "One time a junkie said she'd trade me a pair of tracky pants for a pint."

"Did you buy her one?"

He nodded. "Well, it was before two."

"Price goes up five pence after 2 p.m.," James clarified for me.

Everyone carried on talking. I half-listened, agreeing and laughing in the right places while glancing around the pub, feeling very much a foreigner.

James and I drove a rental car up to Leeds one fall weekend with Sam and Laundry-Matt. Old Pinkhousemates from around the British Isles were meeting for a reunion party. We stopped in Warrington first, and James and I spent time with Eileen on Saturday while the Sam and Matt went to the pub with Harry.

Some British pubs were old-fashioned, timbered buildings with flower boxes, stained glass, and painted wooden signs bearing names like The Beehive and the Queen's Head. However, Harry's favorite pub, the White House, had no sign and a front door that opened straight onto the sidewalk. The plain facade was the shade of a white T-shirt that had been washed with black socks.

Inside, men with hair that same color shot pool on a table with stained felt. Retirees pulled wheelchairs around bare wood tables to play dominos. After a severe fire years ago, the regulars returned the next day—sitting on wooden crates at the charred bar, ignoring the damp air and smell of smoke, drinking beer while water dripped from the ceiling and guys in overalls filled a cement mixer.

We picked Sam and Matt up after a few hours, and they piled into the back seat, laughing.

"That was fucking brilliant, mate." Sam beamed, inspired by the authenticity of a northern working man's pub.

James smiled weakly at me. "I walk in to get them, and they're playing dominos, and Matt's standing up, pointing in a pensioner's face singing, 'You're shit, and you know you are.'"

"Wish I could have such a laugh with my dad at the pub," Laundry-Matt said.

"So, where are we going?" James asked Sam, who was in charge of directions.

"Just go to Leeds and turn left," Sam said, wholly serious, which set Matt off again.

"For fuck's sake," James muttered and handed me his phone to call for directions.

We arrived at a house bubbling with the laughter of old friends. When someone set up a karaoke machine, I clapped my hands together and turned to James. "Not a chance," he said and went to grab another beer.

I found Declan and ran over with a huge hug. "Lazy Leprechaun!" I squealed.

"Hey, I'm working now," he protested. He told me about his new job in Ireland, and I filled him in on the past couple of months in London.

I realized I hadn't seen James for a while, so I searched the house and found him sitting alone on a back staircase. "Here you are!"

He looked up, eyes watery.

"James, what's wrong?"

"It just pisses me off. When people think my dad is so charming. They don't know him." He stared at the bottle of Stella in his hand.

I sat down next to him. "I'm sorry, hon."

"You know he kicked Archie out of the house when he was sixteen, right? Tried to kick me out too, but me mum actually stood up to him then. They split up for a bit."

"Really?"

"Yeah," he continued. "I wish she'd never taken him back." Two fat tears trickled down his face, and he hastily wiped them away. "Anyway, I've given him too much airtime. It's a party. Let's have fun." He walked into the kitchen to replace his empty bottle.

Hours later, sleepy guests lay scattered around the dark house with blankets and sleeping bags. On couches, behind chairs, staggered along the staircase. Anywhere we could fit.

Except James, who was standing, his face illuminated by the TV, surrounded by recumbent bodies. He gripped the microphone, rapping "Lose Yourself" for the ninth time in a row. I crawled out from under the dining room table and loudly whispered, "James!" He ignored me. "Hey! It's time for bed."

He shot me a look like, *Can't you see I'm busy?* and went back to his Eminem impression, head bobbing with each beat.

"James. Literally everyone is trying to sleep."

He reluctantly set the mic down and turned off the karaoke machine. He stepped over the sleeping bodies, intending to be careful, but kicking most of them. Then he dove under the table, lay on the floor, and put his arm around me. I kissed his hand, but he was already sleeping.

One evening in December, I headed down the hall after my shift at the day care ended. As I threw my coat on, I heard Justine call out, "Oh! Stefanie. Before you leave . . ." I stepped back and peeked into her office. She sat behind her wooden desk—open envelope in one hand, British Immigration letterhead in the other. The look on her face told me all I needed to know.

"I'm terribly sorry. They've rejected the appeal." She handed the letter and envelope across the desk with a compassionate head-tilt.

"Okay. Thanks." I left in a daze and read the letter at the bus stop, shivering in the dark December night. They regretted to inform me my visa request was denied. I wouldn't get the back pay, and I could no longer work. They'd allow me to stay until August.

There was such a shortage of teachers in London that they had to recruit from abroad, but having experienced why, I didn't even consider looking for a job at another high school. But we couldn't survive for eight more months without me working. And even if we could, then what? We'd exhausted immigration options that allowed us to live and work in the same country. Well, all but one.

Once home, I lay on the bed and watched *A Place in the Sun* while I waited for James to get home. An English couple toured vacation homes on Spain's Costa del Sol. They bickered about paint colors and spare bedrooms, annoying me with the exaggeration of their tough decision.

James came up the stairs. He walked in and stopped short. "What's up, love?"

As a northerner, he dropped the name "love" often, to me as easily as the checkout girl at Tesco, but he rarely used it as a verb. He'd said it in Sydney, maybe out of instinct or obligation, but not anymore.

I'd given up so much to be with him. It hurt that James wouldn't tell me he loved me, but he always showed me, and I knew deep down that he did.

"The letter came. I have to go home."

James's forehead scrunched up like he didn't understand what I said. He took the paper from my outstretched hand.

"Well, it says you can stay until August!" He smiled, but I didn't.

"I know, but I can't work. And then what?"

"Well, I don't know. We could figure it out then." He seemed annoyed at my pessimism.

That night I lay under our comforter, staring at the dark ceiling for answers. James rested on his side, facing away from me.

We had only one choice if we wanted to stay together. I blew out a deep breath and asked, "What if we got married?"

James lifted his head from the pillow, but he didn't roll over. "Huh?"

"It's the only way we can be together anywhere. I can't work here, and we won't be able to find you a work visa for the States. But if we got married, I could apply for a spousal visa, and we could stay here. Or you could apply for an American fiancé visa, and we could get married and live there, someplace warm, like North Carolina or even California."

"Stef," James said carefully, "We haven't known each other that long. We've only spent eight months in the same country." He lay back and looked up at the ceiling, searching for the same elusive solution.

"I know. But—"

"I told you before, I don't ever want to get married."

"It's the only way we can be together."

"Stef," he repeated, slightly more forcefully. "I don't want to get married."

I rolled onto my side, facing the wall. "Okay."

CHAPTER 35
JAMES

To Ms Stefanie Caroll,
We're so terribly sorry to inform you that even though your employer
couldn't find a suitable candidate to fill your job position, we are unable
to transfer your visa because we are arseholes who don't care about
people's lives or feelings. You must break up with the chap you love and
fuck off back to America. Cheerio!
Yours faithfully,
British Immigration

Just like I'd feared, Stef came to London to live with me, and it all went
tits up. It started with that awful first day at Queensmead. I came home to
find her lying on the bed, sobbing. When she told me about those fuckers,
the anger welled up inside me, but I put my arms around her and forced
myself not to overreact.

The following day at work, I couldn't shake the image of Stef curled
up in a ball, overrun with sadness. I stood at a vending machine in the cold
warehouse, watching coffee drip into a plastic cup. I wanted to march into
the school and scream at them. I'd been naive in thinking Stef's confidence
freed me from responsibility. It was my fault. She'd sacrificed a dream for
a nightmare. Luckily, she found a job at a nursery. After only a day
working there, the smile I loved returned to her face. The one where she
pushed her tongue up against the back of her teeth like she couldn't contain
herself.

For the past few months, we'd been waiting for Stef's new work visa,
taking pleasure in the little things. Going to the chippy for our tea on

Fridays and enjoying lazy Saturday mornings. We'd lie in bed watching Britain's favourite TV hosts Ant and Dec play Wonky Donkey on *SMTV*.

Stef didn't get paid while her visa was processing, so we had to live on my small wage. It covered our rent, bills, cheap meals and two all-day travel cards for enjoying London at the weekends. Stef would map out walking tours, and while we took in the sights, she had that look on her face, the one she had in the Spanish restaurant in Sydney.

Despite our financial situation, being with Stef was effortless. I'd found a mythical unicorn from across the pond. Intelligent, funny, kind, caring and beautiful. And she loved *me*. She told me all the time, but I didn't like saying it back. I'd spent years becoming emotionally guarded. My dad would get drunk and tell me how much he loved me and then find an opportunity to crush me. 'Love' soon lost its meaning.

Stef gave her heart to me, and I would limit her to only glimpses of mine.

One Saturday afternoon, we felt nostalgic, so we called in for a pint at an Australian pub called Walkabout. We chatted with Aussie backpackers about travelling, stayed a lot longer than expected, and got drunk on cheap grog. At a McDonald's near the tube station, Stef munched on a cheeseburger, and drunken revellers milled about around us. I wanted to explain my feelings.

'What I feel for you surpasses love. I feel like a different version of myself when I'm with you. You make me want to be a better person, achieve greater things, so I can provide a future for us,' is what I thought I said.

'I don't like saying "I love you" because it doesn't mean anything to me,' is what I actually said.

Her eyebrows furrowed in confusion. She looked down at her fries.

Now I stood motionless in our bedroom, immigration letter in hand, processing our limited options.

One: We split up, Stef moves back to Pittsburgh and I sit alone in our loft.

Two: We get married, Stef applies for residency and we continue to date.

My parents had been married all my life and were the most unhappy people I knew. I pictured my mum on the sofa watching a war film she hated for the thousandth time whilst my dad sat with his back to her in his chair. I couldn't bear the thought of that becoming us. I couldn't bear the thought of me becoming *him*.

'What if we got married?' Stef blurted later that night. She rambled, and I froze. I heard the words 'visa' and 'fiancé' and 'America.'

'I told you before, I don't ever want to get married,' I said sternly.

But she carried on talking about it. I didn't know what our solution was, but I knew that wasn't it.

CHAPTER 36
STEF

My alarm beeped, and I climbed out of bed. I usually hit snooze a few times while I dragged myself into consciousness, but not this time. I opened my eyes and remembered. No going back to sleep.

I got off my bus, folded my arms against the wind and hustled to the day care in the dark. Lights glowed through the classroom windows, illuminating snowflakes I'd painted on the glass. The conversation from the night before replayed in my mind. If James doesn't want to get married and getting married is the only way to be together, then James doesn't want to be together. At least, not badly enough.

I greeted the ladies in the classroom, already there with the earliest drop-offs. "Hiya, Stef," Suzie said. "Happy Friday."

The doorbell rang, and she hurried past me to open the door. Oliver handed me a plastic truck. "Drive lorrie, Stef!" His sweet face didn't make me smile like it usually did.

I set out snacks. Cleaned up snacks. Set out Play-Doh. I sat next to the kids on a teeny chair, rolling doh snakes and making a mental checklist: call my parents, book a flight, say goodbye. Why prolong the inevitable?

But my chest didn't ache the way I thought it should. My eyes weren't welling up. I felt anesthetized.

On the bus ride home, I wiped the steamy window with my hand and watched the dark streets. Glowing wreaths hung from the streetlights along the sidewalk. Warmly lit pubs were filled with friends, chatting in front of fake Christmas trees with twinkly lights.

"Is there an Asda near here?" asked a man sitting nearby.

"Oh. Yeah. Get off at the next stop, go left, and it's a block down."

"Cheers," he said and rang the stop request bell.

Giving directions made me feel like a local—like I belonged. But now I had to go. James and I had worked so hard to be united, and strangers in an office had unapologetically divided us. I had an answer, though not the one I wanted. I could move forward. I'd go home and come up with Stef's Future 3.0.

CHAPTER 37
JAMES

The morning after Stef suggested getting married, I looked out the window on the train to work, replaying the conversation in my mind. 'It's the only way we can be together.' I imagined Stef's tears in the darkness as she said it. And the hurt in her heart as I rejected marriage. It must have felt like I was rejecting *her*. I hated that this was our only option. I picked up my newspaper and flicked through the sports pages. The words washed over me.

I sat at my desk in the frigid, empty warehouse, a stack of delivery boxes next to me and a pile of paperwork on my desk. I gathered up a bunch of shrink wrap and taped it into a makeshift football. The warehouse became my pitch. What if we didn't get married and Stef went home? *Kick.* Would I stay in London? Would I travel again? Would it even be the same without having Stef to share it with? *Kick.* My chest felt hollow. My alternate life felt hollow.

There was no guarantee that if we did get married, we'd ultimately be happy. *Kick.* Our relationship was still young and under an inordinate amount of pressure. A pressure I'd been feeling since picking Stef up at the airport. I wanted to protect her, but what if I couldn't protect her from a failed relationship? *Harder kick.*

I sat back down at my desk. Would I always wonder what could have been? Would I build up that 'what if' to be the biggest regret of my life, letting it hang over me, tainting all my other life choices?

If I moved to America and we didn't work out, we'd get divorced and I'd move back to England. There would be sadness, but I'd prefer that over a lifetime of wondering.

I pushed the mountain of spreadsheets to one side, brought up Google and typed in 'British Immigration.'

CHAPTER 38
STEF

I opened our front door with my long, old-fashioned key. Nobody was home. I wandered into our bright yellow kitchen and turned on the little radio to fill the silence of the big house. We always listened to music while we made dinner, which was frozen pizza and garlic bread more often than is probably recommended. I sat at the end of the long wooden table and absorbed every detail of that room. The tin box in the center of the table where we pooled our money for bills. The two fridges. The wooden laundry rack hanging from the ceiling.

I heard the front door creak open.

"Stef?"

"In here."

James stepped quickly down the hall and stood in the doorway, looking eager. He carried a thick stack of papers with both hands. "I did some research today."

"On what?"

"Immigration laws."

I studied him from across the kitchen. "Okay."

He set the printouts on the table. "I think we should do it." James tapped his pile of papers. "I've looked it all up. We can get married at the Registrar's office, and then we can apply for a spousal visa for me, and we can go live in California."

James stood there grinning, but I didn't move from my seat. "What made you change your mind?" I asked.

"I thought about it all night and day, and I realized I don't want to lose you. We've come so far, and I'd rather try and fail than always wonder what could have been."

"Okay." I paused. "Are you sure?"

"100%."

I pushed back my chair, walked to the doorway, and collapsed into James's arms. My numbness crumbled like a cement dam, and emotion flooded through my body. I *felt* for the first time that day. I buried my head into his chest and bawled. After a minute, I caught my breath, looked up at James, and wiped my runny nose. "So, we're doing this."

He stroked my hair and kissed me on the forehead. "We're doing this."

I stood in a red metal phone booth a few days later, protected from a steady drizzle. A man and his son shuffled by, bundled in woolen winter coats, carrying shopping bags full of Christmas presents.

I punched the long international number onto grungy metal buttons. With each beep, my nerves grew. I always called home from this booth—James's cell phone was too expensive. But this time, I felt less like I was sharing a happy event and more like the bearer of bad news.

"Yell-o?" Dad answered.

"Dad?" My voice sounded very small.

"Hey there, Steffie! How's everything, honey?"

A bus squealed to a stop and let a couple of chattering teens off. They cowered under the falling rain. "Um, I got my letter from Immigration. I've been rejected. So, James and I. Um . . . We're going to get married."

Silence.

"It says I can stay till August, but I can't work so we won't have any money, and we decided we'd rather settle in the States, so we are going to the JP here in January, or the Registrar, they call it, to get married, and then we'll apply for a spousal visa for James to come live with me in America."

Silence.

"I'm really sorry, Dad. I know this isn't the perfect situation, but we really want to be together, and this is the only way." My eyes filled with tears, and I had no more words to fill the void.

After an eternity, Dad spoke. "Wow, Steffie. Uh, that's big news. Are you sure about this? You two haven't spent much time with each other."

"I know." I shut my eyes, sending streams down my face. My voice wavered. "Eight months. But we've spent every single day of that with each other."

"Hmm. I don't know what to say." I couldn't judge Dad's flat voice. Was he worried? Disappointed? Angry? "Look, I'm not going to tell Mom just yet. Give me some time to process this, okay? I'll talk to you later."

"Okay. Love you. Bye."

"Bye."

I emerged from my metal and glass cocoon and stared down at the sidewalk the whole walk home. My dad had raised me to be sensible. I knew that in his eyes, this was reckless. I ached from the sickening feeling of disappointing him. I'd never felt that before and never wanted to again.

CHAPTER 39
JAMES

'I got a letter from my dad,' Stef said, handing me a stack of handwritten pages as soon as I entered our bedroom after work. She'd called him a week ago to tell him our marriage plan, and it devastated her knowing he disapproved.

My eyes were immediately drawn to the figure $5,000. Was Frank offering to give Stef five grand not to marry me? I wanted to rip the letter into pieces. We finally had a plan, and now Frank wanted to ruin it.

I'd made peace with getting married and began to feel some relief from the stress of making major life decisions. We'd been back to living in the moment. Being ourselves. And now this.

I took a deep breath and slumped onto our bed. I read the whole letter. He said he understood our situation but didn't want us to rush into anything. He offered to loan Stef $5,000 so she could stay in London for a while without having to work, allowing us to continue dating. He wasn't buying me off. He was buying *us* time. I felt bad for making my assumption.

'For a minute there, I was worried that your dad was paying us not to get married,' I said.

'No, that's not what he means,' Stef replied.

'I know, I get it *now*. Tell him that's really generous, but we can't accept it.' I handed the letter back to her.

Stef frowned. 'Really?'

'I know we're still gonna feel the same way about each other when the money runs out, and we'll have the same plan but be five grand in debt,' I explained.

'So, what are you saying?'

'We wanna move to America eventually, right?'

'Yes,' Stef said, sitting next to me.

'Any more time you spend here is time without a job. What if you go home now, start working and saving, and I come over on a fiancé visa? We can get married in the States. That way, we're not starting our new life owing money. It'll be on our terms.' I reached out and hugged Stef.

I could feel her nodding on my shoulder. 'OK. Looks like I'm going home after all.'

CHAPTER 40
STEF

My sister Cassie came to visit just before Christmas, anxious about her first departure from the USA. I'd be heading home just after the holidays, so this was her only chance to travel abroad with a free place to stay and a knowledgeable tour guide.

She arrived at Heathrow looking weary, her messy brown hair partially tucked under a long crocheted scarf.

"Yayyyyy!" I cried, smooshing her into a hug.

She reached into her bag and pulled out another long crocheted scarf. "From you-know-who."

I wound my mom's gift around my neck and guided Cass onto her first Underground ride.

Over the next few days, we ate fish and chips, toured Shakespeare's Globe Theatre, and saw a show in the West End. She tried to stick tight by my side as we navigated the dense crowds in Central London but often fell behind, timidly apologizing to people who'd bumped into her.

James, Cass, and I spent a long day visiting Windsor Castle. "I don't know how you guys do this all the time," Cass said as we walked in the front door. "My feet are killing me."

Our housemate, Mark, opened the door to his bedroom. "Dude!" he declared and fist-bumped each of us. "Stef's sister is here. Let's party!"

We kindly explained we were tired, but he ignored us and ushered us into his bedroom.

"Sit, sit, everyone," he said in his Trinidadian accent and gestured towards his bed. Musky incense filled the dim room in swirling plumes. James, Cassie, and I perched on the edge of his mattress—which I feared would look like a Jackson Pollock painting under a blacklight.

Mark rustled in a cabinet under his TV and pulled out an obscure Christian Slater movie. "James, grab some cups from the kitchen?" Mark opened a full-size fridge by his bed, revealing fifteen bottles of chilled champagne. He poured the bubbly, and we toasted. "Welcome, Cassie," he announced and ceremonially put the DVD in the player. I glanced at Cass. She sat stiffly, drinking her champagne from a teacup, staring in disbelief at Mark's pimp fridge.

Two days later, Cass flew back to Pittsburgh. I was sad to see her go, but it felt good to say, "See you soon."

I wrapped up life in London. We went to Covent Garden one last time, and I ate cheese and onion pasties and Lion candy bars every day, not knowing when I'd have one again. I said goodbye to the ladies at work and squeezed Oliver tight. I bid farewell to my housemates when I happened to see them and fist-bumped Mark one final time.

Before I flew home, we drove to Warrington to spend Christmas with James's parents. Nobody answered the door. We found the key in the shed and let ourselves in. A note lay on the kitchen table, in Eileen's shaky handwriting. "At Whiston hospital. Your dad's got a nosebleed. Hotpot in the frige."

We spent Christmas Day in a cold, sanitized room, gathered around Harry's hospital bed in uncomfortable chairs. Eileen chattered away, and Harry sat quietly, nostrils full of gauze. I felt awkward and was thankful when a broadcast of the Queen's annual speech started on a TV in the corner.

We caught the bus back to London after the holidays, and early the next morning, I hugged James tightly in the dark before he left for work. In a few hours, I'd catch the Underground to Heathrow.

He kissed me and then paused, seemingly searching for the right words.

"See you soon," I said.

He nodded, approving my choice. "See you soon."

Dad met me at baggage claim at the Pittsburgh airport. A grin spread across his face, and he held his arms out wide for a huge hug. Though worried and probably disappointed, he would never treat me with anything but love and support.

My ancient suitcases tumbled from the conveyor chute, and we heaved them off the belt.

"Great to see you, kiddo. Ready to head home?" Dad asked.

"Yes! I can't wait to see everyone!"

"Hey, look, I still haven't told your mom anything. I figured you might want to tell her yourself."

"Okay." I smiled. Mom's reaction would be pure excitement. A wedding! A son-in-law!

As the sliding doors opened, a gust of freezing air stung my cheeks and took my breath away. A few snowflakes danced in the wind. "I didn't miss this weather!" I moaned.

We heaved the baggage into Dad's station wagon and hit the highway. Coming home was a familiar scene. I'd lived in five countries over the past four years. Returning to Pittsburgh usually depressed me—it meant the end of an adventure.

I put my hands in front of the dashboard vents and let the hot air defrost my fingers. A warm contentedness spread through me. Though my time in London ended abruptly, much sooner than expected, I felt good. The start of another adventure, the best one yet, was just months away.

A few days later, Dad motioned for me to come sit next to him on our old wooden coffee table. It still bore a black Sharpie drawing from my childhood—an animal of some sort that looked like those All-Terrain walkers from Star Wars.

He looked at me seriously. "Steffie, I'm just concerned. Are you sure about this?"

"Yes, Dad. I'm sure."

"But you kids can't know each other that well yet."

I frowned. "Yeah, but we're not like a regular couple. We've lived together since the day we met." I looked back at Dad, just as seriously. "I promise, Dad. We know each other."

He gave me a slight smile and a tight hug. "Okay."

I picked James up at the Pittsburgh airport in August, after eight long months of waiting for his fiancé visa and temporary work permit to be approved. Eight months of emails and calling every few days. Eight months of paperwork, and fees, and waiting. It felt eternal, but now he was here.

I found him at baggage claim. "It's so good to see you," I said, burying my face in his chest.

"You too, love." He gave me a kiss and grabbed his bags. "I'm knackered. I didn't sleep at all on the plane, and this girl sat next to me, talking my ear off. And she offered me Swedish fish? Who the fuck brings fish on a plane?"

I laughed. "Swedish fish are candy. Like wine gums, kind of."

"Oh. I thought she was going to pull out a tin of smelly anchovies."

We loaded up the Green Machine, the rusty wagon I'd bought from my dad that shook violently over 55 mph. James looked at the road signs directing us toward the highway. "Moon Beaver? I want to go there!" He looked at me in amusement.

"That's two places. Moon and Beaver."

"Well, that's disappointing."

We fell quiet, the significance of the moment suddenly enveloping us.

"So, I got that job at St. Vincent's school," I said.

"That's great, love. Are you okay with that?"

"I mean, there's no other jobs I'm qualified for, so I guess I have to be. I do feel nervous. Definitely. But not as scared as I thought I'd be. It's middle school, so they're younger. And I went to Catholic school, so I feel more like I know what to expect. Hopefully. It's more than I'm making at the YMCA right now, but it's still not much."

"I guess that's the price for teaching mostly well-behaved students. You just need one good experience to gain some confidence, and then maybe you could try a city school again."

I nodded, and we drifted back into comfortable silence.

Over the next few weeks, James got a job at CompUSA, working in the warehouse unloading boxes for minimum wage. Also, his temporary work permit only lasted for three months, so he'd have to quit work in November, until we passed our immigration interview and his green card was issued. More immigration headaches, American variety. My parents suggested we stay with them until we could afford an apartment in a neighborhood that wouldn't give my dad an ulcer.

On a sweltering summer day, we got legally married at the Justice of the Peace, so we could start our green card application. I honestly don't remember the date. James wore his England soccer jersey. And then we went to Walmart. We'd have been fine to leave it at that.

But Mom brimmed with ideas and still wanted to throw us a real wedding, so we planned a ceremony and reception for October.

She accosted me in our nook of a dining room, holding up a white doily she'd crocheted. "Steffie, do you like this?"

"Yeah, that's nice, Mom."

"I thought we could put them on the tabletops at the dinner."

"Uh, okay, sure, Mom."

"Oh, good, because I made ten."

I fingered the lace, happy to see Mom inspired. But planning this traditional reception almost felt staged. James and I knew we were getting married so we could keep dating.

My petite principal, Sister Josephine, walked into my classroom with paperwork the day before school started. She wore orthopedic flats and a wool skirt that hit mid-calf. I set down my posters and joined her by my desk.

"So, my fiancé and I are legally married already. Can we put him on my health insurance?" I asked.

She glared at me. "I thought you were getting married at St. Teresa's in October."

"We are. But because of immigration stuff, we got legally married at the JP to get the ball rolling."

"Well," she huffed. "I can't consider you married if you weren't married in the eyes of the Lord." She shook her head, her short brown nun hairdo barely moving. "I don't even know if I can allow you to work here."

My mouth gaped open for a second. "Um, well, we aren't considering ourselves married until the church ceremony. It's just for legal paperwork." I hoped that would calm her down.

It didn't. "I'll have to get back to you. Just. Hang on." She rushed out of the room. I sat for an hour, looking around my classroom, wondering if I should continue preparing. Wondering if I'd be fired before I even started.

She finally returned, looking flustered. "So, you're still having a church ceremony."

"Yes."

"And you're honestly not considering yourselves married or acting like you're married until you're married in the church." I shook my head vigorously, ignoring her allusion to premarital sex.

She peered into my soul with her beady brown eyes. "Well. I suppose it will have to be okay. I just hope the parents don't find out. Don't tell anyone." She turned on her heels. "I won't be allowing you to put him on your insurance," she said as she walked out of the room.

I knew if she'd had time to find a new teacher, she'd have fired me. I sat for a moment, stunned by her sucker punch, and finished hanging my posters.

Early the next morning, I stood by my classroom door. My heart wasn't racing, my palms were nice and dry. For some reason, I thought I'd be okay here.

Uniformed middle-school children filed down the hall. Thirteen-year-old girls gathered in clumps, squealing and hugging friends they hadn't seen in ten whole weeks. Boys strutted coolly, exchanging nonchalant nods. A few appeared at my door. They looked at me, smiled, and greeted me as they stepped inside. I let out the long, slow exhale of a breath I hadn't realized I was holding.

The bell rang. I talked. They listened. They laughed at my jokes. They learned.

Hours later, I picked James up from CompUSA. He got in the car and looked at me expectantly. "Well?"

I beamed and bounced in my seat like a kid on Christmas morning. "It. Was. Awesome!" I gushed. "I'm so relieved. They listened. And they smiled at me! It felt really, really good."

His face lit up, and he leaned across the console, wrapping his arms around me. "That's great, love. I'm so happy it went well. Everything is falling into place."

"I know!" I squeezed his hand and squealed with relief. "It's all gonna be okay."

We'd spent so much time working on getting to this point, we just settled into regular life for a bit. We talked about moving to California or future trips we might take, but really, it was a relief not having to *plan* for a while. Instead, we spent our time hanging out with my high school friends and taking road trips to see Christina in Philly. I taught James to mountain bike, and he, my dad, and I would spend hours on the trails. Life was simple.

Rain dulled the stained-glass windows of the packed chapel, where sixty friends and family members sat waiting on a cool October day. Harry and Eileen were the only ones from James's side of the family.

My sister Cassie walked in first, wearing a black dress like my simple white one and black chandelier earrings matching my crystal ones. Dad took my arm. My stomach swirled with anxiety. I wasn't scared to get married—we already were—but I'd never been the center of attention like this.

Dad walked me the few steps down the aisle, where James stood next to Harry. James smiled nervously and grabbed my hand. He leaned toward me, putting his cheek to mine, and I smiled in anticipation of a sweet remark.

He whispered into my ear. "Sam's here!"

My eyes lit up, and I stifled a giggle. I resisted the urge to turn around and find our Pink House friend in the pews.

After the short ceremony, James and I mingled on the church's front porch under an overcast sky.

"You look beautiful, by the way," James said and grabbed my hand. A warm breeze blew, sending red and orange leaves swirling. Eileen stood blowing bubbles, looking adorable in a blue dress and matching hat. Harry looked impatient to get to the restaurant.

Christina and Sam walked over. "I can't believe you're here!" I gushed and threw my arms around Sam.

"Glad to see you, too," Christina joked, squinting her big brown eyes.

"Christina helped me plan everything out," Sam said, and Christina smiled, proud of her well-kept secret.

"I'm glad to see you," I said to Christina, giving her a hug. "Just not surprised. You'd better get your ass here on my wedding day."

She beamed. "I'd never miss it."

After a few photos, we went to dinner at the Grand Concourse—a restaurant in a century-old train station with high ceilings, stained glass, and wide, curving staircases. A dozen pink roses sat on the cookie table, labeled with a card from Declan and some other friends from the Pink House. Christina had arranged that, too.

James and I ate our steaks at a table with our parents. Our moms discussed yarn crafts. Our dads talked about old Western movies.

"People used to tell me I looked like Yul Brynner," Harry said.

Dad nodded. "Well, he's a good-looking guy."

"Never!" Harry waved his beer bottle about. "He's *bald!*"

My dad chuckled uncomfortably and scratched his barren head. "Excuse me," he said and left to find Sam. As one of the few people who knew both the bride and groom well, Dad asked him to make an impromptu speech.

"Hello, ladies and gentlemen," Sam started, entirely at ease. "My name is Sam, and I take full credit for this happy union, as I introduced James and Stef at an Irish pub in Sydney." Our guests laughed, charmed by Sam's words and accent. "They're fun, funny, slightly ditzy blonds. But they're lovely people, and I couldn't be more chuffed for them." He held his bottle high. "To Stef and James!"

In a warm, crowded dining room, my supportive loved ones cheered and clinked glasses to toast our expedited union, and I felt lucky that so many people would want to be there. My Mom and Dad were beaming at me. "Thank you for this," I said. I'd never imagined this moment—sitting in a white dress, having people celebrate my relationship—but it was nice.

Two months later, my symptoms started. My thinking felt foggy, like I'd taken too much cold medicine. Writing my lesson plans and grading papers took forever because I kept finding myself staring out the window or thinking of something else. Choosing a flavor of Ben and Jerry's had me staring at the grocery store freezer shelf for ages.

Dad and I always watched The Amazing Race every week—a reality contest where teams travelled around the globe. One week, I was completely confused and couldn't remember who was on what team, or keep track of all different places they were in.

Sometimes I felt my heart palpitating, and my chest was in a vise. I was anxious and irritable. But what was there to stress about? James was here, we were working, and we were together.

Other times I felt great—elated, even. I'd sing in the car, bopping in my seat as I drove. I thought it was because of James being here or finally having a teaching job I liked and was good at. But soon enough, the fog would roll back in.

I curled up on the living room couch on Christmas Eve. I put my head in my hands and cried. "Dad, what's happening to me?"

He sat down on the coffee table near me. "You wanna go for a run? It'll make you feel better. Put your shoes on."

The park was quiet and enveloped in white. White ground, white sky, sullied only by the brown skeletons of trees and the two sets of muddy footprints we left behind. We ran down the trail, sending echoes of crunching snow into the open sky.

On the car ride home, my dad blasted the heat. I coughed while my chilled lungs reheated. "Feel better?" Dad asked. I nodded, and we rode home in comfortable silence.

On Christmas morning, logs glowed and crackled on the slate hearth as my family littered the carpet with wrapping paper and bows. We drank eggnog and listened to my mom's Dean Martin Christmas CD. Our immigration interview was scheduled for January, after which James could get his green card and start work again. It was the last hurdle before normalcy.

Dad handed James a heavy, roundish gift from the pile by the tree.

James inspected its weight, shape, and size. "It feels familiar, but . . ." Finally, he tore it open as Mom watched eagerly. His face lit up, and she glowed with pride.

I recognized the purple tin. "Aww! Quality Streets!"

"What are those?" Cassie asked.

"Chocolates," James said. "Kind of a Christmas tradition. Thank you, Evelyn. Where did you find these? How did you know?"

She beamed. "I did my research."

The scene I'd imagined two Christmases ago, on Coogee Beach, now played out in front of me. I looked at James and grinned, flushed with the warmth of fire and family.

CHAPTER 41
JAMES

I woke up in a pitch-black room on a creaking sofa bed. The air was stale. I fumbled for light switches but couldn't find them in the unfamiliar space. My eyes adjusted enough for me to gather my clothes from an old sofa and put them on. A beam of sunlight peeked through the bottom of the kitchen door as I slogged up the basement stairs in a jet-lagged haze.

The cramped kitchen glowed with August sunshine. An open window let in the smell of cut grass and the sound of chirping birds. A narrow shelf wrapped around the room below the ceiling, holding miniature wooden buildings in a quaint small-town scene.

Stef was at her day-camp job, and her mum and dad were out shopping. Cassie was working at the video store. I wandered alone in this new home. In this new country.

Popcorn littered the living room carpet beneath my bare feet. Melted pink, white and brown ice cream sat in a bowl atop a side table. I sat on the worn sofa, its threadbare arms digging into me. The Pittsburgh Post-Gazette lay open on the coffee table below fast-food cartons and remote controls. Stef's high school photo, along with her sister's, hung proudly on one of the walls. I stared at Stef's picture, with her cheesy pose and soft-edge nineties glow and smiled. My Stef. I was finally in Pittsburgh with my Stef.

My first weekend, we went for breakfast at a diner called Denny's. Our waitress greeted us with a smile and called me 'honey' in a deep smoker's voice. She chewed gum and had poufy, back-combed hair held upright by half a bottle of hairspray. I ordered something called a Grand Slam.

When three plates were served to me, I figured there'd been a mix up with our order.

'Is this all for me?' I asked Stef.

'Yep. I hope you're hungry.'

'This is a lot of food, but where's the bacon?'

Stef pointed to two thin strips of fat with morsels of meat attached.

'That's the part of our bacon we cut off and feed to the dog,' I explained.

I eyed up the plate of pancakes that accompanied my eggs, bacon, sausage and toast. *I'm not big into pancakes, but that dollop of ice cream on top looks appetizing.* I scooped it into my mouth. The warm, slippery substance startled me, and my tongue repelled a bit back out of my mouth and down my chin. Stef looked on in horror.

'That ice cream is disgusting!' I said, wiping my face with a napkin.

She burst out laughing. 'That's whipped butter, you dickhead!'

I worried about getting to know my future father-in-law, Frank. In England, boyfriends and dads go to the pub to drink a pint and watch football. Frank didn't do either of those things. Also, a military photo of him in the basement intimidated me. He wore a helmet and an army uniform and clutched a machine gun in a field in Vietnam. Mounted next to the photo were a bayonet and various medals.

One Sunday afternoon in August, Stef suggested I go on a bicycle ride around Pittsburgh with her dad. She'd told him that I rode regularly in London. Although I'd met him during my first visit, I'd spent most of that time with Stef. This was my icebreaker. I took a deep breath, threw on some shorts and headed outside.

In the driveway, Frank was loading two bikes onto the back of his car. He wore a bright yellow T-shirt tucked into skin-tight black spandex shorts, a green baseball hat and white sport socks pulled up to his knees. To complete the ensemble, a bum-bag hung around his waist. He cast a far less imposing figure than the one on the basement wall.

I followed behind while Frank led the way along the river towards downtown Pittsburgh. This left little room for small talk, but that was fine with me. Frank would stop to point out a landmark and tell me its history every now and then. Washington's Landing, the Heinz Factory, the Roberto Clemente Bridge.

I enjoyed his passion for his city. *My* new city. An hour into the ride, we stopped for a rest, and Frank offered me a snack called Combos. I reached into the bag and pulled out a small, hard, tubular thing with glowing orange nuclear waste in the middle. I sniffed it, shook my head and put it back in the bag.

Over the coming weeks, Frank and I chatted effortlessly for hours about sport, family and his trip to Australia while on R&R from Vietnam. He even showed me a photo he'd taken of the fountain in Kings Cross. We spent one evening conducting the seriously manly business of making wedding favours. We melted chocolate, dripped pretzels in it, bagged them and tied a ribbon around them.

I wasn't nervous about getting to know Evelyn. One Sunday, at Stef's nan's house, Evelyn cooked a lamb dinner for everyone as she knew I liked it. Not only had she never cooked lamb before, but she'd driven all over Pittsburgh just to find it.

Evelyn and I were home alone one morning while Cassie and Stef were at work, and Frank was on a bike ride. I stared in bewilderment at the toilet. The contents swirled dangerously close to the brim despite me repeatedly pressing the toilet handle. Water overflowed along with soggy paper. I stood motionless and horrified as brown chunks breached the toilet walls. A foul stench filled the room. Water continued to cascade onto the floor, soaking the bath mat.

A knock at the door. "Is everything OK in there, James?" Evelyn asked. I put my hands on my head. *Shit!* Evelyn had gone out of her way to make me feel welcome since arriving in America, but we still didn't know each other well.

'Erm, it's the toilet, Evelyn,' I said after a long pause.

'Can I come in?'

'Wait—'

She opened the door and looked at the toilet. 'Geesh!'

Then she quickly rolled up the sleeves of her long, blue nightgown and fished handfuls of toilet paper from the depths of the bowl. I stood open-mouthed as she hastily tossed them onto the floor.

'I'm really sorry about all this, Evelyn,' I said.

'It's fine. I've seen worse. I was a nurse for thirty years.'

Finally, the pipes gurgled, and the water subsided. Evelyn slipped on the wet tile floor and grabbed the sink to steady herself. She gathered her composure, scrubbed her hands and left the room.

'Sorry! Thanks, Evelyn. Where do you keep the mop?' I shouted as she made her way back into her bedroom.

Eventually, I got a job an hour away in the warehouse of a computer shop called CompUSA. Luckily, my new boss lived near Stef's parents and drove me to work in the mornings. Stef finished teaching mid-afternoon and would have to wait after school for an hour before picking me up at work.

My temporary work permit expired in November, forcing me to quit and wait for my green card.

While in immigration limbo, I started my days by cleaning. Frank worked full-time plus overtime. Cassie came in and out of the house between multiple part-time jobs. She and Frank ordered takeaway often and left the remnants all over the place. Tidying up was the least I could do to contribute.

I spent my afternoons at the family's ancient computer in the basement, listening to the squeal of dial-up internet. I caught up on sport. Not being able to watch football and see it in the news felt strange. The only channel that showed football aired one live match per week and came with an expensive subscription. I hated not being able to get the channel without feeling guilty because I wasn't working.

I tried to teach myself web design. It was interesting, and with the web expanding, I thought it could be a good skill to have. With some basic, slow-running software and old books from the library, I spent countless hours hunched over the keyboard, trying to make sense of CSS and HTML.

Most days, Stef would come home from work all smiles. 'Hi, love,' she'd say from the top of the basement stairs.

'Hello,' I'd manage from behind my book.

'What did you do today?' she'd ask.

'What have you accomplished while I was making money,' you mean? Did you not see the mountain of clean dishes on the draining board?

'Not much,' I'd reply.

I dreaded Stef returning home. I hated feeling like a disappointment to her. She worked so hard and was always cheerful. I grew jealous of her attitude. Envious of her closeness with her dad. Jealous of how her family spoke to one another. They spoke with kindness and love. They appreciated each other.

In mid-January, after six weeks without work, a letter from US Immigration arrived. We'd been invited to attend an interview regarding our marriage and my visa situation. Stef went into full-on teacher mode, filling a thick binder with photographs, email printouts, cinema ticket stubs, letters from her parents and scratched-off phone cards. All evidence of our relationship.

At the interview, we chatted informally with an immigration officer who asked us a few questions and flicked briefly through our wedding photos before giving us the all-clear. I was excited to be allowed to work again, and though Stef was too, she expressed disappointment at all of her hard work going largely unnoticed. Classic Stef. We drove straight over to CompUSA, where I asked for my job back. To our relief, my old boss happily gave it to me and agreed to resume driving me to work.

'You OK, hun?' Stef said, walking down the basement steps one evening.

I looked up from the computer screen. 'I'm alright love, why?'

'We're all upstairs watching Jeopardy. Wanna join us?'

No, I fucking hate that shit. It makes me feel stupid. 'No. Ta love, I'm good.' Although proud of my restraint, it pained me to see Stef's smile fade away.

'What's the matter?' Stef asked.

'Nothing. I told you, I'm alright,' I insisted.

'Why are you down here by yourself?'

'Why are you down here trying to start a row?'

Stef winced. 'I'm not. It's just—'

'I said I'm alright love, I don't know how else to say it.'

I liked and needed my own space. My family rarely hung out in the living room together. When we did, my mum and I would sit on the sofa trying to have a conversation while my dad sat a few feet from the TV, blasting the volume because he refused to wear his hearing aids. Despite the noise, he would somehow manage to catch what we said. Every few minutes, he would clear his throat, and the volume would go up a notch, until he drowned us out entirely. One time, the vibrations sent an owl ornament I'd bought my mum crashing to the floor.

Stef ran up the stairs with tears welling in her beautiful blue eyes. I imagined her sitting back down in the living room and making up an excuse for me. I sensed her embarrassment, as apparently, her husband would rather hang out by himself. I knew it was hard for her, but it frustrated me that she didn't see how hard it was for me too.

CHAPTER 42
STEF

Dad sat on the floor one February evening, surrounded by a smattering of runaway popcorn kernels. I plopped on the end of the couch, and Cassie stretched out across me, reading. Mom had her feet up in her recliner, crochet needle weaving effortlessly, brightly colored balls of yarn unraveling at her feet.

"Plate tectonics!" I shouted.

"Hey! You read too fast, Steffie," Dad complained. "You should have to wait until he's done reading the question."

"But that's my only advantage," I said, and Dad laughed.

Meanwhile, James sat at the computer in the basement, like he did most nights. My family didn't treat him like an outsider, so why did he act like one? During the commercial break, I went to the top of the stairs. "You okay?" I called down.

His shoulders slumped. "Yeah, love. Just felt like going on the internet."

I knew from experience not to keep bugging him. But I felt hurt and embarrassed when he didn't want to hang out with my family.

"Steffie!" Dad called from the living room as the Final Jeopardy song played, and I walked away.

I'd been to several doctors, but no one had been able to tell me what was causing my symptoms. One doctor ordered an EKG for my heart palpitations, which came back fine. No problems, but no answers either. So, I went to a natural health practitioner, who was definitive in his diagnosis. He told me it was my diet. He put me on a strict low-carb, no-sugar, no-alcohol diet.

I followed it to a T and lost twenty pounds. Sometimes I felt like it was helping. I really wanted it to be.

James came home late from indoor soccer one winter night and poked around silently in the darkness of the basement. Soccer was one of the only things that made him happy lately, and he was always buzzing on his return home, excited to tell me how many goals he'd scored. "Hey," I said, rousing myself for his recap.

"I hurt my fucking ankle really bad. I won't be able to play anymore."

My chest ached like I could feel my heart actually breaking. "Shit. Oh, shit, I'm sorry."

"I should probably go to the doctor, but without insurance, it'll be expensive. Fucking health insurance in this fucking country."

CompUSA required a ninety-day waiting period before they offered insurance. Because of his gap in employment, the clock reset, and James had to wait another ninety days. He was currently uninsured.

"That sucks. Man, that sucks." What a worthless response. The thing that brought him joy had just been taken away. And it was my fault he was here, unhappy, in a country he didn't understand. The right words didn't exist. He climbed gingerly into bed, and I lay on my back in silence, tears trickling into my ears.

The next evening, during a *Jeopardy* commercial break, I peeked down the stairs to see him on the computer. Looking up flights to Manchester. I felt like throwing up.

We often bickered, which we'd never done, even through the most stressful of times. "Hey James," I said once while he lay on the couch watching TV, "Could you help clean the bathroom?"

He sat up and stared at me. "Why does everyone always assume the worst of me?"

I leaned back, startled. "Whoa! What? I just asked if you could clean the bathroom."

"You never notice the things I do, just the things I don't."

Little things escalated into fights so quickly. I never started out mad, but suddenly we'd be shouting at each other. I'd never seen my parents fight like that, and I didn't know how it kept happening to us. I'd be confused and anxious for days while James avoided me, and then we'd move on without resolving anything.

I never told anyone we were having problems. I assumed most people thought James and I were crazy for marrying so quickly, and I couldn't bear to give them evidence they were right.

One day, I stood in my parents' big backyard, which was vivid green from April storms. Puffy white clouds slowly floated across a brilliant sun.

Sweat beaded above my eyebrows. I yanked the cord on the old red lawnmower again and again as I replayed our recent fight in my head.

The lawnmower roared to life. Gasoline fumes clouded around me, and I pushed. The scent of freshly cut grass filled the air. Leaves rustled on the trees surrounding the lawn, and birds chirped—but the roaring mower drowned their songs.

"Could you maybe mow the lawn this weekend?" I'd asked James. He looked up at me from the couch, instantly irritated. "You've never offered to," I continued. "I do it every weekend. It's the least we can do for living here."

James stood up and gestured around the room. "I'm *always* tidying up. I clean the scum under the draining board. Your and Cassie's hairs out of the shower. You never notice any of this. Why don't you get on Cassie?"

"Well, she's not my husband."

"You really do think I'm an asshole, don't you?"

"No! I don't think you're an asshole." I started to cry.

James threw his hands up in frustration. "Oh, for fuck's sake. You always make me feel like shit for making you cry."

I wiped my cheeks with my hand. "You're not *making* me cry. I'm just crying a bit!" We'd faced each other in the living room, looking at strangers.

I pushed harder. Shredded grass spewed onto the lawn as I forced the thundering mower in concentric rectangles, spiraling inward, winding me tighter. Was I right? Was he?

James and I had lived in other countries with little money and been happy. We'd spent months and months long-distance and been happy. We fought so hard for this life together, and we were more unhappy than we'd ever been.

CHAPTER 43
JAMES

During the winter, Pittsburgh became even more foreign to me. The sun disappeared, and I'd never seen so much snow. Though a novelty at first, eventually dirt-covered piles of it, taller than me, lined the roads. Then there was the bitter cold. People pointed out on several occasions that I was 'from England and should be used to this.' Almost any one of these winter days would have shut down the UK.

Stef found a men's football league, which I joined. Once a week, I got to be with like-minded people to play and talk about football. *My* football. I'd lost some pace and was a bit rusty, but playing meant that once a week, I got to feel like myself again. My teammates were friendly, and one was originally from England. We became fast friends, and he regularly invited me over to his house to watch matches on TV.

On a snowy February evening, I planted my foot down on a hard gym floor while making a tackle. My foot stopped, but my leg kept on going. Seething pain shot up my leg as my ankle buckled under the force. Teammates rushed to fill plastic bags with snow and ice from the car park for the swelling. On the sidelines, I choked back tears of pain and sadness. Luckily, the car was an automatic as I could only use my left foot. The drive home took twice as long, watery eyes and blizzard-like conditions compounding my efforts.

The following day, the swelling was up to my calf, and my leg turned every shade of purple. I was in agony and couldn't put any weight on it. Stef was devastated. She'd been so excited I'd been playing football and making friends. I called off work and spent the day on the sofa, but the pain worsened. I needed to go to the hospital, but because of Sr Josephine's sanctimonious bullshit, I had no health insurance through Stef's job, and I still had a couple of months before I could get insurance through CompUSA. I found myself in red-tape limbo, yet again.

I hobbled around on crutches. The descent into the basement proved particularly tricky with its low-hanging ceiling.

I researched the potential medical bills online. Emergency room visit, x-rays, possible MRI and maybe even physical therapy. It could cost thousands. My head spun with the ridiculousness of it all. I took back everything bad I'd ever said about the good old National Health Service in the UK. They have long wait times, but you don't have to refinance your house to pay medical bills. Not only had I been robbed of my favourite pastime, but our fledgling joint bank account was in danger of being ransacked.

The idea of disappointing Stef and her family saddened me. I panicked and searched 'flights to Manchester' online. It worked out cheaper to fly back to the UK and receive treatment there. I had a backup plan.

A few days later, I told a teammate about my predicament. He said he was a chiropractor, and he would x-ray my ankle for free. His generous offer humbled me. The x-ray showed no break, but he diagnosed me with a high ankle sprain with severe ligament damage. He predicted a long road to full recovery. Our bank account was safe, and I was extremely grateful for his help, but I'd have to quit playing for a long time. Football had become my own piece of happiness away from the house. An escape from the NFL water-cooler chatter at work. And now it was gone.

A week later, I was back in a warehouse unloading trucks, hobbling around in a large medical boot. Back to my unfulfilling job and web design in the basement.

'So, I was talking with my dad, and we were wondering if you've ever considered going to college?' Stef asked one day on the ride home from work.

Despite both of us working full-time jobs, the low wages kept us staying with Stef's parents, and I relied on Stef and my boss to drive me to and from work.

I'd worked hard in Australia and supported myself. I hadn't needed anyone. Now I needed my wife, her parents and a stranger from down the street. I felt buried in guilt, but her question got my back up immediately. I clearly wasn't good enough for her now. Her manly mover had turned into a basement loser.

'No, not really,' I replied calmly.

'Well, what're you gonna do for the rest of your life?' she asked.

I knew we didn't have the money for college, and I didn't know what I wanted to study anyway. It would be a waste.

'I don't know. Be a backpacker,' I said jokingly. Up until this point, I was just trying to get through the day to day, and maybe save money for a big trip sometime in the future. I figured that's what we were doing. Now all of a sudden, I needed to go to college.

We were driving past the petrol station on McIntyre Road when she uttered, 'Well, I guess I'll make the money then.'

My chest tightened. My stomach tensed. I was fuming, hurt, sad and humiliated all simultaneously. She'd belittled me in a way I never thought her capable. We didn't speak for two days.

Consumed by inadequacy, I felt helpless and unable to communicate it. Growing up, we never talked things out in our house. Reasoning with my dad was futile, and questioning was interpreted as a declaration of war. We kept our feelings locked away until we could no longer contain them. A screaming match would ensue, followed by snarky insults and swearing. Doors were slammed, and silence would descend on the house.

Next followed a prolonged period of ceasefire. My dad would hide behind his newspaper if I entered the room. I'd hide in my bedroom as much as I could until he went to the pub. Then I would go downstairs and speak to my mum.

After a few days, the silence was usually broken with a casual remark. 'Did you see the Manchester United match?' Regular service would resume without resolution, and any lingering issues swept firmly under the rug with the rest of them.

Now with Stef, I saw every question and every discussion as an attack against me. Her words ignited the hatred I harboured for my father. A hatred I'd been suppressing since early childhood. I was punishing Stef for all the years of hurt caused by a manipulative dad with a wicked tongue.

Stef and I were sitting at the computer in the basement one evening in spring, after another long week of work and petty squabbles. I decided we needed to start again.

'We should go travelling soon,' I said.

'How?'

'Well, we could use the money we got from the wedding. Then start saving again later for furniture and all that stuff.'

'When?'

'I don't know. I really want to take you to Thailand, love. We could learn to scuba dive...'

'While we're in Asia, could we see the Great Wall?' Stef asked.

'I'd love to see the Terracotta Warriors.'

Stef's eyes brightened. 'I want to finish this school year and do day camp over the summer. We can fly out in the fall?'

'Fuck it. Let's go.' I said.

I wrapped my arm around Stef as she typed furiously and booked our tickets. A flight to Beijing in October, then three weeks later, a flight from Hong Kong to Bangkok. Flight home TBD.

Since booking the Asia trip, Stef and I had something to be excited about. I made an effort to spend less time isolated in the basement and more time in the living room with Stef's family. *My* new family. I was still shit at *Jeopardy* but made my peace with it.

We'd completed a TEFL (Teach English as a Foreign Language) course so we could teach in Thailand. The thought of Thai kids picking up my northern English accent amused us. The school year ended, which gave Stef time to plan our trip. She took charge and loved it. She bought a guidebook, and we'd sit in bed while she read all the places we should go.

We got even stricter with spending. A big Friday night out consisted of a beer, water and fifty ten-cent wings at a local bar called The Barking Shark. The wings were tiny, and Stef would sometimes ask for fries, even though she'd only eat a few of them.

'Fries are $2.75. We could get twenty-seven more wings for that!' I'd say.

We'd laugh at our frugality but always left a fifty percent tip. Then back to the house to watch a DVD. Dinner and a movie for under ten bucks.

Over the summer, I battled a persistent ear infection. First, I tried ear drops, then multiple courses of antibiotics, and most recently, steroids. At least my health insurance from CompUSA had started, and these treatments only required copays.

Despite my assurances to Stef, I knew something wasn't right. One day the pain increased and woke me up in the middle of the night. It resonated up from my lower neck and thrust deep into my ear like a jagged-edged knife, each heartbeat pushing it further and further in. I walked from room to room, my hand cupping my ear. Eventually, I bent over the kitchen sink in agony, tears falling.

'Hello,' I answered the phone a few days later.

'Yes, hello. This is Doctor Mitchell. I'm calling about your CT scan.'

'OK.'

'You have a cholesteatoma.'

'A what?'

'A cholesteatoma. It's a cyst that has formed in your middle ear. The problem is, it's become extremely potent and made its way through your skull. It's pushing on your brain's outer membrane.'

I froze. I could still hear the doctor's voice, but the words were muffled

199

as though I were underwater. I stared out of the dining room window into next door's garden where the first autumn leaves were on the lawn. I always thought it odd there wasn't a fence separating the properties.

'You need to come into the office at 8:30 on Monday morning to discuss your surgery,' he finished.

'Yes, OK. See you then.' I hung up the phone and broke the news to Stef, causing floods of tears to stream down her sun-freckled face.

My ears had been a problem since birth. I spent my second and eighth birthdays in hospital, having my ears drained and grommets put in. Now we'd found out my narrow eustachian tube wasn't regulating the air pressure inside my ear. This had caused the top of my eardrum to break away from the ear canal, leaving space for protein cells, water, sand, dust and anything else to accumulate. Over a long period of time, this matter formed a cyst, or cholesteatoma, which can eat through bone.

Stef and I sat in the doctor's sterile treatment room as the doctor described, matter-of-factly, that he'd drill through my skull behind my ear to gain access. Then he would remove the cyst and assess the hole.

For fuck's sake, please stop talking.

He explained the cyst would be virtually impossible to remove completely the first time and would almost certainly recur, resulting in a repeat of this procedure in about two years.

I felt a tingle in my nose, then a sting in my eyes. He wanted to remove everything the cyst had come into contact with, including my eardrum and maybe some bones. He'd fashion a new eardrum from scar tissue and replace any tainted bones with prosthetic implants. I'd be deaf in my right ear until the second surgery, by which time the scar tissue eardrum would be strong enough to be reconnected, and I would partially recover my hearing.

Please let that be it.

The eardrum in my 'good' ear showed signs of retraction, which might require similar surgery to reinforce it from the inside to avoid a cyst.

As I processed this, he informed me the surgery would be in four days. Aside from the obvious risks of exposed brain surgery, the cyst could have wrapped around a facial nerve, creating a chance of facial paralysis if the nerve was damaged during removal.

I wanted to leave the office. I needed some air.

'You're lucky you got that ear infection, actually,' the doctor said as we stood to leave.

'Why?' I asked.

'Well, that's the reason we found the cyst. Otherwise, it would have silently eaten through to your brain. Another six months, and this could have killed you.'

Back at the house, I sat in the bedroom with my head in my hands. My brain couldn't figure out which potentially disastrous scenario to process first. Our Asia adventure was only five weeks away. Would we have to cancel? The doctor understandably gave no assurances. I pondered this for a second before reminding myself of the most critical issue. I allowed myself to contemplate my mortality, sobbing loudly like a child, then composed myself and went to be with Stef. She'd just finished telling her parents and was shaken up. We hugged, and she cried into my chest.

During the car ride home after the surgery, driving over Pittsburgh's potholes sent vibrations through my ear. Frank helped me walk gingerly from the car, through the garage and into the basement. The solemn look on his face told me how bad I looked. Noises in the house disorientated me. I had no idea which direction they were coming from.

The inside of my ear crunched and cracked. I reached up to touch it. My finger expected the soft skin of my earlobe, but instead, I felt a cold plastic cup. I couldn't handle it. I sat on a chair and declared that was where I'd be staying.

I waited for Stef to return from the pharmacy with my medication. It felt like my ear now housed a bowling ball. The noises inside it gave me shivers. Somehow, the *pssshhht* from the ring-pull of my ginger ale can was painfully loud. The room began to spin, so Frank helped me onto the sofa bed and propped me up with pillows.

After the post-surgery morphine wore off, the gravity of my situation became more apparent.

What I *was* told:

1. I was still alive.
2. The surgery was a success.
3. My face wasn't paralyzed.
4. I'd have a headache.

What I *wasn't* told:

1. Drilling had dislocated my lower jaw.
2. Having my mouth clamped open split the sides of my lips like I'd tried to eat a knife sideways.
3. The breathing tube made my throat so raw, even water hurt.
4. The headache they mentioned was a massive fucking understatement.

The intense pain meds made me spacey—not sleepy, a kind of in-between place. Asleep with my eyes open. Twice a day, I'd endure pain to swallow a few pieces of thinly sliced ham. I stared at the TV all day with Stef by my side. Overnight, we'd leave MTV on, and the drums from Green Day's 'When September Ends' seemed to play on a loop those first few days.

Stef was always there for me, to prop up my pillows, to administer my medication and to hold me up while I suffered the indignity of peeing into a plastic bottle. She hid her shock when removing the plastic cup covering my ear. I avoided a mirror for the first week. After I finally looked, Stef admitted that I resembled Sloth from The Goonies for the first few days.

Most of all, she comforted me. I'd never felt further from my family. My jaw made talking painful, so phone calls home were brief and frustrating.

After days of insomnia, I finally fell asleep. I awoke a few minutes later, sweating and panicked. The sight of Stef soothed me, but the narcotics had to go. I switched to Tylenol. Each heartbeat throbbed like an earthquake through my ear and into my brain. But mentally, I felt more like myself again.

What about the trip? This question dominated my thoughts. During some of the most painful moments, I pictured the beautiful beaches of Thailand and how I longed to show them to Stef. I imagined the smile on her face as we sat on plastic stools eating street food. Her look of awe as we scuba dived through schools of rainbow fish. She needed this trip. *We* needed this trip. A surgeon had rebuilt my ear, and this trip would rebuild our marriage. I *had* to get better.

After a week, I ventured upstairs to the roar of a neighbour's lawnmower—which sounded like it was in the living room. When Stef dropped a fork into the sink, the high-pitched sound reverberated around my head. I turned around, grabbed the stair rail and ambled back into the depths of the basement.

Three days later, I returned to the doctor's office for a follow-up. Aside from letting Stef remove the cup, I'd not let anyone within arm's length of my ear. I lay partially upright on a dentist-like chair while a nurse inspected my stitches. Without warning, she ripped off the strip of gauze covering them. I became light-headed, and my eyelids drooped. She waved smelling salts under my nose and apologized.

The doctor inserted something into my ear. I tensed up and held my breath as he removed rolls of gauze. Intense ringing began in my ear, and the crackling sounds grew louder. The doctor told me he was pleased with the procedure and my progress. He needed to see me two weeks before our flight so he could give me the final OK to travel.

PART FOUR:

THE WAY HOME

(2005 – 2006)

CHAPTER 44
STEF

"Holy shit! What is he doing?" I exclaimed, looking through the windshield of the bus. A car ahead had slowed on the steep mountain incline. A pickup truck accelerated to pass him on a bend in the road. Our bus driver floored it to overtake them both simultaneously, putting us entirely in the wrong lane as we rounded a blind corner on the mountain.

James slowly opened his eyes as we crested the hill, and everyone returned to their lane of origin. Unconcerned, he went back to sleep. A bright pink scar behind his ear peeked through his buzzcut. His T-shirt hung loosely on his gaunt frame.

After a year of misunderstanding, planning the trip to Asia started to guide us back to the same page. I know they didn't mind, but I felt terrible that after my parents had let us stay with them to save money, we went and used the cash from our wedding gifts on a trip. But though neither James nor I said it out loud, we knew we needed this to fix whatever had broken between us.

When not only the trip but James's health was threatened, it overruled everything. For the past month, I had helped James recover. Stacking pillows, getting water, dumping pee bottles. We ignored our past issues and focused on the immediate.

We lived in limbo for weeks, not knowing if James's health would force us to cancel the trip. The doctor had told James he'd have to wear earplugs in the ocean, and scuba diving was out of the question. He'd shared his concerns about James flying at first, but at an appointment two weeks before departure, he gave James the all-clear.

We'd just arrived in Beijing, after two days of travel. Exhaustion beckoned, but excitement shooed it away. I relaxed into my bus seat, observing the rainy countryside. Farmhouses nestled in valleys. Cobs of corn dried on their roofs. Women sold pomegranates at roadside stands, and men rode donkey carts by the side of the road.

A break in the trees revealed the Great Wall, tracing the crest of a steep crag in the distance. It was beautiful. I nudged James with my elbow. "Look."

He glanced out the window. When he noticed the wall, he sat up, grinning with a sudden burst of anticipation.

The driver dropped us in a parking lot below the bluff, by the base of a cable car whose existence I despised. But we only had a few hours to explore, and James was still somewhat weak, so we took the ride to the top.

I stepped onto the crumbling barricade and ran my fingers along the unrestored bricks, trying to channel their history. To see what they'd seen. The wall undulated across dark hills, seeming more ancient and mystical with the brooding weather. James and I hiked uphill to a square watchtower far from the tourist chatter. I ignored the ice cream carts, cable car, and other anachronistic annoyances and looked out a window, imagining Chinese guardsmen standing right where I stood, watching over Mongolia, setting smoke signals to warn of incoming threats.

"Hey," James said. "Nobody's up here. Fancy a wildy?" He smiled mischievously.

I smirked at him. "There is absolutely no way I am ever having sex with you outside."

He frowned, pretending to be disappointed. Well, maybe actually disappointed, but pretending he thought there was a chance.

Two middle-aged Chinese women appeared on the stairs, rustling plastic bags of souvenirs. James and I moved along. They followed, never speaking to us but hot on our heels. When we turned around and smiled, they smiled back, and we hiked together.

They were forty and fifty years old, and both lived in Simatai, the village near this part of the wall. Forty taught me to count to ten in Mandarin, complete with finger signals that in no way correlated with the numbers. I taught her the English equivalents. James recorded the lesson on our new camcorder, laughing as I simply pushed her fingers up one by one. Fifty took us by the elbows as we walked down the down the perilous steps and shared some tart orange berries that she'd just picked off a nearby shrub.

I was glad we gave in. They were sweet and fun, and we came away with twelve dollars' worth of postcards, a photo book, and a prestigious certificate stating, "I climbed the wall at Badaling," which we treasured even though it was geographically untrue. We paid more for these items than the entire bus trip, but we considered it support for our buddies from Simatai.

They left after our purchase—no doubt our time with them had expired, and they were off to make new friends. I took photos of the misty cliffs while raindrops spattered on my head. I felt exhausted, bewildered, thankful, and happy. A part of myself—my favorite part—had reawakened. I wiped the water from my camera and looked over at James. He lowered the camcorder and smiled. We were on our way home.

CHAPTER 45
JAMES

'Son of a bitch!' I shouted after smashing my head on the train's ceiling for the thousandth time. My head throbbed, and my body ached from the flu. I looked over at Stef on the opposite bunk.

She made a pouty pity face. 'I'm sorry you feel ill.'

'No, you're not,' I replied.

Due to the Chinese National Day holiday, every train out of Xi'an was fully booked. We had to stay for four and a half more days than we'd planned. I'd spent the last few days inside our Xi'an hotel, out of the cold and endless rain, to avoid getting sick. Stef refused to waste any precious time for exploration and continued to walk the walled city, during downpours, in a thin raincoat and sandals. She got sick and then kindly passed it on to me just in time for our mammoth train journey to Shanghai.

'I told you to fuckin' stay in. Why did you have to—' I started, but the smell of freshly cooked spicy noodles made its way along our carriage. 'I'm off to get noodles,' I said.

I *did* want noodles, but mainly I *didn't* want an argument. There'd been a ceasefire. We focused our attention on the trip to allow the relationship time to heal itself. Our love remained constant, but our friendship had suffered. Recently, I'd seen us becoming close again. I'd seen Stef again. On the Great Wall, she laughed and smiled with two local women as they taught her how to count in Mandarin, her enthusiasm plain to see.

Though annoyed at her for getting me sick, I bit my tongue.

The absence of a ladder made it difficult to climb down from the top bunk of three. I paid particular attention to the elderly ladies beneath us, one of whom I'd accidentally kicked in the head the previous night.

At the end of the carriage, a group of older women congregated around a hot tap. Each of them cradled a small bowl of steaming noodles, laughing in unison as one of them told a story. I'd grown accustomed to hearing the local language. A few weeks had passed since we'd heard anyone else speak English. I pictured my Mum, Nan and Auntie Dorothy on their weekly meetup, sitting in a cafe eating jacket potatoes and laughing at nothing in particular.

The next few hours consisted of naps and noodles, interspersed with coughing and sneezing. I followed every sneeze with a scowl in Stef's direction. While sitting on a low seat in the aisle, a local teenager sat across from me. He rested his arms on the small table between us and picked up my MP3 player without looking at me or asking. He stared at it, inspecting it as though it were gold bullion. I removed my earphones.

'I'm Li,' he said.

'Hello, I'm James,' I replied.

'What?' His forehead scrunched up as he sat back in his seat.

'J-A-M-E-S. James.'

'Oh, OK. I study English at university in Xi'an, but from Shanghai.' He presented me with an English textbook from his backpack.

'Your English is very good,' I told him, and I flicked through a few pages of his book.

He grinned. 'My friends will never believe I talked to English speaker.'

'I'll write a message for them.' I chose a page and wrote a note introducing myself and explaining the conversation we'd had. His dark eyes lit up, and he admired my words like they were a celebrity autograph.

Though I wanted to talk more, fatigue forced me towards my bed. 'Stef, come and meet Li,' I called out.

She came down from her bunk and took over so I could sleep.

For several hours we rotated shifts, answering Li's never-ending questions. He soaked up all the conversations he could. Each chat grew more inquisitive and informal. I enjoyed the exchanges but suffered in silence between fevers and cold sweats.

With Stef on Li duty again, I lay in my top bunk. Unable to see out of the window, my thoughts turned to the reason we had visited Xi'an: The Terracotta Warriors. A site I'd been even more excited about seeing than The Great Wall. For over two millennia, 8,000 battle-ready clay warriors stood buried in a field, faithfully watching over their emperor in the afterlife. We marvelled at the vast rows of exhumed soldiers, each with a unique face. What a wealthy and powerful empire China must have been to produce such extravagance. A sense of the surreal hit me when I studied a group of soldiers surrounding a chariot, complete with horses. It was the furthest I'd felt from my old life.

We stayed in a hostel, far removed from the lavish abodes of former emperors. The cold, humid room swarmed with mosquitos. The shared bathroom down the hall had a hole in the floor for a toilet and a pipe in the wall for a shower, which trickled out lukewarm water.

Despite the miserable weather and hotel, it felt good to be out of Pittsburgh, as it now represented a low point for Stef and me. Though, I was looking forward to getting out of the malaria suite and moving on to Shanghai.

I awoke after a nap to hear Stef and Li still going strong. 'Politics is not our business, so we don't worry about it. There's nothing we can do to change it.' Li said. 'Approval rating for Prime Minister always one hundred percent.'

I signalled to Stef that I'd take over. She stood up, gave me a weary look and climbed onto her bunk. I set my bottle of water and MP3 player down on the table.

'What you listen to?' Li asked.

'Eminem. Have you heard of him?'

He smiled. 'I like Eminem,' he said. 'But can only listen to a couple of songs online. Can't buy here.'

I offered him my earphones. 'Would you like to listen?'

He wiggled in his seat like an excited child as he grabbed the earphones and placed them in his ears. His head bobbed, and his fingers tapped the table. He tried to sing along without knowing the words. He mumbled loudly, blissfully unaware of his volume. A few minutes later, he removed the earphones and cast me a confused look. 'What it mean, "My pee-pee go, da-doyng doyng?"'

I almost choked on my water. 'Umm...well, it means when...' I clenched my right fist and raised my forearm forcefully, hoping the gesture would describe an erection. His eyebrows furrowed deeper. I made the gesture again, this time pointing towards my crotch. His eyes widened. *He's gonna have fun explaining that to his friends from English class.*

After 32.5 hours, the train crept into Shanghai station.

'Do you have hotel?' Li asked me.

'No, we don't have anything booked,' I replied.

He grimaced. 'Shanghai is busy. Big holiday. When my Dad pick me up, we help you find hotel.'

'That's OK, we'll be alright.'

His smile convinced us to follow him.

Li introduced us to his dad, who had thick, slicked-back hair and long Elvis sideburns. He spoke no English. Li told him of his offer. He took a moment before smiling and gesturing for us to follow him.

We exited the station into a dark, seedy street crowded with shopping trolleys, cardboard boxes and dirty wet blankets. Homeless people wandered by.

Our presence drew a crowd. A local screamed at me in Mandarin and grabbed my backpack. Li's dad shouted and ushered him away. Li's grin faded, and he didn't stray from his dad's side.

'You OK, love?' I asked Stef.

She nodded and grabbed my hand. We followed Li and his dad to an incongruous luxury hotel. It had one room available at a budget-destroying $300 a night. This was now Plan B.

Further into the neighbourhood, decrepit multi-storey housing rose high into the foggy night sky. Window AC units dotted the towers, balanced precariously on rusty wall brackets. Laundry dangled from windows, looking like it had been left drying, soaking in the rain and re-drying for years. Food vendors dotted the street. The aroma of sizzling meat skewers punctured the smell of rubbish.

Li's dad led us into one of the high rises. 'Please thank your dad for his trouble,' I told Li in the lift.

We went from floor to floor, and each time the proprietor of a guest house told Li's dad we couldn't stay there. Occasionally, Li would spout out random words from his Dad's conversations to keep us in the loop.

'No vacancies.'

'No insurance for not Chinese guests.'

'They don't say why.'

At the fifth place, Li's dad's voice grew louder, and his conversation with the owner escalated into shouting. We looked at Li for answers, but he could barely keep up with translating.

'What if we can't find a place?' Stef said, sobbing. 'What if we're out on the street tonight?' She rubbed her hand on her chest amidst shallow breaths.

'It's OK, love. We'll be fine,' I wrapped my arms around her. 'If all else fails, we'll use the credit card and get that fancy room for the night and find somewhere else in the morning.'

When the shouting finished, Li translated for us. 'They have room for you. Too expensive! But my dad got better price for you.'

'Li, please thank your dad again for us. And thank you, too.' We hugged them both before letting them go and enjoy their much-deserved family time. The room was basic but had its own bathroom. I collapsed on the bed. Stef peered out of the window, the yellow haze of streetlights illuminating her.

I laughed out loud as a memory popped into my head. Stef looked at me.

'What's so funny?' she asked.

'Pee-pee go, da-doyng doyng.'

CHAPTER 46
STEF

James and I had already spent several days in our room at the Shanghaishizabeiquzhengfu hotel. Because of the National Holiday that kept us in Xi'an longer than expected, we also couldn't get a train back out. We had to skip a planned trip to see the limestone peaks of Yangshuo. Now we had a week to kill in Shanghai, and the constant drizzle kept us holed up.

The last dry day felt like ages ago. We'd joined Beijing citizens of all ages, gathered in a park outside the imposing walls of the Forbidden City. The sun burned behind a smoggy haze. A group practiced Tai Chi, their limbs moving in slow unison. Accordion music lilted, an impromptu dance session springing up around the musician.

A group of middle-aged locals stood in a circle, kicking a kind of shuttlecock in the air like a hacky sack. They used their ankles, knees, and heads to keep the rubber disk in the air, its colorful feathers flying. James gestured that he'd like to play. They nodded and made a space. They cheered when James would chase after the shuttlecock, flicking it back with an overhead kick. If he missed, he'd pull goofy faces that made them laugh. And when he sent it over an iron fence, a petite woman climbed over to retrieve it, groaning and pretending to be annoyed.

We grinned and waved goodbye, brimming with happiness. I'd never traveled anywhere I didn't speak the language, and here was a genuine connection without the help of a single word. As we walked away, I looked at my funny husband. He was beaming.

Unfortunately, these light moments had become overshadowed. We couldn't understand China, and it was wearing us down. Drivers ran red lights consistently. Several times we had to sprint to avoid being flattened by speeding sedans, and on the bus ride back from the Great Wall, we sat in a jam for an hour because the traffic from an intersecting street refused to stop, while the vehicles on our road backed up for miles.

Sales techniques sometimes felt like harassment. Rickshaw drivers followed us for blocks, refusing to accept our polite "No, thank you." Once, I stopped to look at what a vendor was grilling—long tubes of white meat spiraled around skewers. When I smiled and walked away, not ready to try snake on a stick, he yelled at me until I bought one. It seemed like eye contact and a kind declination were not only ineffective but taken as a challenge.

I watched a bus driver clean wax from his ear with his key and saw a man hock a loogie onto the floor of a restaurant and grind it into the carpet with his shoe. Locals stared at us, even if we caught them looking, well past the point of awkwardness.

The hotel room became a welcome respite from both the cold rain and the culture shock. We spent the first three days playing shithead and interpreting Mandarin infomercials. My favorites: a table you can strap yourself to and crank yourself taller and sticky pads that suck fat out through your feet.

I sat by the smudgy window one day, peering down at the daily bustle of Shanghai life. A woman hunched under a wooden yoke—woven baskets piled with green-skinned oranges dangled from each side. A man on the sidewalk flipped smoking lamb skewers on a charcoal grill. A teenager came out of a 7-11 with a bottle of Coke and a vacuum-sealed chicken foot.

The constant pour slowed to a momentary sprinkle. "Let's go out. It's not bad right now," I said.

James lay on the bed, watching an infomercial for skin-whitening cream. A beautiful woman smiled at the camera, caressing her alabaster face. He grabbed the remote and clicked off the TV.

We checked out Nanjing-Lu, the pedestrian shopping district. Tall, futuristic buildings buzzed with neon, flashing in colorful choreography. Columns of fluorescent Chinese characters blinked from myriad signs, reflecting a dynamic rainbow onto the shimmering glass towers. The wet pavement glistened with swirling colors.

We infiltrated a sea of locals flooding the walkway, but vendors immediately spotted our blond hair and bombarded us with shouts of "You want Prada? Shoes? Bags? Dior? Versace?" We looked away, put up our hands, and shook our heads, interacting with the Shanghainese solely with the word "No."

"Hey," I said. "I saw in the guidebook that there's a pub called

O'Malley's in Shanghai."

James's eyes lit up. "A Guinness would go down a treat right now." He put his arm around me. "Should we pay tribute to the place we met?"

"Considering our anniversary's coming up, I think it's only right."

We headed in the direction of the pub. As we wandered down damp, dark streets, some of my symptoms appeared. Mist rose from the pavement, and it felt like it was filling my mind.

I stopped to look at the map in the guidebook. I turned the book in different directions, trying to orient myself. I couldn't make sense of the crisscrossed streets with similar names. We wandered for about twenty minutes, unable to find the pub. It was then I realized I'd been leading James around the wrong side of town.

"Love?" James asked.

I looked up from the map, feeling like an idiot. "I don't know."

"Let's just head back," James said. The moment had passed.

We got some lamb skewers and walked toward the subway station. A guard blew her whistle at a crosswalk and held up a white-gloved hand, forcing drivers to stop and let pedestrians pass.

There were no orderly lines in the dank underground station, just a pressing horde of shouting and hands flying. It looked like the New York Stock Exchange. We waited in the back, and as those in the front of the mob were served, others pushed past us to take their place. People stepped on my feet. The man behind me exhaled hot breath on my neck. I wanted to scream.

"We'll be here all bloody night." James's British, queue-loving brain was about to explode. Someone elbowed him in the ribs, and his face hardened. "Let's go," he said, and we fought through the mosh pit.

We purchased tickets, wriggled our way out, and stood on the edge of the platform. The train pulled in, and the doors opened right in front of us. Fifty Chinese commuters shoved their way on and off the train at once, pushing our bodies from all directions, and we were the last two people to wedge into the car. The tide of humanity pushed us apart. My jaw clenched and my heart beat faster. I spotted one empty seat. As I started to sit, someone violently bucked me out of the way. I whipped around to find a middle-aged, suited businessman had stolen my seat, literally, right out from under me. He nonchalantly settled in for his commute.

"WHAT the FUCK is WRONG with you?" I shouted, glaring into his dark eyes. James heard the English profanity over the din of the crowd and wrestled his way to me. "He body-checked me and stole my seat!" I raged.

James's head turned crimson as he unleashed a stream of obscenities. The offender sat and looked straight ahead, unfazed and probably unsure of what had been so upsetting.

I touched James lightly on the shoulder, and he stopped. We waited. The doors parted, the locals rushed, and we barely made it out.

"I can't take this!" I exclaimed.

"I liked it better in our hotel room," James agreed. We hurried back to the Shanghaishizabeiquzhengfu to call it a night.

The following day, James and I boarded a fully booked overland train to Suzhou for a day trip. We had to sit separately. I plopped down in my seat and grabbed a tightly sealed water bottle from my bag. The young man beside me watched me struggle to twist it open. "May. I. Help. You?" he asked.

I handed it over and smiled gratefully as he gave me back the opened bottle.

The AC filled the train with a damp cold. Fat raindrops slashed horizontally across the steamy windows. I opened my backpack to retrieve my jacket, and some of its fabric caught in the pack's zipper. I yanked on it unsuccessfully. An elderly woman in the seat facing me snatched the bag and wrangled with it. Then she elbowed her gray-haired, snoring husband and plopped the bag in his lap. He looked at the bag, and then at me, and said something I translated as, "Wow, this is really stuck."

He eventually liberated the jacket from the zipper's teeth. "*Xie xie!*" I cheered.

He smiled and nodded. "*Bu ke qi.*" You're welcome.

I bundled up and peered at the countryside through clear streaks in the fogged glass. I knew I'd been judging the Chinese by *my* perception of acceptable behavior. But Chinese norms and human kindness weren't mutually exclusive. Would the kid who opened my water have pushed in front of me in the ticket mob? Would the sweet old man who freed my jacket have hurled me out of the way on the subway? Would his helpful (if aggressive) wife have bullied me into buying a snakecicle?

Before I arrived at an answer, we arrived in Suzhou. The rain stopped for us, and we got to wandering. We crossed under keyhole arches, past pagodas, into gardens filled with the fresh scent of wet leaves. We stood on arching stone bridges and looked down murky canals edged with whitewashed homes with slate-tiled roofs. Steps from their back doors led straight to the water, where local women scrubbed laundry. Wind rustled the branches of weeping willows, sprinkling us with their tears.

At the Confucian temple, I ran my fingers over a stone stelae carved with intricate Chinese characters and wished I could read what wisdom it held. A teenage girl sat in a doorway, sketching a gate in the courtyard with a charcoal pencil.

Up the road, a park buzzed with playful children and beaming parents.

Based on the Chinese one-child policy, few of those kids would be playing with a sibling. A girl blew bubbles from a sudsy wand. A two-year-old boy squealed, running after them in baby chaps that revealed his little bum.

James and I sat on a low stone wall and listened to a band of older gentlemen playing traditional songs. Guitar and keyboard players accompanied a man playing a string instrument. It had a hexagonal box on the end of a long wooden stick, and as he drew his bow, sonorous tones emerged, complementing the singer's voice. The frontman wore large, nerdy glasses and a white Yellowstone Park souvenir baseball cap. When he caught us watching, he smiled warmly.

As dusk fell, the band packed up, and we gathered our bags to move on. A woman with glossy hair pulled into a ponytail stopped right in front of us. She looked about forty.

"Hello," she said.

"Hello," we replied.

She looked up to the sky, seemingly searching for the right words to say next. "Uhhhh," she muttered, looming over us for ages.

I raised my eyebrows at James. He responded with a barely detectable shrug.

Finally, she found it. "Where are you from?"

"America and England," I said.

She replied with a blank stare. She'd worked so hard to come up with a question, even though she wasn't able to understand the answer. I appreciated the effort. It was more than I could say in Mandarin.

White Cap came to the rescue. He translated our answers for Ponytail, who nodded in understanding. A crowd pressed in around us as we spoke, trapping us on the wall. We tucked our day packs under our legs.

The onlookers interviewed us through our interpreter. Where do you live now? How did you meet? How tall are you?

James and I stood up to show them our height. Ponytail asked if my hair was naturally wavy and blond. I explained that it lightens in the summer from the sun, and she covered her mouth with her hand and giggled.

White Cap spoke better French than English. Translating an English answer from James to our translator in French and from him to the crowd in Mandarin was like a weird game of polyglot Telephone.

"Tell him we liked the music," James suggested.

White Hat grinned with pride. "Those are old folk songs. During the Cultural Revolution in the '60s, nobody was allowed to perform such songs."

I'd read about Chairman Mao's attempt to modernize China by banning the Four Olds: old customs, old culture, old habits, and old ideas. But hearing about it and its aftermath first-hand made it more real. Erasing a country's entire heritage is not progress.

"Now," our new friend explained, "we are having a Cultural Resurrection. If you want to sing, you sing. If you want to dance, you dance." He beamed, his joy contagious. "Every Saturday, we come to the park to enjoy our freedom to do such things."

The sun had now set, and we had to catch the train back to Shanghai. We threw our packs on our shoulders, bid our new buddies goodbye, and hiked back over the arching stone bridges, under the weeping willows.

"That was brilliant," James said. "I proper enjoyed talking to them."

"Yeah, me too."

We lined up to board the train, and a man cut right in front of us and jumped on first.

"For fuck's sake," James muttered.

I shrugged. "I guess that's just how it works here."

James looked at me, surprised.

"Well, we're the strangers," I said. "We're not going to change anything by being pissed off."

"Get you, enlightened one. You learn that from Confucius?"

I stuck my tongue out at him. "Ha. No, I just don't feel like being annoyed for another week." And I hopped on the train for the journey back.

A stoic Chinese man stamped my passport and slid it back across the counter with several papers tucked inside—my train ticket from Shanghai to Hong Kong, a reminder I'd need a new visa to reenter China, and a laminated card printed with: "Give to frontier agent."

Another stone-faced employee waved us into a stuffy waiting room crammed with metal chairs in rows so narrow my knees nearly touched the woman's across from me. James sat with his left arm tucked into his lap and his right elbow jutting into my lap.

The woman clipped her nails as we waited. Slivers of keratin flew through the air and bedazzled my sweatshirt. I gave her an ineffective dirty look and brushed them onto the floor.

Suddenly every waiting traveler rushed to the exit on the other side of the room as if they'd heard an announcement in a frequency only locals could detect. On our way out, a man I assume was the "frontier agent" collected the card.

Once in our cabin, a ticket collector exchanged our paper tickets for plastic cards with our cabin and bunk numbers on them. We happened to have the cabin to ourselves, and we settled on the bottom bunks for the long trip to Hong Kong. After a few rounds of shithead, James lay down for a nap. I put the cards away and gazed out the window, pulling the bunk sheet around me in the arctic air conditioning. The Titanic theme song played almost imperceptibly on the PA system.

As we chugged south, the view changed. The sun peeked through the clouds, and eventually, the sky cleared completely, for the first time since we'd been in China. I could sense the change in climate, as folks outside wore lighter clothes, and temperate trees gave way to rice paddies.

It was our one-year anniversary, but our wedding day seemed like a much more distant memory. So much had changed since that lighthearted day that I'd assumed marked the end of all our troubles. I reviewed our fights and awkwardness. My mental issues. James's ear surgery.

I cried as the memories came back. Since we'd flown around the world, I'd pushed them from my mind, though they really weren't that long ago. James woke up and gave me a small smile. He sat on my bunk and pulled me close, never asking what was wrong. We just sat together in silence, watching the world rush by and hoping the next year held better things.

Just before arrival in Hong Kong, another ticket collector returned our paper tickets and took the plastic card. For good measure, one final employee checked our paper tickets as we disembarked. Chinese bureaucracy ran like a well-oiled Rube Goldberg machine.

That night we walked the promenade at the edge of Kowloon, looking across Victoria Harbour at the skyscrapers of Hong Kong Island. Music played, and buildings lined in neon lights flashed in tempo. James looked at me as the harbor sparkled. "Happy anniversary, Love."

"Well, *we're* coming from Egypt. The pyramids were just *spectacular*," said the twenty-something with a dramatic flourish of her hand. She perched next to her husband on the airport shuttle's plush seat. Pristine his and hers travel backpacks rested at their feet.

"We loved the pyramids," the young man across the aisle replied for himself and his wife. "It's a shame they have gotten so touristy, though." He cocked his head to the side and made an exaggerated annoyed face.

James rolled his eyes. "*You're* a tourist, dickhead," he muttered.

James and I had just flown to Thailand after a few days in Hong Kong. I looked out a rain-soaked window at the dark streets of Bangkok, letting the strains of pretension fade into the background. James had stayed on Khao San Road with Rick and Keith during his first visit to Bangkok. I'd heard his stories, seen the photos, and imagined the frantic bustle—but nothing prepared me for being there. I swung my dirty pack onto my shoulders and stepped off the bus into the night, into a wall of heat and humidity.

James pointed down the street. "There's some cheap guesthouses down there." He marched forth, through the mob of international backpackers, with me following quickly behind. A Thai man straddling a scooter blared his horn to part the crowd. Tuk-tuks lined up at the end of the road, their drivers waiting to take explorers to the far reaches of the city.

Signs of all colors jutted from buildings and hung over the street in a canopy of marketing—bars, hotels, laundry, internet, tattoos. Outside a McDonald's, a grinning red-and-yellow Ronald statue pressed his hands into a traditional *wai* to greet backpackers craving burgers.

Vendors up and down the block offered far better food options. The thick air carried mouth-watering smells of jasmine rice and grilled meat. An old man stood behind a cart of tropical fruits unidentifiable to me: long, flame-colored slices with shimmering black seeds, pink grenades with speckled white flesh, small translucent orbs covered in barbed red rinds. Nearby, a woman pulled a cob of corn off a grill and smeared the char-flecked kernels with a paintbrushful of butter. I stopped in front of a young man frying quail eggs in a pan and marveled at their cuteness.

I wiped my brow and dried my hand on my tank top. A slick shine of sweat covered my chest. Tuk-tuks and motorbikes spat fumes into the ether, and I could feel the pollution sticking to me as if my skin were flypaper.

I hustled to keep up with James, but something new caught my attention every few feet. Open-front bars lined the sidewalk, each one blasting dance beats to patrons sitting by the road on short plastic stools. They drank bottles of Chang beer or sipped from straws plonked in a communal bucket of booze.

Hawkers eagerly announced their wares as we passed: pirated CDs and DVDs with poorly photocopied labels, silver hippie jewelry, incense burners, Red Bull tank tops.

"What's 'Same Same?'" I asked James, having seen about six different T-shirts bearing the slogan.

He laughed. "'Same same but different.' They say it a lot around here."

Khao San was a crossroads of excited travelers who had just arrived and worn-out wanderers having their last hurrah before a flight home. I couldn't understand how a place could be so frenetic yet so chilled out at the same time. And how it could make me feel the same way. I understood now why James had wanted to bring me here since his first visit two years ago.

James glanced back and gestured with his hand. "Over here, behind the 7-11." He led me toward a narrow alley, where I expected to see nothing but roaches and garbage cans. We turned down a passageway, revealing two guesthouses, a steamy laundromat, and a beauty salon. Cardboard paved the way over the disintegrating sidewalk.

We entered a guesthouse, uneven wooden stairs groaning with every step. Our spartan double room cost 150 baht—about three dollars. We dumped our bags on the mattress and glimpsed a cockroach scurrying under the bed. James wrinkled his nose and shut the door. "You hungry? Central Khao San has good food."

We sat at a table in the front, overlooking the street. A girl with fat blond dreadlocks sat at the next table, philosophizing with a guy wearing a Che Guevara T-shirt. We ordered yellow chicken curry and a Chang beer, cashew chicken without rice, and a water. I felt annoyed at my dietary restrictions. I was traveling the land of rice and noodles and couldn't even try them.

When James scooped the last bit of yellow curry from his plate, he said, "The Irish pub on the corner has AC."

"Oh, hell yes."

He guided me back up Khao San Road, and I noticed the couples from the bus still wandering with their backpacks amidst the crowd. We opened the door to Gulliver's Pub. Cold air and Usher's song "Yeah!" blasted me in the face. "Come on," I said, breaking out my sexy club moves in a long, tiered peasant skirt and sport sandals. "You never dance with me."

"You know that's not gonna happen," James stepped up to the bar and ordered a Guinness.

A young Thai woman approached me. "You are very pretty."

"Thank you! You're very pretty, too," I said, surprised by the compliment.

Another Thai woman walked up and touched my hair. "Very beautiful."

"Thank you! I like your hair, too." The three of us smiled and danced like we were old friends.

James started talking to a French guy. James had taken French in high school and exclusively remembered *Voulez-vous verifier les pneus?* though "Do you want to check the tire pressure?" is rarely useful.

After a few beers, James insisted on speaking to the man in French. James leaned over to me and whispered, "How do you say, 'You are the first French person I've spoken French to'?"

"Vous êtes le premier français avec qui j'ai parlé français."

"Right." James looked at the man. *"Vous êtes…le…parle français."*

"We can speak in English," the man said.

James ignored him and asked me, "How do you say, 'I'm sorry my French isn't very good?'"

I sighed. *"Je suis désolé, mon français n'est pas très bon."*

James nodded. *"Je suis désolé…uh…"* Then he pointed to himself, said *"français,"* and gave a thumbs down.

The French man frowned. "Okay. We must leave now. Good night."

The lights flicked on, and everyone fled like the roaches in our hostel bedroom. We exited onto the misty road. Most travelers and vendors had gone to bed, and Thai men with brooms and dustpans swept up the vestiges of the night's revelry.

James gushed, "That was the first French person I've ever talked to in French before!" as if it were brand-new information.

"Oh, yeah?" I laughed and looked at James—the old, silly James I'd fallen so in love with. We hadn't had a night like this in a long time.

"I think you need some food." I bought him a Styrofoam plate of steaming pad Thai noodles sprinkled in chopped peanuts. We sat on the empty sidewalk, and he gobbled them down before we headed to the room.

James lay on the bed and mumbled "*Je m'excuse le francais un peu,*" before passing out.

Excuse me French a little, I translated in my head before falling asleep, exhausted and exhilarated, too.

A few days later, after James showed me around the city, we took an overnight train from Bangkok to the tourist town of Patong, on the island of Phuket. We'd come to visit James's childhood friend, John, and his girlfriend, Lamai. John was short, with a round belly. "Have a good journey?" he asked in a strong northern English accent.

"Yes, thanks," I lied, my stinking shirt and bloodshot eyes evidence of the sweltering train that rocked at an 8.5 on the Richter Scale all night.

"No, you never!" John guffawed.

I laughed.

Lamai smiled shyly. "Welcome to Patong."

We climbed onto benches in the bed of a pickup truck, and Lamai told the driver in Thai where we wanted to go. The wind blew her long, shiny black hair. She was petite, feminine, and bafflingly unsweaty.

We drove through the tourist area by the shore. Locals in straw hats wandered a long beach hawking fruit, beer, ice cream, sarongs, pedicures, and massages to vacationers on beach loungers. Aussies and Europeans on holiday moseyed up and down the main street, drinking and flirting. I tried to guess the Brits by the rosiness of their complexions.

With soft sand, swaying palm trees, blue sky, and bluer sea, Patong was a paradise that catered to Western tourists, but that's not what I wanted. I'd recently received an email from the director of a school in Chon Buri, a province along the Gulf of Thailand. He offered me fifteen hours a week, and though he didn't have a placement for James yet, he said one would probably open up in the future. I couldn't wait to go to a town, teach kids, and immerse myself in Thai culture. I was just waiting for James to say yes.

But John offered James a job at his business in Phuket, selling vacation club memberships. He promised James would make good money and said we could stay with him and Lamai as long as we liked. Lamai worked there, too, as a receptionist.

James wanted to do it. I emailed the school director and thanked him but told him I couldn't take the teaching job.

I couldn't find teaching work in Patong. John offered me a sales job, too, but the idea dredged up memories of selling Girl Scout cookies door-to-door. I heard every "No, thank you," as "You suck, little girl." I felt anxious just thinking about it.

My days were a cycle of run, shower, buy grilled chicken from the guy on the corner, and read while the afternoon monsoon poured.

I hoped Lamai could be my cultural link, but she rarely talked to me. She stayed in the kitchen for the first week while James, John, and I talked and ate dinner in the living room. If John stayed late at the office, she'd timidly nod as she came in the front door and then sprint up the stairs.

One evening after work, John, James, and I sat in the living room. They talked sales. I stared out the window. Roaring rain smacked the street. Lamai approached, dropped her umbrella, and left her sandals on the porch. She opened the door, whispered hello, and walked to the kitchen carrying a plastic baggie. I followed her, whether she wanted me to or not. Lamai set the bag on the dark wooden table and hesitantly asked, "You want some food?"

"Sure!"

Her eyes widened like she didn't expect me to say yes. I grabbed a fork from a drawer and sat across from her. She dumped the contents of the baggie onto a white plate. Julienne cucumbers, cherry tomatoes, red chilis, and bits of purple garlic swam on her plate in a thin brown sauce. It smelled unpleasant. "What is this?" I asked.

"Cucumber salad," she answered. "From Isaan. In North, where I'm from." She speared a cherry tomato and delicately bit into it. "It have *naam pla*—fish sauce." Fish sauce is salty juice from year-old fermented anchovies. It's found on every table in Thailand, in nearly every recipe.

I scooped some cucumbers and chilis and took a hesitant bite that set my mouth on fire. I got up and grabbed a bottle of water from the fridge. Lamai snickered. "Spicy?" she asked.

I gulped some water. "Mmm-hmm."

"In Thailand," Lamai added, "we say '*Mai phet, mai alloy*,' It mean 'not spicy, not delicious.'"

I swallowed another bite. Now I tasted the fish sauce. I didn't like it, but I told Lamai I did. "*Alloy!*"

She smiled, looking relieved, surprised, and pleased all at once. "John call this 'shit food' cause it stink. He make me sit in the kitchen to eat it. John just eat fry rice."

I laughed. "Really?"

"Yeah. But you could visit my village and eat Isaan food, for sure!" She beamed.

I wanted real Thailand, and it doesn't get more real than rotten fish juice. I scooped another bite and unearthed a teeny crab. "Do you eat that?" I asked, and Lamai laughed harder than I'd ever seen. Possibly harder than she ever had before.

"No, no! Just for flavor!"

A month passed. James hadn't made a sale, meaning he hadn't made any money. When he came home every evening, I'd chatter his ear off, desperate for human contact. Meanwhile, he'd just spent eight hours making small talk with tourists who never bought anything, and he just wanted to watch TV.

One evening, Lamai came home from work early. She held up a plastic baggie of something new. I shut my book and followed her to the kitchen. She pulled plates from the cabinet, and I grabbed forks and spoons. After scooping rice from the steamer on her plate, she poured out the dish with a flourish. "Frog stew!"

I stuck my fork straight in. "*Alloy*," I said and meant it. "How do you say 'very delicious?'"

She grinned. "*Alloy mak mak.*"

We'd shared many authentic Thai dishes in her kitchen by this point. I dipped slices of green mango in fish paste. I sprinkled *prik naam pla,* fish sauce with small chilis, over fried eggs. Lamai taught me to use silverware the Thai way—fork in your left hand, pushing food into the spoon in your right. She even taught me how to make fried rice, and I wrote her recipe in my journal to save for a future when I wasn't on this low-carb diet.

Through it all, we'd talk about her village, or Pittsburgh, or her day at work. She taught me useful Thai phrases and the names of all of my favorite dishes, and I taught her American slang. And often, we just ate in comfortable silence.

I felt annoyed that James and I had saved up, gotten certified to teach English, and flown across the globe—just to kill time in a tourist town. But it was either James worked here or I worked in Chon Buri, which was the same situation. I tried to suck it up. And getting to know Lamai made it better. She reminded me I *was* in Thailand. I just had to look harder for it.

CHAPTER 47
JAMES

'Pitch the bitch,' my boss Fred said with pride, drawing laughter from the group. 'Happy wife, happy life,' he added.

I sat, unamused, listening to more bullshit jargon during our daily sales meeting. Fred was a tall, loud Australian man in his fifties. He always wore Hawaiian shirts and had exaggerated features, from his owl-like eyebrows to his enormous hands, which caused me to wince during our first handshake.

John stood up. 'Now, let's make some sales, everyone!'

I'd have loved to make *a* sale. But I'd been there a few weeks, and I'd earned a grand total commission of zero baht.

Immediately after the meeting, I greeted my first customers of the day, young Australian newlyweds in cheap T-shirts and flip-flops. I remembered my training and took them out onto the large balcony of our fifteenth-floor office. Their eyes widened at the view, and I gave them a moment to snap pictures of the beach and the deep blue Andaman Sea.

After a few minutes of small talk, I sat them down at my computer and dove into my pitch. I showed them luxury hotels in international locations and told them how Holiday Club members had access to the best deals on holidays. The man sat back in his chair while his wife leaned forward towards my screen.

'What's going on here?' the man asked, frowning.

'What do you mean?'

'We're just here for our free holiday, mate,' he said, shuffling in his chair.

'You have to listen to the presentation to get your holiday,' I informed

224

them.

The man rolled his eyes and folded his arms. My muscles tensed, and sweat poured down my back, soaking my shirt. I glanced over at John's all-glass office, where he and Fred watched on.

After an uncomfortable forty-five-minute presentation, Fred appeared. He introduced himself, wrote a dollar amount on paper, and presented it to them. He looked at them, raised his owl eyebrows and gestured towards the paper with his head.

The man scowled. 'We're not interested, mate.'

'You liked the deals, though, right?' I asked the woman in desperation. She smiled slightly but said nothing.

'I said we're not interested!' the man repeated, and they stood up and walked out, taking my commission and dignity with them.

After work, I waited, dejected, for a scooter taxi. Not just sad about the lost sale, but because it could be a few days until I even got to pitch again. There were five members of the sales team on a rotation. Some days I sat in front of a computer all day without any clients at all. And when next in line, I'd look at the door every five minutes, anxiously awaiting my turn.

John had told me I could potentially make some serious money at his company. We appreciated the job and he and Lamai welcoming us into their home. I wanted to provide for Stef and me. Our conversation in the car back in Pittsburgh about how I would make money was etched into my mind. That's what was driving me to make this job work.

Usually, on these rides home, I focused my attention on the erratic oncoming traffic, trying desperately to subdue a scream whilst my driver weaved in and out of it. This time, though, I looked to the side. We passed tourists and market stalls selling fake designer T-shirts. Soon, the view changed to locals and street vendors selling bagged papaya salad and whole skewered fish.

I made it home in one piece and walked under the security barrier into John's housing complex with my hands in my pockets and my head down. Another day but definitely *not* another dollar.

Stef sat in the living room of the house, rereading a magazine. She offered a faint smile in my direction.

'How'd it go today?' Stef asked.

'Same same, love.' I noticed her glossy eyes and gestured for her to follow me upstairs.

'What's wrong?' I asked.

'Nothing.'

'Obviously not. You're bored, aren't you?'

The tears began to fall.

I hate it when she cries! 'It's nothing to cry about,' I said. 'If you're *that* bored, let's just go!'

'That's not what I want,' Stef said, wiping her face. 'If you want to stay, we should stay for a while. It's only fair.'

'Well, we can't stay now with you bawling your eyes out over it! Just admit it. You've hated it here since day one.' Her silence verified my theory. 'I wish you'd just been honest with me. If you'd told me from the start, we wouldn't have stayed. But now I'm involved in this, and I want to see it through.'

'Are you blaming me for this?' Stef asked.

Knock, knock. 'Mate, are you coming to dinner?' John asked through the door. I looked at Stef, and she nodded. 'Um, yeah mate.' Stef wiped her eyes and grabbed her purse.

Stef's eyes were red at the restaurant, and her cheeks puffy. Two more work colleagues joined us. Stef sat in silence while we talked about our lack of sales. We got home late and continued our conversation in the bedroom.

'If you took that job teaching in Chon Buri, how long would I have had to sit around while you worked?' I asked Stef.

She shrugged. 'Exactly, I don't know. I know it's the same thing. I figured, what's the point in telling you I didn't like it here? That would just make you feel bad.'

I didn't know what to say.

'I was only trying to do the right thing,' Stef said, her tears returning. 'And now somehow, everything's my fault.' She covered her face with her hands.

'I love you, love. I don't want you to be unhappy.' I said. I hated seeing her like this, but we had to be up early. We climbed into bed.

After only four hours of sleep, we left John and Lamai's house. With our visas about to expire, we had to leave Thailand to extend them. A local travel agency offered one-day trips to southern Myanmar, the closest border, for this exact purpose.

With last night's argument stinging like an open wound, we set off down Nanai Road. Tension replaced conversation. Annoyance, guilt, sadness and embarrassment were just a few of the emotions vying for my attention. I couldn't make sense of it. I walked in front of Stef the whole way to town. I couldn't risk looking at her face and wanting to talk. I knew that a bus full of people on a long trip was not the right place to get into it.

Stef sat by the window with a guidebook open on her lap. I put on my headphones and closed my eyes. Sleep proved elusive. I replayed our argument in my mind. I didn't like this job but didn't want to waste an opportunity to make decent money. There were worse places in the world to be living than this. Why did she not see this? Feeling responsible for her happiness weighed heavy.

After an hour, I gave up on sleeping. I opened my eyes but kept my headphones on as I wasn't ready to talk. Stef stared out of the window with a huge grin. She marvelled at everything that went by. Kids playing in the streets, local markets, trees, hills. *How could she be this excited to be sitting on a fucking bus?*

This was the most enthusiastic I'd seen her in a month. The wet season had restricted Stef to morning runs on the beach and rainy afternoons in the house. In the evenings, if I was tired, we did nothing.

I'd been so preoccupied with trying to make money for our future that I'd neglected our present. I'd lost sight of our original plan to teach English. Stef really wanted to do it, but deep down, maybe I always knew it wasn't for me.

I'd weighed up both scenarios based on money instead of the experience. We could be in Chon Buri with Stef earning very little money vs living rent-free with John and Lamai with significant earning potential. It had seemed like an easy decision to me.

We arrived at the Kraburi River in Ranong, Thailand, six hours later. Our chain-smoking Thai guide disembarked with a wave of his hand, and our group followed him down to a dock through a pungent fish market. He walked fast, never looking back to check on his flock. He had thick, centre-parted hair down to his ears and skin littered with faded tattoos. He spoke in broken English, revealing three nicotine-stained teeth.

We stepped past a customs sign. It stated that no drugs were to be brought back into Thailand, and only one carton of cigarettes was allowed per person. At the river's edge, our guide stepped confidently across three docked boats onto a somewhat larger one with an orange canopy. We all looked at each other before following him cautiously, our group of fifteen helping each other clamber across the wobbly boats. The crowded vessel creaked, our weight forcing the boat deeper into the water. A couple inches more, and the river would have come spilling over the edge.

We sat bunched up on low wooden benches, sweating in close proximity.

My knees were tucked up by my chest, and the flapping canopy did little to fend off the midday heat. Relief came in the form of an occasional water spray from the side of the boat. My head was in my hands while Stef's was on a swivel. I'd seen this trip as a huge inconvenience, but it was an adventure to her. My stomach sank.

Thirty feet from shore on the wide, brown river, our guide began collecting everyone's passports. I shot Stef a curious look. I didn't like the timing of this. A small group of Vietnamese women with long, perfectly straight black hair handed theirs over while chatting loudly to each other.

One by one, different coloured passports piled up in his hands. He came within inches of me and held out his hand. I hesitated for a moment and handed him ours, clutching them tightly for a few seconds before letting go. Filled with paranoia, I imagined him selling them in Myanmar on the black market and leaving us stranded. I felt naked without them, and I watched him like a hawk for the remainder of our journey. Stef grabbed my arm, smiled and wiggled her whole body with excitement at the thrill of it all. I returned the smile.

The boat pulled up to a rickety bamboo hut perched atop the river on skinny wooden stilts. Of the original nine, three stilts had rotted out either from the top or bottom. Their stumps remained like stalagmites and stalactites. A wooden sign on the door read *Thailand Immigration*. Our guide climbed a ladder up to the office with our passports, returning a few minutes later.

We continued on, past many boats of various shapes and sizes, amidst choking clouds of engine smoke and the smell of burning fuel. As we approached the other side of the river, our guide invaded my personal space again with a big smile and tobacco breath. He kneeled in front of me and scribbled 'Viagara' on his palm with a plastic biro. He thrust his hand inches from my eyes while nodding expectantly.

I shook my head. I wanted to correct his spelling but instead waved him away. He moved on to the next man in the group.

The driver tied our boat to another one at the dock. Our guide took off before the lines were knotted. He hopped over many moored boats like stepping-stones, up a rusty ladder onto the concrete of the jetty and into a wooden shack, which must have been the Myanmar immigration office. The group of Vietnamese women went next. They bypassed the shack and a metal barrier at the end of the jetty and went into town. I looked at Stef and shrugged my shoulders. She nodded, and we made our way onto dry land.

Border towns can be the collision of two countries' seedy underbellies. They fill me with anxiety. They're where backpackers come to get new visas or continue their journeys, where people from one country can come to escape legalities back home, and where chancers hang out, preying on the vulnerable.

A group of us milled about, unsure of what to do. On the other side of the barrier, a gang of kids in shorts and flip-flops huddled. Some of them sold trays of baked goods, shiny bracelets and the like. Stef pointed out some local women walking by with triangles or circles of yellow mud painted on their cheeks. I knew she longed to venture off, but we didn't know how long we would be there. Concerned for our safety and worried about our guide ditching us, I convinced Stef we should stay on our side of the barrier.

Our guide appeared from the shack with the stack of passports. He handed them out quickly and vanished into the hustle and bustle of Kawthaung Town with no instructions on what we were to do.

Stef opened her passport to check out her new Myanmar immigration stamp. I inspected mine thoroughly for any signs of tampering before grabbing Stef's to do the same. I half-expected our photos to have been ripped out and replaced.

A middle-aged English man approached us. He had short, trendy grey hair and an earring. 'Don't bother going into town,' he said sternly.

'Why?' Stef asked.

He pointed towards the barrier. 'The kids with the bracelets distract you while the others rob you.'

'Really?' Stef asked.

'Yeah. I've done this loads of times. Trust me.'

Just then, the Vietnamese women came back, each of them carrying a couple of cartons of cigarettes. They approached each person in our group and held out a carton.

'You take for me?' each one asked.

'No, thank you,' I said.

Our guide returned later with a large plastic bag. I pictured erection medication and an assortment of contraband. His glazed eyes suggested he'd partaken already. Back on the boat, the Vietnamese women tried desperately to offload their excess cigarettes. They asked us at least ten times on the way back.

Armed with a new thirty-day visa, we set off on the long bus ride back to Phuket. The air still needed to be cleared, but it had been a very long day. Stef rested her sleepy head on my shoulder.

Icy cold air streamed from AC vents above us. Stef snuggled up against me, raised her knees onto her seat, and closed her eyes. I watched her peaceful face intermittently bathed in yellow light as we passed through villages. Catching sight of our reflection in the window, I recognized us. We'd regained some closeness after a rocky first year of marriage. But last night showed me we still needed to work on our communication.

Stef and I both wanted the best for each other, and since Pittsburgh, we'd both been trying hard to avoid confrontation. But it had backfired. By not wanting to upset each other, we'd both suffered.

Stef's tears always conjured memories of my mum crying during my arguments with my dad. Despite being in the wrong, he never backed down. He argued and shouted for as long as it took to upset my mum. He knew I couldn't stand seeing her cry, and I'd concede, sealing his victory.

Living with Stef's parents had allowed us this escape, but I had to step up. I wanted to stick at this job for a bit longer but knew I needed to talk to Stef about setting a deadline for moving on. I needed to bring balance back to our relationship.

Stef and her Dad had broached the subject of college to me on a few occasions, but I always took offence to it, and it made me feel pressured. Also, I never really liked school and had no idea what I'd study. However, this wasn't just about me anymore. If I went back to school, I could help make a better life for us both. I'd do it for us. I'd make Stef proud and give her the life she deserved.

CHAPTER 48
STEF

I had just run for forty-five minutes down the golden, freshly groomed beach, past early-rising tourists and optimistic locals selling parasailing trips. I walked home along Nanai Road, in the locals' neighborhood, as I had every morning for weeks. Two mechanics welded motorbikes by the side of the road, and some women hung clothes to dry outside a fresh-smelling laundromat. A Thai woman walked out of an internet café, past a pile of flip-flops, to a gold spirit house on the sidewalk that resembled a tiny temple on a pedestal. She placed a bottle of red Fanta on the ledge, a gift for the spirit residents inside. Helmetless drivers whizzed past on scooters, carrying one to three additional people and occasionally a chicken or a baby. Tons of people surrounded me, but I felt alone.

On the way home from my run a few days prior, a white man and a Thai woman called out to me from a small bar. The barrel-chested, gray-haired German held up a bottle of Heineken. "I can buy you a drink, yah?" he asked.

I declined the drink but sat at the picnic table with them. The Thai woman sat with her foot on the bench, arm balanced on her knee, cigarette dangling from gold-ringed fingers. The man talked about a deep-sea fishing trip he'd been on and offered to show me photos. He flicked through the pictures on his digital camera—blue sea, white boat, big fish, naked Thai woman on a bed. "Ooop!" he exclaimed, putting the camera down.

I stood up. "Okay, I better go. I have to take a shower."

"Well, I like to help you with that, but okay," the man said. "Bye-bye."

That's what I got for trying to make friends.

It didn't feel like Thanksgiving as I plopped on the couch and tortured myself with an American channel's Turkey Day coverage: tips on cooking the bird, diet advice for the holidays, an early blizzard that covered the Northeast.

During the first month of our trip, James and I had grown closer again and had begun to feel like our old selves. But now we were back to the frustration and awkwardness. After some discussions about staying or leaving Phuket, James and I agreed to give it one more month. We'd move on after Christmas. James kept saying one sale could bring in some good money for us, but I didn't hold out hope.

John, James, and Lamai filed through the front door that evening after work as the last tinges of pink were fading from the sky.

John saw my pouty face. "What's up, Stef?"

"It's Thanksgiving, and I'm missing it."

"What *is* Thanksgiving, anyway?" he asked.

James laughed and taught John what he'd learned, though I'm sure John didn't care about the history of colonial America or our affinity for green bean casserole.

"Right," John said. "I'm starving. Let's go out."

We piled in his car, and he drove us up the mountain, far from the bustle. The glow of Patong looked distant and beautiful. The Tavern on the Hill was open in front but obscured by trees and vines. Warm yellow light bulbs glowed in bronze fixtures, and hefty dark wood tables filled the terra-cotta tiled floor. A chalkboard displayed the special: "Roast Turkey and Lots of Things." I gasped.

John grinned. "Hey, look at that!"

We sat by a wall of jungle, and I asked our waiter about the special. "Yes, we have turkey and corn and pumpkin pie."

My eyes filled with tears of happiness and surprise.

"Ah, she's gone all emotional, now," John teased. "So, what is this pumpkin pie?" he asked.

"It's a bit like a custard," James explained, "but I don't like it."

"Pump-kin." Lamai practiced deliberately, her head bobbing forward with the effort of each syllable.

"You can just say 'punkin,'" I advised. I turned to John. "Don't listen to James. It's delicious."

Lamai whispered "pun-kin," while John mentioned he wanted to try the pie.

"No," scolded Lamai, "you like hippopotamose." She pretended to pop his big belly with a toothpick, making a hissing sound and sending James and me into giggles.

The waiter placed plates full of turkey, carrots, sweet potatoes, and broccoli in front of me. He returned to the kitchen and came back with corn, mashed potatoes, cornbread, stuffing, gravy, and cranberry sauce. The Lots of Things took up half the table, and I didn't know where to start.

John and James eyed up my feast with jealousy, but Lamai was quite satisfied with her papaya salad. We sat for ages, enjoying the company and delicious food. I hadn't talked and laughed so much in a long time. I'd been so frustrated by the stagnation of our adventure that I'd forgotten I was spending every day *doing nothing in paradise.* Any sane person would have traded spots with me in a heartbeat. I should have been eternally grateful, but I felt like a jerk. I don't know why I cared so much about sticking to plans—I had yet for one to work out.

The waiter brought out a huge slice of pie, topped with a dollop of whipped cream. Lamai forked off a bite, and her face crumpled in horror, making the rest of us laugh.

"*Mai chop?*" I asked.

She vigorously shook her head no.

John took out his camera. "Smile, Stef!" I posed with my beautiful pie, thankful for the thoughtfulness of my temporary Thai family and grateful that life was pretty damn amazing.

CHAPTER 49
JAMES

After already travelling for countless hours from Phuket to Bangkok to fuck-knows-whereville on the Cambodian border, I was in no mood to be pissing about. At the station, a man told us they'd overbooked the bus to Siem Reap and that we needed to ride in a taxi they'd paid for.

I sat in the back of the Toyota Camry with only one arse cheek on the seat, my left hand raised, clutching the handle above the window with my shoulder squashed against the glass. Stef sat next to me in a similar position but practically in my lap. Next were two young Korean ladies. One sat on the front edge of the seat while the other leaned in behind her. The passenger seat up front housed a large, bald Italian man with questionable hygiene.

'How long to Siem Reap?' Stef asked the driver.

'Three hours.'

Marvellous!

After a few minutes, the paved roads of the border town disappeared. They'd been replaced by the surface of Mars. No lanes, just a wide expanse of orange dirt with sinkhole-sized craters. We hit the first one at 60 mph and my head crashed against the window. 'For fuck's sake!'

Stef said nothing but grabbed my leg. The two Koreans squealed, and the Italian let out a nervous laugh. The driver turned around and smiled.

There were no seatbelts in the backseat, so the four of us swayed in unison through each bump and hole in the road, and soon my bum went numb. Cars kicked up the dry dirt, filling the air with orange clouds. Periodically, two headlights would shine through the dust, heading right for us. Our driver would swerve at the last minute, causing the car's suspension to groan. Each time he smiled.

At a snail's pace, this would be tedious. At lightning speed, it was terrifying. The driver weaved back and forth at maximum velocity, continuously blaring his horn. He flew over bumps and dipped into holes, with no concern for the car or its frightened passengers.

We sped past pickup trucks piled high with boxes, furniture or chickens in crates. Threadbare rope strapped the cargo down, and usually, a few men sat nonchalantly on top. One people-carrier was bursting with two dozen people. The short-straw passenger sat to the driver's left with his cheek smushed against the window. His eyes followed us as we zoomed past.

Occasionally, we crossed a stream, but instead of a bridge, two loose planks of wood lay somewhat parallel over the water. Our driver was unfazed by this and barely even slowed down, confident nothing was coming the other way through the rust-coloured fog.

Bang! Creak! We hit another crater. With each one, I tightened my grip on the handle.

'What happens if we get a flat, mate? Do you have a spare tyre?' I asked the driver.

'No, no spare tyre!' He laughed at the notion.

Stef was looking out of the side window at the sun setting over an infinite, flat, barren landscape, trying to enjoy the view. As always on these trips, I had an overwhelming urge to protect her. Aside from my own natural instincts, the concerned face of her dad was etched in my mind.

'Don't worry. I'll take care of her, Frank,' I'd said during an uncomfortably long, firm handshake in Pittsburgh International Airport.

Stef was my wife. My friend. My love. Innocence and naiveté were some of the qualities I liked in her. She balanced me out. She hadn't become jaded by the world and always, always saw the good in people. But those qualities sometimes made her vulnerable. Where I saw death, she saw rainbows.

I'd read that bandits were known to attack tourists on Cambodian roads at night. I pictured scores of them surrounding us as we sat by the side of the road with a puncture. What would we do? How would I protect us? Riddled with panic, I needed a distraction.

I thought about the last few months. I never earned a single penny working at John's company, but it hadn't been in vain. It gave me some direction.

And Stef and I had found each other again.

Since leaving Phuket, we'd lain on the beach, kayaked, snorkelled and gotten drunk on the island of Ko Phi Phi, the site of my infamous 'Thai Buckets' night out. It felt good to show Stef the Thailand I knew. The

Thailand she wanted to see.

With the phrases Lamai had taught us, we could avoid the local tourist traps and eat at locals' restaurants. Listening to Stef order food in a new language took me back to our proper date in Sydney at the Spanish restaurant. She smiled with pride as waiters and waitresses complimented her Thai pronunciation. Our grasp of the language also meant we could hold our own when haggling in the local markets. Stef's intimidation was replaced with confidence. Locals would be hard-pressed to sell her snake on a stick now.

Night-time made all aspects of the drive more dangerous, but our driver was relentless. Maybe he wanted to avoid the bandits, too. In any case, he didn't slow down. On the plus side, I couldn't see the craters anymore, though I was unable to brace myself for impact. Instead, I took the head-smashing and wobbled around with my seatmates.

Suddenly, I felt a strange sensation. I loosened my grip, and my body didn't move. I realized we were now on a paved road. But I had the feeling I was still swaying, like the feeling you get on land after being out at sea. Despite what seemed like chaos, we'd made it in one piece. Every car made it in one piece. We didn't witness a single crash all day. Maybe these drivers had a system that worked for them, and we were the only ones who considered it dangerous.

I took a long, deep breath for the first time since leaving the bus station. Instead of dust clouds, the headlights now illuminated the silky-smooth road into Siem Reap.

Extravagant hotels lined the streets at the outskirts of town. Fountains bubbled in their curved driveways amidst bright lights that erased half of the stars.

'You stay here?' our driver teased. 'Thousand dollars a night.'

'Keep driving, mate,' I said, prompting an acknowledging laugh from the driver and other passengers.

The driver dropped us right at the door of an eight-dollar-a-night guesthouse. I hobbled out of the car, tipped the driver and let out a celebratory sigh. I stretched my legs and massaged some feeling back into my arse. Stef grabbed our bags, and we dragged ourselves inside for the night.

CHAPTER 50
STEF

Dara, a young professional sporting a button-down shirt and impeccable hair, attached the carriage of his tuk-tuk to his motorbike. "Where you frommm?" he asked, his question and singsong pronunciation both typical of the Cambodian locals we'd met so far.

"America and England," James answered while I rooted through my day pack. Camera, check. Film, check. Camcorder, check. I'd dreamed of visiting Angkor since high school when I'd seen it on the Travel Channel, and I couldn't wait to document the 900-year-old temples. Most structures had been cleared off, but some were left as found, strangled by the irrepressible wild. I felt like I could burst from anticipation.

Dara gave us a thumbs-up and patted the cracked vinyl seat of the tuk-tuk. We settled in. The air smelled of diesel and sounded of motors and horns. Vendors paced the dirt streets of Siem Reap in the clear morning sunshine, balancing large, flat baskets piled with fruit or snacks in clear bags. We sputtered past the gas station—a table of gasoline-filled two-liter bottles and a plastic funnel—and approached a busy intersection.

Scooters, bikes, trucks, and tour buses from four directions forged ahead simultaneously, and nobody had a stop sign.

"Oh, shit," James muttered.

I gripped the side rail with a frozen fist. Dara seemed unfazed. Inside the maelstrom, drivers weaved around each other in dreamlike symbiosis. Suddenly, we popped out of the other side. I looked back at the mess behind us.

"How the hell did we do that?" I asked.

Dara laughed. Just like our driver the night before, he navigated

Cambodia's challenging traffic with nonchalance.

We joined a long line of idling tuk-tuks and tour buses behind the entrance gates. Dara took a plastic comb from his pocket and ran it through his shiny hair. We'd learned that his crisp white shirt and long, immaculate fingernails broadcast his status here. He was no farmer.

Once inside the complex, Dara pulled over at the first temple and let us explore. I ran my fingers over carvings of dancing nymphs—hands overhead, fingers arcing precisely. Hundreds of giant faces, likenesses of the Khmer king Jayavarman, watched over us like they did his subjects centuries ago.

Tourists filed off a large, air-conditioned bus and swarmed the site. They wandered into every photo and chattered loudly throughout our video footage. James and I exchanged eye rolls and jumped back in the tuk-tuk, grumbling about the ambiance murderers.

Dara drove down the road and stopped again shortly, near the forest's edge. "We stop here." He pointed to a barely discernible path. "Back in woods. Quiet temple."

I grinned. "You're the best, Dara."

He gave us another thumbs-up.

We delved into the trees and found a maze of crumbling walls. Gnarled branches snaked between carvings of Hindu gods. "This is more bloody like it," James said, panning across with the camcorder.

I shot a photo of colorful, threadbare prayer flags dangling from a tiny alcove. From the corner of my eye, through an intricately carved window, I saw a giant black animal lumbering out of a pond.

"James. James, there's a bull." I froze, not taking my eyes off the beast. "He's, like, just there. Out. He could gore us."

"That's a water buffalo, you dickhead. You've spent too much time in Spain."

I glared at James and looked back at the buffalo, peacefully munching on vegetation by the water.

Dara drove us to the well-known sites and some well-kept secrets. We finished our afternoon at the main temple, Angkor Wat, where some barefoot children milled about. James held up the camcorder. "Where you frommm?" he asked a young girl.

She looked caught off guard and giggled. She was probably about to ask him the same thing. "Cam-bodia," she said and scrunched her nose at him.

I watched James goof around with the local kids. A few months of green curry and garlic pepper pork helped him return to a healthy weight. He was blond and tan, just like when we first met in Australia. As he joked with the kids, I felt a flutter in my chest. The frustrations and miscommunications of Pittsburgh and Phuket seemed far away.

A boy of about eight approached, black hair cut into a bowl, skin glistening in the intense sun. "You buy water, miss?"

"I'm sorry." I held up my water bottle. "I already have some."

He pulled a thin bamboo bracelet from his pocket and handed it to me. "For you."

"Oh, no, thank you." I'd have had bangles up to my elbow if I bought one from every kid selling them.

"No, for you. Gift." He tucked it into the pocket of my shorts and walked back to some other children by the temple walls.

I looked at James and pouted. "I feel bad. Maybe we could buy a bottle for Dara."

"Yeah, go on, then."

I looked over to see the boy watching us with a confident grin. "You buy water from me, now?"

We burst out laughing.

"Cheeky bugger!" James said, impressed.

I smiled at the young entrepreneur. "Yes, I'll buy water from you now!"

We climbed back in Dara's rumbling tuk-tuk, and I presented him with the water bottle, which he immediately cracked open and chugged from. "You have good day?" he asked.

"Yes, the best!" I said.

He gave us a thumbs-up and pulled into the chaos to take us home.

We walked around town the next day. Thousand-dollar-a-night hotels towered next to tiny four-dollar guesthouses. Massive, shiny tour buses squeezed down narrow, jammed streets. Siem Reap was in transition, scurrying to keep up with a tourist boom.

Children followed me, tugging on my skirt hem, asking for dollars or just staring with big, glassy eyes. A girl about five years old, hair in a messy ponytail, arched backward to keep from dropping the baby in her arms.

Every American kid who grew up in the '80s and wouldn't finish their dinner knew there were starving children in Cambodia. But that was another world to me then. One I couldn't fathom. Seeing these children in front of me made my heart hurt and filled me with guilt. It wasn't fair.

One boy, about nine years old, stepped up with a confident smile. "Hello, what's your name?" he asked.

"Stef. What's yours?"

"Thom. I'm earning money for school. Where you from?"

"America."

His eyes lit up. "Oh, I know many things about America. Last state:

Hawaii. Second to last state: Alaska. Capital of New York: Albany. Capital of Texas: Austin. You buy a bracelet? Ten for two dollars."

I told him I didn't need any bracelets, so he pulled out a pack of temple postcards, naming and sharing a fact about each one. "Stef, you buy something from me?"

I wanted to give all I had to every child in that town and felt selfish for not doing just that. "I'll give you two dollars, but I only want one bracelet. Thom, you're a really smart kid. Make sure you stay in school and study hard."

He grinned. "Okay."

James and I walked away, and he put his arm around my shoulder as I took a deep breath. "You can't help them all, love."

I nodded and quietly put the bamboo bangle on my wrist next to the one from the day before.

We traveled onward, from Siem Reap to the Cambodian capital, Phnom Penh. I sank into a wicker armchair one afternoon, on cushions worn to comfy perfection, sipped a pineapple smoothie, and looked across the large wooden deck of the Lakeside Guesthouse. A slatted roof shielded me from the sun's rays, but I still felt its heat and saw its reflection in the glittering Boeung Kak.

A boxy TV sat on a table by the wall. On-screen, two elderly Cambodian men approached a deteriorating building surrounded by concrete walls and barbed wire. They stood stiffly amid the ruins with creased and weary faces. They hunched over and trembled, sobbing into their hands, seemingly reliving the pain of their torture.

The men in the documentary were at S-21, a Khmer Rouge prison up the road. Their leader, Pol Pot, turned Cambodia into a communist, classless society in the '70s. His ideology was the opposite of Chairman Mao's—abandon the new and return to the old. He closed schools, hospitals, and factories. He burned currency and confiscated private property. He forced the urban population to work on countryside farms.

The former prisoners turned toward some middle-aged men standing nearby. Previous prison guards with faces hardened, maybe by thirty years of suppressed guilt.

"How could you torture us?" the old men asked.

The guards didn't apologize. They insisted they were victims, too—brainwashed and threatened as teenagers to inflict pain upon traitors of the state.

Fifteen billiard balls scattered with a loud clack. James held a pool cue by the felt table, chatting with another guest. He bent forward and drove a ball toward a corner pocket.

"Bollocks!" James threw his hands up in disgust. "Fucking terrible."

The other backpacker laughed.

A few young female travelers sat at a table by the lake, drinking and soaking up the sun.

A clean-cut guy in his early twenties stopped near me. He gestured toward the TV and grimaced in disapproval. "I don't understand the people who watch this shit," he announced to no one. "Fascinated with death. I don't need to go see that type of thing." Then he sat down to read his copy of *On the Road*, carefully choosing the chair most visible to the sunkissed girls.

I needed to go see that type of thing. I thought it was important to understand what they experienced, to empathize, and I couldn't do that if I refused the discomfort of even thinking about it.

S-21 had been made into a museum and memorial. Later that afternoon, James accompanied me on a long walk through dusty, sticky Phnom Pehn, though he didn't want to visit the prison, either.

"Am I demented?" I asked him.

"No. Not for this, anyway." He gave me a nudge on the shoulder that I ignored.

"Seriously. This is a huge deal, and I never even knew it happened. In our lifetime."

"It's okay," James said. "You don't have to justify yourself just because I don't want to go, love."

I paid for my ticket at an underused kiosk, and James sat on a bench to wait for me. I stepped inside, past the concrete wall and barbed wire. A feeling of sadness and fear enveloped me, and I was glad to be alone.

On a large sign, curlicue Khmer script detailed prison regulations next to awkward English translations. Number Three: "Don't be a fool, for you are a chap who dare to thwart the revolution."

These were the enemies of the state: professionals, intellectuals, government officials. Teachers, students, engineers, monks. Some were arrested for wearing glasses, as it implied literacy and education.

Before becoming S-21, this battered building burst with life, laughter, and knowledge. As a high school, teachers and students once walked freely down the corridors. The same corridors that later housed shuffling prisoners and shouting guards.

I walked slowly down an empty hallway, and my footsteps echoed. I entered large cells devoid of decorations or desks but still recognized them as classrooms. Heavy iron shackles sat on the floor, and blood stained the checkerboard tiles. I imagined an enthusiastic teacher engaging her class, later shackled to the same floor. Punished for the crime of educating.

In one room sat a large wooden table with two legs and a steeply slanted tabletop. Ankle shackles up top, wrist restraints below. A rusty metal watering can sat alongside, used for pouring out confessions.

Photographs lined the long walls. Thousands of prisoner intake shots. Not just men and women. Children. Killed because their parents were killed. I looked into their eyes, but they didn't look defiant. They looked defeated. Out of 17,000 inmates, eight survived.

I wept for them until my eyes stung. This was real. They were real. I walked out of the prison, somber and shaken. James stood up for our hike back to the guesthouse.

"You all right?"

I wiped my nose. "I don't know. But I'm glad I went."

"Okay, good." He put his arms around me and gave me a comforting squeeze. "You're a good person, love."

I smiled weakly and let out a quivery breath. "Thanks."

I didn't feel like a good person.

I'd finally had a successful, enjoyable year teaching just before our trip to Asia, but I'd quit my first two teaching jobs because I was too sensitive to handle the kids, feeling at the time like I couldn't possibly survive the stress. But I wasn't fucking tortured for it. I felt embarrassed and guilty for every complaint I'd ever made and vowed never to whine about anything ever again, knowing as I made the promise, I'd never keep it.

James rubbed my back soothingly. "Shall we get a curry for dinner?" He asked.

"Yeah. Sure."

And life carried on.

James handed our clunky MP3 player to a young American guy behind the shop counter, along with five dollars and a handwritten list of ten albums. "Cool, man." The guy looked down at the paper. "Give us like, an hour to load them?"

"Sure. Cheers, mate," James said. We walked back down a narrow dirt alley toward our hostel on the lake.

"Wow. No way that's legal," I said, shaking my head.

James smiled. "I think a lot of illegal things get overlooked in Phnom Pehn."

One long, skinny passageway lined with guesthouses, shops, and restaurants made up the capital's backpacker district. Travelers milled about, chattering. A Cambodian man sat behind a wooden table in the alley—a few maps taped to a wall designated the space as his travel agency. A guy slowly rolled past on a sputtering scooter. A woman sold cold drinks from a Styrofoam cooler.

A sign in a café window stated: *Add Happy $1.50.* "What's 'Happy?'"

I asked James.

"That's where they put weed on your food."

"For real?" I raised my eyebrows, recalling the booming sign at the Cambodian border announcing, "Drug Penalties Are Punishable By Death."

We hung out on the deck at the hostel for a while, and after we picked up our newly loaded music machine, we stopped for a late dinner at a café called Oh My Buddha.

"I'm going to try a happy pizza," I said to the waiter before I realized I'd decided to.

James's eyes widened. "Really?"

"Um, yeah! Why not?" I replied. "You want some?"

"Go on, then," he said.

Our casualness belied our inexperience. We had no idea what the hell we were doing. The happy pizza arrived, looking like an average pie dusted with extra oregano. We chowed down and waited. Thirty minutes passed.

I frowned. "I don't feel that happy. Do you?"

James shook his head. "No, not especially happy."

"Hmm. Maybe it *was* just a shitload of oregano," I said. "Let's get a happy smoothie, just to make sure."

After I ordered the green-specked smoothie, the urge to laugh rose up from my chest, tickling my insides and threatening to give me away. I bit my lip to keep it in. I didn't want everyone in the restaurant to know I was stoned.

The waiter set the shake on the table. I chugged it to alleviate my dry mouth.

"Fuckin 'ell, Stef!" James blurted when I passed him the nearly empty cup.

The laughter burst out of me. James giggled at me giggling. It felt nice to be silly together.

I held my finger to my lips. "Shhhh. Don't tell anybody."

In Spain, my life didn't really start until after sunset. I was twenty-one and went out often, drinking gin with the girls at a *discoteca*, or wine with Miguel at his chalet. When James and I met at the Pink House, we spent a lot of tipsy, funny nights together. I started the early shift at Kathmandu still slightly inebriated a couple times, rehanging fleeces and drinking iced coffee to sober up before customers arrived. When we lived in London, we'd spend Saturdays at cozy pubs, drinking cider, watching football, eating steak and chips, and making new friends. Everything was easygoing. I was easygoing.

In America, that stopped. I felt tense—about navigating immigration,

James fitting into my family, his medical scares and lack of insurance, and what our future would look like if we couldn't make more money. I followed the rules of my diet strictly, never having ice cream, or chips, or alcohol, or anything fun, ever, though it didn't always seem to be helping my anxiety or concentration issues. In Phuket, I couldn't relax and enjoy myself because I couldn't handle deviating from the plan.

James and I had recently gone on a jungle trek. One evening, the other trekkers and our guides played a drinking game called Drunken Hamsters, where cards were drawn and rules were made up along the way. James decided that if someone drew an eight, they had to stand up and say, "God save the queen," just to tease the two Scottish trekkers with us. As the night wore on, the game got sillier and rowdier, with people forgetting the rules and everyone shouting at them to take a drink.

Jacqueline was Canadian. She cracked jokes all night, and when she proved she could stick her whole fist in her mouth, James laughed really hard. Toward the end of the night, she drew an eight and accidentally said, "God save the drink," cracking everyone up. I sat there and watched the game with my water bottle and couldn't help feeling left out. I was twenty-seven, and I didn't need alcohol to have fun, but sometimes, I missed that feeling of letting go.

I walked to the bathroom at Oh My Buddha, grinning at everyone along my route. I sat on the toilet for ages, staring at the wall, until I finally realized I'd finished peeing. I cracked up. "I'm so funny right now," I announced, snickering and then audibly shushing myself.

I emerged from the bathroom, making sure to smile again at the café patrons I passed. James looked up. "Did you fall in?"

Lots of giggles.

"Oh, dear," he said, laughing. "Let's go."

We walked home in the dark, humid night. I complained about still being thirsty, so James bought a water bottle from a roadside vendor. He plucked it out of an ice-filled cooler and handed it to me. I ran my fingertips up and down the plastic container. Each drop of condensation felt huge and slimy.

I walked to the door of the hostel and turned the knob.

"Stef—what the fuck?" James pulled me away by the arm. "This is somebody's house!"

"This is our hostel," I insisted, going for the door again.

"It's not!" James took my hand and led me away. "Bloody hell, you almost walked into somebody's living room!" He steered me to the empty deck at the back of our hostel. I sat on a bench overlooking the lake.

I danced in my seat to a song playing in my head. I pointed at James and made a serious face. "You're not as happy as me. Go get a happy shake, so you can be happy like me!"

"Hang on, love, I need a wee," James patted me on the shoulder and walked off.

The lake looked like an infinite pool of ink. I puzzled over lights glowing from the far shore. They danced erratically and left messy reflections in the black water. I lifted my arm. It looked wiggly, like a scrambled picture on an old television. A slight breeze came off the lake. The world went silent. I was alone.

Lights shouldn't dance.

Arms should not be wiggly.

My hands trembled. I clutched my chest, rocking forward, unable to breathe.

"Stef, love?" James said, hustling back from the bathroom.

"Make it stop," I pleaded. "I hate it, I hate it. Please, help me."

James put his arm around my back and helped me across the wooden deck to our private room. The floorboards stretched on for miles, the door to our room a tiny rectangle in the distance. Suddenly, we stood in front of it.

James unlocked the door.

I dove inside and collapsed onto the squealing double mattress. "Uhhhh. What time is it?" It felt like 6 a.m.

"Eleven." It had been an hour since I drank the shake.

I lay down flat, my head at the foot of the bed, and stared at the ceiling, hyperventilating, trying to ignore the heart palpitations. I knew I was going to die. Or be brain-damaged forever. I imagined James trying to explain this to my parents.

"James," I pleaded, "can you take me to the hospital? Please?"

"Stef, love, you know I can't. We'll get in trouble."

I gasped for air. My fingers tingled. I looked at the ceiling and visualized a cheerful Lisa Frank landscape of unicorns and rainbows. It didn't help.

I suddenly worried that James had called the police. I imagined an angry squad of officers bearing machine guns and plastic shields crashing through the wall—like a cross between a SWAT team and the Kool-Aid Man.

James sat next to me on the bed and tenderly stroked my hair. "Stef, you'll be okay. You had too much, but it will wear off."

"Are you sure?"

"Yeah, love. I'll be right back—I'm gonna get you a pop. I've heard sugar can help."

James rushed to the street vendor and bought me a Sprite. I chugged it, and in a fleeting moment of clarity, flew off the bed and puked it into the toilet. I hugged the bowl, sobbing and retching. James helped me up and guided me back to bed.

"It'll be okay, Stef. You'll pass out soon and wake up in the morning with it out of your system, just like alcohol. It's okay," James reassured me.

"Do you promise? When will I pass out? I just want to pass out."

He sat on the edge of the bed and squeezed my hand tight. "So, how about the Steelers making it to the Super Bowl?" he asked.

A half-smile crossed my lips, and I weakly chanted, "Here we go, Steelers, here we go."

He asked me a few more questions to distract me, though he was struggling to stay awake. Every time his fingers slipped away, my eyes flew open, and I woke him up. I needed him. I wouldn't allow him to let go.

I stared at the oscillating fan, stuttering in place for what seemed like hours. I knew I just had to trust James. *Trust James*, I repeated over and over until I drifted off.

I opened my eyelids a bit. Morning light flooded in, and the room spun. I shut my eyes and moaned.

"Love?" James asked. "You okay?"

"Mmm. No. Not really."

I slept the entire day, waking only to pee and eat some snacks James brought me from the café downstairs.

"Stef, love?" James tapped me lightly on the shoulder. "You should eat some dinner." He handed me a plate with an omelet on it.

"Thanks, hon." I sat up on the bed to eat.

"So, I was talking with this bloke downstairs—he and his girlfriend were just in Goa. And they ate marijuana in something, and a bit later, she sprinted to the balcony and tried to jump over the railing."

I gasped. "Are you serious?"

"A lot of people say the weed's more potent down in these places."

I fell back asleep after I ate, slept through the night, and felt marginally better the next morning. It would take a few days to stop feeling swirly and confused. My pursuit of happiness was a huge mistake, but it would have been far worse without James. I felt so grateful he was by my side the whole time.

CHAPTER 51
JAMES

As usual, Stef had the window seat, and I sat by the aisle. An aisle crammed with locals on small blue plastic stools. A few chickens roamed the floor. For the last six hours, we'd baked on this air conditioning-free bus. Cambodian karaoke videos provided the soundtrack, their volume pushing the capability of the bus's speakers to their limit, the only plus side being that it drowned out the chorus of clucking chickens and wailing babies.

I doubted the bus could handle the excess weight, and it came as no surprise when we broke down. Stef and I stood in the midday heat at the side of a road in the middle of nowhere. Dust swirled around us in the warm breeze while smoke rose from the engine.

At the temples of Angkor, Stef bore a permanent smile as she talked with the local children. We strolled around the ruins of Ta Prohm, marvelling at the way the jungle had reclaimed the buildings. We rocked in hammocks at a budget guesthouse as monks walked the streets around us. We talked.

Now we were on our way to Laos. Specifically, a place called Si Phan Don. A cluster of islands in the Mekong River. The name translates to 'Four Thousand Islands,' though only a few were habitable. Our guidebook promised tranquillity in this rarely visited destination.

After Stef's 'happy' incident, it was just what we needed. Her extreme reaction to the pizza and shake didn't worry me. I just tried my best to calm her. When my 'happy' kicked in, it bypassed the giggly stage and went directly to the feel-like-shit stage. Each time I fell asleep, Stef grabbed my hand. She needed me.

247

Eventually, with the bus engine fixed, the driver waved us back on. Hot, stagnant air greeted us. Seven hours later, we threw our backpacks on the floor and our bodies onto squeaky beds in a guesthouse near the Cambodia-Laos border.

With whiny karaoke songs still ringing in our ears, we crossed the Mekong River the next day in a wooden boat. Next came a long, bumpy minibus ride on narrow roads through thick jungle. We eventually stopped at a roadblock. The driver opened the door. "Immigration," he said, ushering us out of the minibus. The sound of rapid gunfire punctured the silence as a man with a machine gun shot at the tops of the trees. If it was an intimidation tactic, it worked.

A shed next to a car-park barrier acted as an immigration office. Inside, an older man stood in full military uniform, complete with a colourful assortment of shiny medals pinned to his green jacket. He looked at me with a stern expression and said nothing. I got the sense he was bitter about spending his twilight years on border patrol after once being a decorated soldier. A long, silent moment passed without him so much as glancing at the passport and visa I'd laid out for him.

'Two dollar. You need two dollar,' our driver said.

'But we've got visas,' I replied.

'You need to give two dollar or no go to Laos.'

I slid two crisp US dollar notes across the counter. His face softened, and with much enthusiasm, he stamped my passport and tipped his hat. After Stef did the same, he raised the gate, and we continued our journey into Laos.

A few days later, I awoke in our riverside hut with a pounding head, upset stomach, parched mouth and bursting bladder. Our two-dollar-a-night accomodation didn't have a toilet. I leaned over the side of the bed and found a plastic bottle on the floor. After drinking the remaining lukewarm water, I peed a tiny trickle into it. By the time Stef woke up, my eyes felt swollen and my headache made it painful to open them. My body felt like a furnace and a freezer simultaneously.

'Are you OK, hun?' Stef asked.

'I feel terrible, love.'

'Are you hungover?'

'I only had a few beers last night. Not enough to make me feel this bad.'

Stef grabbed our tattered guidebook from the floor and flipped to the back.

'The symptoms of malaria include fever, chills, headache, sweats, fatigue and nausea,' she read out loud.

My pulse quickened.

'Malaria has similar symptoms to flu, and if not treated quickly, can be life-threatening.'

It no longer felt exciting to be so remote. It felt stupid and scary.

My skin was clammy, but internally a fire raged. I stepped outside for some fresh air while Stef went to ask Mr Vang, the owner of our bungalows, for advice. They returned to find me slouched against the hut. I saw the concern on Mr Vang's face. The first time I'd seen him without a smile.

'You no look well,' he said.

'What should we do?' Stef asked him. Floods of tears streamed down her cheeks.

'I get boat for you. There is hospital on other island. They have electricity there.'

Stef frantically packed our bags, and we waited on the riverbank.

A tiny, seatless boat pulled up to the shore, its engine chugging away at the back. Stef and Mr Vang helped me into the boat, and we set off slowly upstream. Though I didn't know how long the trip would take, I found comfort in knowing we were making progress. Stef sat behind me on the floor of the boat, propping me up. Wooden planks cut into my legs. A cool breeze hit my face, forcing the tears out of my eyes.

I turned my thoughts to the previous morning in an attempt to calm my racing mind. I had awoken early in our bamboo hut while Stef slept beside me. The morning sun pierced the gaps in the walls, illuminating the room with glowing rays of light swirling with floating dust. Birds chirped outside our window, and the Mekong River below rhythmically lapped the stilts of our hut. The smell of jasmine rice from Mr Vang's open-air restaurant filled the room. I picked up my book and tiptoed outside, the floorboards creaking under my feet.

Crisp morning air greeted me. I lowered myself into an old woven hammock which swayed me gently. It hung just below the sloping roof of the hut, framing off my own personal view of the Mekong. On the river, a fisherman stood adeptly balanced on the bow of his small wooden boat. He cast his traditional net by throwing the bundled mesh high into the air. As it came down, it spread out majestically, like a blooming flower, landing on the water with a crisscrossed splash. Resisting the temptation to stand and applaud, I opened my book and began to read.

The choking sound of the ancient engine plucked me back into the present. The boat ground to a halt amidst a strong current that pulled us in different directions. Stef's voice wavered as she asked the driver what happened, but he didn't understand English. He pulled a cord repeatedly, trying to resuscitate the engine, but the suffocating sounds suggested we'd be there for a while.

I fantasized about a sterile hospital with pristine rooms and state-of-the-art equipment. Smiling doctors lined up outside waiting for me. I'd become so sick in such a short space of time. Just the day before, I had the strength to spend the afternoon bike riding around the island.

Stef and I had hired bicycles with baskets and bells. We pedalled them over an old concrete bridge, a remnant of a French colonial railway. On a nearby island, tin shacks and fishing boats dotted the shoreline. Stef wanted to stop by the local school. The kids gleefully kicked a football around the playground. When it flew over the fence, I kicked it back to them, and they cheered. We rode our bikes back, ringing our bells to alert the locals on the narrow path.

Two lively, muddy little girls who looked about four years old appeared on the trail. We stopped, and they immediately gravitated towards Stef. She knelt down to let one try on her sunglasses. Giddy with excitement, they smiled at each other and giggled at nothing in particular. Stef gave them the bamboo bracelets from her wrist before waving goodbye.

Back in the stricken boat, the deep aching in my stomach worsened. Without the breeze, my fever returned with a vengeance. I could no longer hold up my heavy head, and I let it fall back onto Stef's nurturing shoulder.

Around us, life continued. The river was the lifeblood of the island. The locals bathed in it, restaurant cooks washed pots in it, and fishermen gathered food from it. I'd watched a man brushing his teeth in the exact same spot a woman had just gutted a chicken.

Mercifully, the engine coughed back to life as though the driver had shocked it with defibrillators. An acrid plume of black smoke surrounded us, and we resumed our course at last.

When we pulled up to the island, a steep dirt bank lay before us.

'Where's the hospital?' Stef asked, but the driver pointed back down the river and held out his other hand for payment. She gave him some bills, and he departed. Barely able to walk, I threw my arm around Stef, and she practically carried me up the hill, where we found a group of ramshackle buildings. We needed to ask for directions to the hospital and wandered around the complex, past open-front rooms where people lay on wooden beds. This *was* the hospital.

I slumped on a bed in an empty, fanless room while Stef went to find help. '*Sabaidee*? He is sick! *Il est malade!*' Stef's screams in three different languages echoed down the corridor as she paced. Sickness consumed me. My weakness felt weightless. If not for my heavy backpack anchoring me, I was convinced I'd float away. Stef's voice grew louder and more agitated, but her calls for help in Laotian, English and French went unanswered. Outside, the rosy sky was just as beautiful as the previous evening.

We'd marvelled at the sunset the night before from a tranquil spot at the tip of the island. Tiny, tree-covered isles dotted the Mekong as far as the eye could see. The glassy river reflected the fluorescent pink sky, disturbed from time to time by the silhouettes of families travelling on narrow boats. Only the sputtering of engines broke the stillness of the air.

An absence of electricity meant no wires, no neon signs and no loud music. The soundtrack of the island was the chatter of locals and birds and the burbling of the river. We let this way of life wash over us, embracing its charm. When we returned to have dinner at Mr Vang's restaurant, he always sat with us to chat. We conversed mainly in English and Thai, and he took great pride in teaching us some basic Laotian words. His disproportionate enthusiasm suggested he didn't meet many travellers. During our short stay, he'd grown fond of us and invited us to a family wedding on a nearby island in a few days. We gladly accepted.

We sat under the makeshift roof at a worn table, feeling a light breeze blow through. While we talked, his shy young wife rustled up local recipes. One dish had a delightful special sauce. After ordering it several times, I asked for her secret recipe, expecting to see a rare locally sourced ingredient. She fetched it from the kitchen, carrying it proudly: a bottle of tomato ketchup.

Stef returned short of breath with a nurse who didn't speak English, Thai or French. The nurse put her cold hand on my burning forehead. Then she found a dirty thermometer in the back of a cupboard and tried to put it in my mouth.

'No way!' I jolted back from her. She seemed surprised by my reaction but not overly concerned by my condition. Even with the language barrier, surely, she could see my discomfort. She pointed the thermometer at my armpit, and I raised my arm in the air. She took my temperature, but her expressionless face revealed no answers. I got the feeling she thought we were overreacting.

Stef threw her arms up in annoyance and went in search again. I'd lost my perception of time, so I had no idea how long she'd been gone. She returned with a man she found in a cow field who could understand us.

'You go stay Mekong Guesthouse. Doctor come see you tonight,' he translated, pointing down a path.

'Test him now!' Stef pleaded.

'Doctor no here. He home, in shower.'

I gave up and walked out of the hospital, wandering in the direction of the guesthouse, which I hoped had a huge fan with an Arctic breeze. My trembling legs barely supported me.

'You're fucking kidding me,' Stef said to nobody specific and quickly caught up to me.

Two local ladies in their sixties ran the guesthouse. They'd lived in Canada, so they spoke English well. They welcomed us in, gave me acetaminophen and Vitamin C, and offered us an air-conditioned room. However, we opted for one with a fan. Even in these desperate times, we were conscious of our budget. I lay under the fan and savoured the cool relief for a few minutes until the power inexplicably went out. The room went black, and the fan slowed down and whirled to an agonizing stop.

After dinner at Mr Vang's the night before, we'd found a hole-in-the-wall bar with a stuttering generator. It provided dim light and powered a small fridge stocked with ice-cold beer. We shared drinks and travel tales with other backpackers for a few hours until the generator gave out and the lights faded. Determined to keep the night alive, the owner filled the bar with candlelight. Under the yellow glow, we made friends with an English couple. We talked and laughed and arranged to meet up to go tubing down the river the next day. Eventually, the candles flickered and extinguished one by one, and we walked home under the bright, white moonlight.

I lay in the blackout, sobbing. How could a place so serene be so deadly? I couldn't help but recall my time spent recovering from ear surgery in Pittsburgh. Had I gone through all that just to meet my end in a guesthouse in Laos? Even if the doctor did come to see me, my experience so far made me distrust the local hospital. After a long wait, the power kicked back on. Just then, one of the sweet owners knocked on our door. 'Doctor here.'

We went downstairs only to see the same damn nurse from the hospital. She offered no pleasantries and didn't even look at me. She sighed as she lifted a medical bag onto the kitchen table. We didn't bother asking about the doctor.

The two owners helped us navigate the language barrier. The nurse wanted to take a blood sample and test it for malaria. To my surprise, she pulled out a sterile syringe in a sealed bag. She pricked my finger, collected a drop of blood, and asked for two dollars for the test. After she left, we asked the owners how long it would take, to which one replied, 'In Laos, things very slowly here.'

I lay still on the bed while Stef sat beside me for a few silent hours until one of the owners knocked on the door. Stef stood up sharply.

'Be happy for no malaria,' the owner said, 'But white blood cells high, some kind of infection.'

Stef covered her mouth with her hand and sat back down on the bed. Sensing her relief, the owner smiled widely.

Though initially elated at the news, I felt like a fake. They must have all thought we were hysterical. Exhausted and with frayed emotions, a sense of disappointment took over. I'd caused such a commotion for everyone and so much worry for Stef, and I didn't even have malaria.

'Nurse knew no malaria. Your temperature not high enough,' the owner mentioned casually. This was consistent with our experiences in Asia, where we often felt left in the dark. No wonder the nurse was so nonchalant. She gave me an unnecessary malaria test because we made a big fuss, but it never occurred to her to tell us she already knew I didn't have it.

Stef squeezed me tight as the feeling of relief washed over us both. The owner suggested I rest and took Stef a few doors down to buy me some antibiotics.

Stef screaming and swearing in the hospital was out of character for her, but hearing it showed me how much she cared. She propped me up both physically and mentally, and we had gotten through it together. Too bad we'd miss the wedding.

'Here we go, Steelers, here we go!' My football (soccer) teammates had sat around me in a sports bar in Pittsburgh, their eyes glued to a large TV showing the first game of the 2004/2005 NFL season. The crowd, adorned in black and yellow jerseys, waved small yellow towels around.

The game was taking forever, and I just wanted to get home and find out the Manchester United score. The room erupted again with cheering for no apparent reason. One of the players was down on one knee, acting out the motions of loading a bow and firing an imaginary arrow.

'Did they score?' I asked.

'No, he made a tackle,' one of the lads replied. *They celebrate every play? How am I going to fit in here?*

Eighteen months later, Stef and I plonked our dusty backpacks and weary bodies down at a table in Central Cafe, Bangkok, a few hours before dawn. There were more waiters than customers. We'd just arrived after an overnight bus journey from Laos and were killing time until Super Bowl XL kicked off between the Pittsburgh Steelers and the Seattle Seahawks. A waiter stroked his long black hair in a mirror. We asked about the game. He confirmed it was to be shown before pointing to an old tube TV on wheels. He quickly returned his hand to his hair.

I pictured everyone in Pittsburgh preparing. Stef's dad, Frank, would be wearing his jersey and hat, his Terrible Towel laid ceremonially on top of the TV. I longed for some game-day atmosphere in the sleepy bar.

Just before kick-off, two singing Seattle Seahawks fans entered Central. The two young men wore green jerseys, and one had a green baseball cap on backward. Their faces were painted green with the words 'Super' and 'Bowl' written on their cheeks in white. They were loud and enthusiastic, and we loved it. Some people rolled their eyes. *Here come the loud Americans*, I imagined them thinking.

My second Steeler game experience was at Stef's nan's house.

'What are we having for dinner, love?' I asked Stef.

'Kielbasa in sauerkraut, and pierogies in butter and onions,' she replied.

'What in what? And what?' I asked, fidgeting in my seat.

'Polish food. My mom's side of the family is Polish.'

I didn't care for the sauerkraut but very much approved of the kielbasa sausage. The pierogis reminded me of ravioli without the sauce and with fluffy mashed potato inside. Also delicious.

Evelyn's side of the family sat around the dining table, passing plates and scooping food. The men chatted about the upcoming game and about a rookie quarterback called Ben Rothlisomething or other. I sat back in my chair and thought of the time I had dinner with the Italian family in Australia when I worked as a fruit picker. Stef looked my way and smiled.

After dinner, Frank and Stef's uncles gathered around the TV. Frank took the time to explain the many rules and nuances of American football. At first, I constantly compared it to rugby, a sport familiar to me and hugely popular back in my hometown.

It irked me that they called a game that is played almost entirely by hand football. In rugby, there is one team of players who run consistently for sixty minutes without helmets or pads, not an offence and a defence that each play only half of the match. If you put someone out of bounds, you get the ball back. If you score, the opposing team kicks the ball back to you. You only get six attempts to go the whole length of field, and you *definitely* don't celebrate each play.

Every Sunday through the autumn and winter, we'd gather in Stef's parents' living room for the game. Frank wore the carpet beneath his feet by constantly pacing the living room. He rapturously applauded first-downs. Touchdowns brought a shake of the fist and a 'Hey-hey, alright!' He threw his hat on the ground after turnovers and opposition touchdowns. By the end of a close game, he knelt on the ground, slumped over the sofa about two feet from the TV. The one thing I could relate to was the passion of the fans, and the emotional toll games had on them. It was then that I made my peace with the differences and accepted American football for what it was.

With the Thailand sun rising over Bangkok, Super Bowl XL kicked off. Since the game started tentatively, loud commentary from the Seahawks fans provided our entertainment. Towards the end of the first half, our quarterback dove into the end zone for a touchdown. 'Here we go, Steelers, here we go!' we shouted.

The Seahawks fans groaned while the rest of the customers remained focused on their travel guides.

In my head, I could hear Myron Cope's raspy-voiced excitement announcing the touchdown on Pittsburgh radio. It felt nice to think of Pittsburgh fondly, to begin to disassociate it with the lows of our first year of marriage.

The screen on the old TV flickered erratically. More groans from the Seahawks fans. The one with the baseball cap approached the TV and banged lightly on its side. It brought the picture back to life with Seattle lining up a field goal attempt. 'Let's go, Hawks!' The two lads chanted.

Before Seattle kicked the ball, one of the many waiters stood in front of the TV. He admired the shiny fingernails on one of his hands while he pointed to the street with the other. 'You leave now,' he said faintly.

'What?' the Seahawks fans asked in disbelief.

'You go now.'

'Come on, man,' they pleaded.

The waiter walked away, and they threw their arms in the air in frustration at the failed field goal. The clock ran down to halftime. Another waiter approached them and did the same as the last. They pleaded their case again and remained in the bar. The owner, an older stern-faced man, confronted them next.

'You leave now!' he ordered.

The one in the cap approached the TV and recreated what had happened. 'I was only trying to make the picture better,' he said.

The owner disappeared behind the bar. He leapt over it a few seconds later, carrying the business end of a pool cue.

'They should just go,' I whispered to Stef.

The owner raised the pool cue in the air, pointing it towards the street. 'Go! Now!' he shouted.

Still, they didn't leave.

We'd learned in Phuket that Thai people can sometimes get violent if they lose face. One of the salesmen at John's company had a girlfriend who roundhouse-kicked him in the head for coming home late. Newspapers covered stories of tourists being attacked for arguing over tuk-tuk prices. And we'd heard stories of women cutting their cheating husband's knobs off.

'Yeah, that guy looks mad,' Stef said. 'Should we say something?'

Before we had a chance, the other fan approached the owner with his hands together. 'We just wanna watch the game.'

'You go now.' The owner's face reddened.

'But—'

And with that, a group of waiters surrounded the Seahawks fans, grabbed them, and pushed them into the street. The owner followed, landing a sharp right hook to one of the fans, sending him tumbling against the side of a parked car and then to the ground. Stef gasped. I craned my neck, and others stood up to watch, open-mouthed in disbelief.

'Oh my God,' Stef said, covering her mouth with her hand.

People in the street scattered around the melee. The one with the baseball cap ran down the street without looking back. The formerly placid waiters kicked his friend from head to toe. He managed to scramble to his feet. The owner swung the pool cue, smashing him in the leg. He cried out in pain and fell to his knees. The owner wound up for another blow.

'Fuckin 'ell. That's harsh,' I commented.

The fan finally found the strength to get back on his feet while the owner took a swing and a miss. He fled the scene, running and limping.

The staff re-entered the bar, and we all quickly returned to our seats. Some buried their heads in their books while others stared at the floor like Stef and me. The owner went into the back, and the waiters crowded around a mirror fixing their hair. I put my hand on Stef's lap.

'Why'd they do that?' she asked me.

I turned to see her pale face and glossy eyes. 'I don't know, love.'

We took a few minutes to compose ourselves. I moved our bags closer to us.

Sufficient daylight signalled the inside lights to be turned off. Chilled music began to play from the many speakers hung around the bar. The owner re-emerged with a cigarette in his mouth. He scanned the room before approaching the TV and switching it off.

'Excuse me. It's only halftime,' Stef called out.

I squeezed her leg. 'What the *fuck* are you doin' love?' I muttered under my breath.

'*Mut lao*! Super Bowl finished,' he answered.

I threw some baht down on the table. 'Grab your bag, love. We're leaving.'

CHAPTER 52
STEF

Heavy beats of drum and bass music blared from the nearest open front beach bar, and colorful lights shone into the darkness. Young revelers, arms and cheeks swirled in glowing paint, danced barefoot in the sand—spinning round, feet pounding, and hands clenched tight to their buckets of Red Bull and Thai whisky. Backpackers in Chang tank tops and baggy fisherman pants posed for photos in front of a large stone sign carved with the words "Full Moon Party."

Several drunken partiers stumbled into the warm froth to pee, and many others had already passed out, scattered along the shore. One tan girl lay face down on the beach, arms and legs splayed at funny angles, wet sand clumping in her bleached hair. A wave lapped at her toes.

"She looks like a skydiver whose chute didn't open," James said.

"Tomorrow, she'll feel like one, too," I added, crouching down to check that she was breathing. "Where the hell are her friends?"

James had told me about the famous Full Moon Party when he was on Koh Pha-ngan with Keith and Rick, and I wanted to experience it. Once he recovered from his mystery infection in Laos, we headed back to Thailand in time for the rowdy festivities. We made some instant and temporary travel friends at our hostel and stayed up until the sky turned pink, illuminating the empty bottles, straws, and other carnage along the coastline.

A day later, the post-Full Moon exodus left the island quiet and the sand pristine again. Our new friends had moved on to their next destinations, but we'd decided to stay for a bit. We moved to a rustic bungalow, perched on a wooded hillside framing the main beach, dropped our bags, and headed out for a day of lounging on the sand.

After the sun set, we popped into an empty beach bar. I grooved in my seat to "Gold Digger" by Kanye West.

James glanced at the tiny dance floor. "You wanna go dance, don't you?"

I smiled. "No, not by myself."

He took my hand. "C'mon, love."

My mouth dropped open and transformed into a huge grin. The two of us took up the floor, shuffling and twirling around like idiots, laughing like crazy.

We walked home along the empty beach under a waning but still brilliant moon. The dark ocean lapped beside us, and clusters of palm trees hugged the edge of the beach.

James and I finally felt in sync again, albeit after a few disasters, but those times of stress brought out the best in our relationship. For two people with a history of running away from problems, we knew that even through the worst of times, we'd never, ever, run away from each other.

I grabbed James's hand, and we playfully swung our arms in unison. He looked over at me and smiled. I stopped walking and looked up at his handsome face, lit up by moonlight. He leaned down to kiss me and even in the tropical air, I could feel my face flush. I pulled back and whispered to him, "Let's have sex on the beach."

James looked at me in surprise. "Really? Are you sure?"

I glanced around. "Yeah, there's nobody here." I led him back under a bunch of palm trees. We knelt on the soft sand in the dark, and he touched my cheek while we kissed. My heart raced from arousal and danger. We lay down and I looked up, watching the palm fronds rustle. Bright stars twinkled through the leaves of the trees. The world was quiet except for the crashing waves.

I gazed up into James's eyes. He sweetly brushed some sand off my forehead. Something moved behind him in the darkness. A flash of white. I tilted my head to look. Someone stood in the shadows, about five feet behind James.

I gasped. James looked back. A short Thai man wearing jeans and a baggy white T-shirt glared at us. We leapt to our feet, spraying sand around, adjusting our clothing. The man continued to stare with dark, angry eyes.

"*Kor tot, kah.*" I folded my hands and bowed my head in a *wai.* "*Kor tot, kah,*" I repeated.

James joined in. It meant, "Excuse me," but it's the closest we knew to "I'm sorry."

I turned around, fumbling to pick up my flip-flops from the sand. The coarse grains scratched my fingers.

I apologized once more, bowing and slowly backing away. *Wai*-ing like my life depended on it. The man stepped forward and grabbed me, wrapping his fingers tightly around my forearm. I wrenched myself away and fled down the beach beside James. My hands shook furiously as we ran. I looked behind us, but I couldn't see him anymore.

"He had a gun," James whispered. Beads of sweat glistened on his forehead.

"What?"

"He had a gun."

"What?" I said again. It didn't compute.

"He had a fucking gun, Stef! He had a gun! He pulled up his shirt and showed it to me in his waistband while you were picking up your sandals." James burst out.

We ran to the base of the hill alongside the beach, crouching down, creeping behind stone walls, and ducking under tropical plants. We avoided any lights, fearing he'd follow us. When we reached our bungalow, we crawled in and gingerly shut the door behind us. James stood up and tried to lock the door. The inside latch dangled, broken. In a desperate panic, we pushed a chair behind the door and piled our backpacks on it. We sat on the bare mattress in the dark, tucked against the wall. Silent but for our rapid breaths. Moonlight streamed in through the gaps in our hut, striping the black room in blue. We watched the door all night.

We finally allowed ourselves to fall asleep well after the sun had come up and didn't wake until the afternoon. I sat up and looked at the makeshift barrier behind the door. "Jesus, that was scary," I muttered. "Why do you think he showed you that gun? Like, what was he planning to do?"

"Mug us, maybe? I don't know." He looked down and shook his head. "I don't want to think about it."

"I'm glad I didn't know about the gun. I think I would have frozen instead of running away."

"I might be ready to go home," James said, glancing at me for my opinion.

Behind him, our window overlooked the lush hillside. Yellow sunlight beamed, illuminating a cloudless sky. Bright tropical flowers hugged the slope. At the bottom, electric blue ocean and pure white beach. Paradise.

I looked back at James. "Yeah. Me, too."

A few days later, James and I took our last bus to Bangkok and checked into a hotel in a high-rise downtown. After my happy pizza trip, James's malaria scare, the Super Bowl beatdown, and our brush with a gun-wielding Thai man, we'd had enough adventure. We craved safety. Stability. I lay my dirty, ripped, orange-and-navy backpack on the ground by the bed. James checked his carry-on again for our tickets and passports. We'd fly out in the morning.

The sun began to set. We went down to a roadside stand on the sidewalk for dinner and ate garlic pepper pork at a plastic table while perched on stools. Skyscrapers soared around us. At the end of the busy avenue, a slice of sky reddened and faded to black.

James bought a bottle of Singha from a 7-11 on the corner, and we took it up to the rooftop of our high-rise. My eyes adjusted to the dark, making out a dirty, empty swimming pool. A haphazard tower of chairs and tables leaned on the wall.

I laughed. "Not quite the ambiance the guy at the front desk advertised."

"Yeah, I won't miss that," James said. "Not getting the full story. Here, film my last drink in Asia." He handed me the camcorder.

"Okay," I narrated, panning across the skyline, "It's our last night in Bangkok." Silver towers surrounded us, their illuminated windows filling the night with a white glow. I stopped on James. The camera struggled to focus on him in the dark. He held up his beer bottle, and I peered through the viewfinder at a blurry image of him toasting the continent.

"Cheers, Asia. It's been an adventure!" He took a big gulp of Singha.

I stopped recording. "Cheeseball." I handed the camera back to James, who made a face and walked over to take some shots from the other sides of the building.

I leaned my elbows on the concrete ledge and looked down. Far below, men and women in suits hustled home late from office jobs. A man stood behind a hot plate on the sidewalk, tossing noodles in a frying pan. A teen squatted on a stool nearby, scarfing from a Styrofoam tray.

Our grand adventure was over. I'd be leaving with equal parts relief and sadness. Back in high school, I'd pined for lands I'd never seen. But the things I'd seen in Asia, and the history I learned, opened my eyes to how good I'd always had it. I felt a new affection for home and the comfort I always took for granted.

I declared the trip a success. James and I had been drifting apart, and now our bond was more solid than ever. We both had our idiosyncrasies, and we'd both made questionable decisions, but we never judged each other. We had weird health issues and did stupid shit. We were misfits together, and I couldn't imagine being as comfortable with anyone else. "We're lucky we found each other, love," he said once. "Nobody else would have us."

We felt like us again, which was comforting and scary at the same time.

Going back to normalcy scared the shit out of me. What if "James and Stef" only worked on the road? I pushed the doubt down deep.

There on the roof, I didn't know that James would go to college and become a graphic designer, and I would happily teach at a public middle school for thirteen years.

I didn't know that my eventual diagnosis of cyclothymia would fill me with relief because it meant my anxiety and cognitive issues were real and could be treated. Or that James would have surgery on his nose, ear, hand, and back.

I didn't know James's job would get behind on his paycheck, always offering stock options and promising a big payday when they sold the company, which never happened. The amount we'd lose, coincidentally, would be around the same amount as the debt he'd accrued all those years ago. Karmic equilibrium.

I didn't know that no matter how happy our life would be, there would always be a void. An emptiness that nothing but travel would fill. On short vacations, we'd catch glimpses of our former, adventurous selves and long for the days of quitting jobs, booking one-way tickets, and not knowing what the fuck was about to happen.

I didn't know that fourteen years after standing on that roof in Bangkok, in the middle of a global pandemic, we'd hunker down in our living room and write all about those good old days. And after a year of isolation, we would sell our house, give away our belongings, quit our jobs, and drive around the United States for a couple months, sleeping in a tiny trailer named Bill and feeling more like ourselves than we had in a long time.

Between us, James and I had a lot of travel experiences. I was glad I'd had my own, but I also loved that, for the past few years, we'd shared them. And hopefully would continue to, forever. A melancholy reel of memories ran through my head. That first night I saw him in Sydney, through the window of the Pink House, felt like a long time ago.

James came up behind me and wrapped his arms around my waist.

I smiled. "What if we'd never had Mondays and Tuesdays off together in Sydney?" I mused.

"What if I'd never pissed that girl's bed and jumped out the window? I could be here with Amanda," James said.

I giggled. "Yeah, I don't see it."

"Me neither, love," James said with his deep laugh. "Me neither."

Below us, cars and buses and scooters and tuk-tuks vacillated between traffic lanes. The blare from their horns sounded muffled from twenty stories up. The humid night air clung to us, but high atop the city, a breeze

261

blew gently against our faces. James rested his chin on my shoulder, and for a silent moment, we just stood, looking out at our glittering world together.

GLOSSARY

AAA— (USA) American Automobile Association

Abbatoir— (UK, AUS) slaughterhouse; James's worst nightmare

Acetaminophen— (USA) pain-relieving medication

A-levels— (UK) qualifications you study between ages sixteen and eighteen before university

Aussie— (UK) 1. a person from Australia; 2. referring to Australia

Baht— currency of Thailand

Bintang— Indonesian beer

Biro— (UK) ball-point pen

Bits and bobs— (UK) 1. odds and ends; 2. male genitalia (slang)

Bitter— (UK) a type of beer

Blackcurrant— (UK) 1. a small berry; 2. cordial made from blackcurrant

Body check— (USA) to slam someone out of the way, mostly used in hockey

Boiler suit— (UK) haz-mat suit

Boot— (UK) car trunk

Braces— (UK) straps that go over the shoulders to hold up pants, suspenders

Butties— (UK, northern) sandwiches

Caravan park— (UK) trailer park

Cheers— (UK) thanks

Chips— (UK) fries, (USA) crisps

Chippy— (UK) a shop that sells fish and chips

Citizens Advice Bureau— (UK) a place where people can get free advice

Climbing Frame— (UK) jungle gym, playground equipment

Comforter— (USA) duvet

Couch— (USA) sofa

CSS and HTML— web design programming languages

Dodgy— (UK) sketchy

Dual carriageway— (UK) four-lane highway

Duvet— (UK) bed comforter

Eejit— (IRL) Irish word for idiot

Ensuite— (UK) master bathroom

Erm— (UK) Um

Flat— (UK) apartment

Football— (UK) soccer

Frat— (USA) short for fraternity

Fuck me drunk— (AUS) holy shit

George Best— (UK) one of the greatest football (soccer) players ever

Give someone two fingers— (UK) Give someone the finger, but in Britain they use two, like a reversed peace sign

Go tits-up— (UK) fail, go badly

GPA— (USA) Grade Point Average, a way of measuring overall academic achievement

Graft— (UK) work

Grog— (UK, AUS) alcohol

Grommets— (UK) tubes inserted into ears to help them drain

Hard Day's Yakka— (AUS) hard day's work

Having a laugh— (UK) 1. having fun; 2. kidding; 3. taking advantage

Headmaster— (UK) school principal

How ya going?— (AUS) How are you doing?

Hostel— cheap hotel with shared bedrooms, bathrooms, and common areas

Jeopardy— (USA) long-running trivia gameshow

Jumper— (UK) sweater

Kiwi— (NZ) 1. referring to New Zealand; 2. someone from New Zealand; 3. NZ national bird; 4. A small brown, furry fruit that resembles the national bird

Knob— (UK) 1. penis; 2. idiot

Lip Smacker— (USA) popular brand of lip balm

Loveseat— (USA) two-seat sofa

Magaluf— (UK) popular tourist destination for Brits on the island of Majorca in Spain

Manchester United— (UK) the greatest soccer club in the history of the world

Marks— (UK) grades earned on schoolwork

Mate— (UK) 1. friend; 2. US equivalent to dude

Me— (UK, northern) my

Metropolitan University— (UK) cheaper version of regular university, community college

Meself— (UK, northern) myself

Minging— (UK) gross, nasty

Missus— (UK) girlfriend or wife

Mobile— (UK) cell phone

Mozzie bites— (AUS) mosquito bites

Newsagent's— (UK) convenience store, newsstand

NHS— (UK) National Health Service, national healthcare

Only Fools and Horses— (UK) Beloved British sitcom

Page 3 Girl— (UK) a topless woman found on page three of some newspapers

Pants— (UK) underwear; (USA) trousers

Paracetamol— (UK) pain-relieving medication

Pasties— (UK) pastry pockets

Pavement— (UK) sidewalk; (USA) tarmac

Pebble-dashed— (UK) 1. house exterior covered in cement and stuck with small pebbles; 2. how the toilet bowl looks after a messy shit

Pensioner— (UK) retiree

People-carrier— (UK) van

Petrol— (UK) gasoline

Pissed— (UK) drunk; (USA) angry

Pissing it (down)— (UK) raining really hard

Pitch— (UK) football field

Pound— (UK) British currency

Principal—(USA) school headmaster

Purse—(USA) handbag; (UK) women's wallet

Quid— (UK) slang for pound (currency)

Removal man— (UK) furniture mover

Retail park— (UK) strip mall

Rupiah— Balinese currency

Saucy Bangers— (UK) beans and sausages in a can

Scouse— (UK) 1. a stew popular in Liverpool; 2. Liverpool accent

Scouser— (UK) someone from Liverpool

Semi-detached house— (UK) duplex

Severance— (USA) redundancy payment

Shout— (UK, AUS) round of drinks

Sign on, sign on, and you'll never get a job— (UK) altered lyrics by Manchester United fans to the song "You'll Never Walk Alone," the anthem for the Liverpool Football Club

Singlet— (AUS) tank top, vest

SMTV— (UK) Saturday morning entertainment show

Sofa— (UK) couch

Sound— (UK) good

Spag bol— (UK) Spaghetti Bolognese

Spotted Dick— (UK) traditional British dessert

Stubbies— (AUS) small bottles of beer

Sweet tea—(USA, southern) iced tea brewed with sugar in it

Ta— (UK) thanks

Ta-ra— (UK, northern) goodbye

Taking the piss— (UK) 1. teasing; 2. taking advantage

Tea— (UK, northern) the last meal of the day

Tennis shoes— (USA) sneakers

Tesco— (UK) chain of grocery stores

Torch— (UK) flashlight

Trackie pants, Trackies— (UK) tracksuit pants

Trainers— (UK) sneakers

TripTik— (USA) booklet of maps specified for your trip, distributed by AAA

Trunk— (USA) car boot

The Tube— (UK) London subway

Twat— (UK) 1. jerk (not as bad as in the U.S., rhymes with bat); 2. vagina

Twatted— (UK) beat up

Twin mattress— (USA) single mattress

Ute— (AUS) pickup truck

Van— (USA) people-carrier

VB— (AUS) Victoria Bitter, a beer

Wellies, Wellington boots— (UK) rain boots, galoshes

Wonkey Donkey— (UK) a game segment on SMTV

CPSIA information can be obtained
at www.ICGtesting.com
Printed in the USA
BVHW032304060422
633621BV00005B/33